DATE DUE

Jean-Jacques Rousseau

Volumes of the *Continuum Library of Educational Thought* include:

St Thomas Aquinas	Vivian Boland OP
Pierre Bourdieu	Michael James Grenfell
Jerome Bruner	David Olson
John Dewey	Richard Pring
John Holt	Roland Meighan
John Locke	Alexander Moseley
Maria Montessori	Marion O'Donnell
John Henry Newman	James Arthur and Guy Nicholls
Plato	Robin Barrow
Lev Vygotsky	René van der Veer
Rudolf Steiner	Heiner Ullrich
Jean Piaget	Richard Kohler
Jean-Jacques Rousseau	Jürgen Oelkers
E.G. West	James Tooley
Mary Wollstonecraft	Susan Laird

See www.continuumbooks.com for further details.

Members of the Advisory Board

Robin Barrow, Professor of Philosophy of Education, and former Dean of Education, Simon Fraser University, Canada.

Peter Gronn, Professor of Education, Department of Educational Studies, University of Glasgow. (Formerly of Monash University, Australia.)

Kathy Hall, Professor of Education, National University of Ireland, Cork.

Stephen Heyneman, Professor of International Educational Policy at the College of Education and Human Development, Vanderbilt University, Nashville.

Yung-Shi Lin, President Emeritus and Professor, Department of Education and Institute of Graduate Studies, Taipei Municipal University of Education.

Gary McCulloch, Brian Simon Professor of the History of Education, Institute of Education, University of London.

Jürgen Oelkers, Professor of Education at the Institute of Education, University of Zürich.

Richard Pring, Lead director of the Nuffield Review of 14–19 Education and Training for England and Wales; Emeritus Fellow, Green College Oxford; and formerly, Professor of Educational Studies and Director of the Department of Educational Studies, University of Oxford.

Harvey Siegel, Professor of Philosophy, University of Miami.

Richard Smith, Professor of Education and Director of the Combined Degrees in Arts and Social Sciences, University of Durham.

Zhou Zuoyu, Professor of Education, Beijing Normal University.

Jean-Jacques Rousseau

JÜRGEN OELKERS

Continuum Library of Educational Thought

Series Editor: Richard Bailey

Volume 13

continuum

Continuum International Publishing Group

The Tower Building   80 Maiden Lane
11 York Road   Suite 704
London   New York
SE1 7NX   NY 10038

www.continuumbooks.com

British Library Cataloguing-in-Publication Data
A catalogue record for this book is available from the British Library.

ISBN: 978-0-8264-8412-3 (hardcover)

Library of Congress Cataloging-in-Publication Data
Oelkers, Jürgen, 1947–
Jean-Jacques Rousseau / Jürgen Oelkers.
p.   cm.
(Continuum Library of Educational Thought)
Includes bibliographical references.
ISBN-13: 978-0-8264-8412-3 (hardcover)
ISBN-10: 0-8264-8412-3 (hardcover)
1. Rousseau, Jean-Jacques, 1712–1778.   2. Education.   I. Title.   II. Series.

LB517.O38   2008
370.1–dc22
2007030630

Typeset by Aptara Books Ltd.
Printed and bound in Great Britain by Biddles Kings Lynn, Norfolk

"What will a Child learn sooner than a song?"
(Alexander Pope, *Imitations of Horace*)

Contents

Series Editor's Preface

Education is sometimes presented as an essentially practical activity. It is, it seems, about teaching and learning, curriculum, and what goes on in schools. It is about achieving certain ends, using certain methods, and these ends and methods are often prescribed for teachers, whose duty it is to deliver them with vigor and fidelity. With such a clear purpose, what is the value of theory?

Recent years have seen politicians and policy-makers in different countries explicitly denying *any* value or need for educational theory. A clue to why this might be is offered by a remarkable comment by a British Secretary of State for Education in the 1990s: "having any ideas about how children learn, or develop, or feel, should be seen as subversive activity." This pithy phrase captures the problem with theory: it subverts, challenges, and undermines the very assumptions on which the practice of education is based.

Educational theorists, then, are trouble-makers in the realm of ideas. They pose a threat to the status quo and lead us to question the common sense presumptions of educational practices. But this is precisely what they should do because the seemingly simple language of schools and schooling hides numerous contestable concepts that in their different usages reflect fundamental disagreements about the aims, values, and activities of education.

Implicit within the *Continuum Library of Educational Thought* is an assertion that theories and theorizing are vitally important for education. By gathering together the ideas of some of the most influential, important, and interesting educational thinkers, from the Ancient Greeks to contemporary scholars, the series has the ambitious task of providing an accessible yet authoritative resource for a generation of students and practitioners. Volumes within the series are written by acknowledged leaders in the field, who were selected for both their scholarship and their ability to make often complex ideas accessible to a diverse audience.

It will always be possible to question the list of key thinkers that are represented in this series. Some may question the inclusion of certain thinkers; some may disagree with the exclusion of others. That is inevitably going to be the case. There is no suggestion that the list of thinkers represented within the *Continuum Library of Educational Thought* is in any way definitive. What is incontestable is that these thinkers have fascinating ideas about education, and that taken together, the *Library* can act as a powerful source of information and inspiration for those committed to the study of education.

Richard Bailey
Roehampton University, London

Foreword

Rousseau is generally considered not only a pedagogical classic, but also perhaps one of the originators of modern thinking. For example, the understanding of childhood as a period in which knowledge acquisition and the development of moral reasoning and judgment ought to take place as a quasi-natural development is considered to have developed thanks to him. Children should be socially educated, for which a secure space provided by the educator is vital. Such a space is a prerequisite for a "negative education" by providing children with room for development instead of using all the time available only for instruction. Educational reformers and psychologists as well as philosophers and politicians have been fascinated by Rousseau's postulates, not least because they are still controversial, irrespective of the contemporary debate. Rousseau's work has been received highly selectively and usually without adequate awareness of his admittedly inconsistent complete works. Even those who are fairly well acquainted with Rousseau's *oeuvre* are challenged by his varied and contradictory life and works.

In this introduction to Rousseau, Jürgen Oelkers succeeds in revealing Rousseau's way of thinking by concentrating on a few focus points, especially by a contextualized and careful presentation of the central topic of education. He manages to show, on the one hand, how Rousseau dealt with religion, for example in his attempts to marginalize the impact of the idea of original sin, and, on the other hand, his role as an independent intellectual who accepted loneliness and even social ostracism. Oelkers thus manages to contextualize the usually fixed renarration of the 1762 publication *Emile or On Education* within the theoretical and political discourse of the time.

Rousseau refers to "natural religion," to nature as the original measure of man and the starting point for social criticism. He sees large cities, and in particular Paris, as a negative foil since they harbor favoritism, over-reaching, competition, and intransparency. His idea of an education free from original sin in a quasi-imaginary space clearly marked off from society shows just how much Rousseau's thinking was influenced by political conditions. He transformed the Christian religion into a civic credo without any intention of decreasing the importance of Christianity. In their natural state, in their secure space, the children develop free from sin, yet they have to be introduced to a society that does not follow nature.

As becomes clear by this introduction, Rousseau was not so much an inventor of ideas, but much more a keen thinker who came across different topics and gave them his own spin. Public announcements played a central role in this process; confessions became part of a way of life, so to speak.

As far as I can see, Jürgen Oelkers makes Rousseau's voluminous correspondence accessible to the development of educational theory for the first time, and he furthermore points out the importance of Rousseau as an *homme de lettres*. Rousseau's hallmark in his writings is the paradox, which becomes particularly obvious in his letters, where he often contradicts his own theoretical assumptions. His way of thinking was characterized by variations and counterpoints, which his contemporary readers and also opponents were much more aware of than we are today. This is evident from the fact that despite his anti-philosophical habitus he was considered a philosopher, an intellectual in the modern understanding who did not shy away from commenting on a variety of topical issues and events. Although his ideas have proved inspirational, they were never intended or presented as a system or corpus of theory. In this respect, Jürgen Oelkers describes Rousseau not only as a classic, but as a "great outsider," whose work still offers fruitful insights to all who are willing to delve into it.

Professor Dr Philipp Gonon
Chair for Vocational Education and Training
University of Zürich

Preface

There is probably more research and writing on Jean-Jacques Rousseau than on any other author of modern educational philosophy. The various bibliographies list as yet uncounted thousands upon thousands of titles; not all, but many of these works are of importance for research, as often are older works on more obscure themes. Certainly, there is no problem that has not already been dealt with. Every year, all over the world, hundreds of contributions are published in different disciplines and languages, which certainly raises the challenge of writing another work on Rousseau's views of education.

The challenge behind this book is two-sided: on the one hand, Rousseau's philosophy of education has been examined surprisingly little compared to his other main topics and at the same time in a more or less stereotypical way. Generally, Rousseau is considered the founder and first classic of "natural education," from which the child-centered, modern education of the twentieth century is said to have developed. On the other hand, the explicit connection or at least the inner coherence of Rousseau's educational point of view has always been assumed. What interpreters have been looking for was an educational doctrine or even the unity of his way of thinking.[1]

Rousseau fought against doctrines and refused authoritarian theories, yet he wrote a philosophy of education that has become a doctrine. He never wanted or could be a *philosophe*, but nevertheless was perceived as one. Behind his theory of natural education, there is no "philosophy" in today's sense of the word, but his countless readers have always claimed its existence. Yet that which is called "natural education" is artificial and has no concrete empirical background, something which Rousseau would have demanded from every other educational theory. From this point of view, it is the number of paradoxes that makes Rousseau and his reflections on education a matter of interest.

There is more than this. If we consider his readers and their motivations, there must have been something about both Rousseau the man and his work that is still challenging and fascinating today. Voltaire's judgment in his famous letter of October 24th, 1766 to David Hume does not grasp the facts and has proved a complete misjudgment. Concerning Rousseau, Voltaire says, there are only "minor miseries" which deserved no attention and would definitely be forgotten soon. "Les folies de Jean-Jacques, et son ridicule orgueil ne feront nul tort à la véritable philosophie; et les hommes respectables qui la cultivent en France, en Angleterre et en Allemagne, n'en seront pas moins estimés" (Voltaire 1983, p. 691).

Just the opposite was true. Not only did there develop a cult of Rousseau as a person and of his work as early as in Rousseau's lifetime, but also the controversy persisted. Rousseau's theories have always been contested: he had and still has devoted followers and pugnacious opponents (in France, Trousson 1995; see also Cottret and Cottret 2005); even now his ideas divide the "respectable" readership, but they are not perceived as "follies" and all attempts to discredit his character and his work have failed. Today, Rousseau is an irrefutable classic of several disciplines, and thus also in education. But why is it so? What did he write to justify this position?

At first sight both questions seem to be completely absurd; after all, in 1762 Rousseau published *the* book on education to which all the following discourse has again and again referred. If one reads *Emile* today, however, this point of reference is surprising. Obviously, it is due less to reading than to its assumed status as a "classic," to which some fundamental quotations, like "back to nature," are ascribed and which then seem to have fulfilled its function. But *Emile* is not simply a theory of "natural education," and this book is by no means Rousseau's only or "true" statement on education.

Whoever wants to interpret and assess Rousseau's philosophy of education cannot simply refer to the first three books of *Emile*, where most of the quotations are found on "child-centered education." What Rousseau says about education must be deduced from his complete works and their different contexts, taking Rousseau's paradoxical style into account, as well as his original intellectual biography and unconventional way of life. And there is not simply *one* fundamental text written by him to contain the philosophy of education as a whole.

By "works" I do not mean only Rousseau's well-known books and essays, but also his letters, which hold a primary importance in this book. In a very literal sense of the term, Rousseau was an *homme de lettres*; he wrote more than 16,000 pages of letters alone, and thus lived and thought by them. "Contexts" are not only the complex events of Rousseau's life as an outsider of society, but also the discourses and theories surrounding his main topics. Rousseau was neither the first nor the only person to consider "natural education," nor the inventor of the "genius of childhood," nor, finally, the *sole* reference for promoting the development of "modern education."

It is the goal of this book to shed a different light on Rousseau's philosophy of education. I assume that Rousseau's fundamental question has little to do with child-centered education, which was developed more than one hundred and thirty years after *Emile* had been published. Basically, he deals with a theological problem referring to the question of how man could live without sin, believe according to his own convictions, and be himself. This is a fundamental contradiction to Christian doctrines, which as late as the eighteenth century assumed that man's sinful nature is repeated and continued by every newborn child. In contrast to this, Rousseau in *Emile* constructs his first child without sin or the model of a post-Augustinean philosophy of education.

This is only *one* of Rousseau's topics, although an essential one. But there is no coherent theory behind what he writes upon education. Very often he made statements on questions of education not seldomly in such a way that we must state contradictions to positions supported in *Emile*. His educational reflection is often rather *occasional* and does not follow any doctrine, except where it is formulated – in *Emile* – and even there it is not without paradoxes and contradictions. On the other hand, Rousseau is hardly likely to have made the effort of writing a thoroughly composed book of more than five hundred pages if there were not a message in it. The question is what must be supposed to be that message and how is it related to the other passages in his work where Rousseau makes statements on education.

What I present here is an introduction to the way in which Rousseau takes up educational topics, combines them with his philosophical problems, and achieves solutions of his own. I will try to do justice to his solutions, but this can only be done from today's point of view and thus there must be critical distance. My own conclusion at the end of the book will be a mixed one. On the one hand, Rousseau's theories on education are untenable in some or even many respects; on the other hand, we must be lucky that he wrote them. They mark a standard of philosophical reflection below which we must not fall, even if – or because – his solutions often look strange. But every discipline learns from its great outsiders.

My point of view is that of the history of modern education. I am interested in the role Rousseau plays in this history, for which the eighteenth century has particular significance. Often, his role is understood to be that of a radical change toward modernity, whereas Rousseau himself had been orientated by political and social concepts of authors of pre-Christian antiquity. He wrote the most controversial critique of "progress and modernity," but is still considered to be the pioneer of modern education. Individuality seems to be the fundamental feature of modern education, which is interested in the single child. But one of Rousseau's essential problems is not "individuality" but *love of oneself* and how it should be related to "society" in a way which might do justice to it.

This view of the problem is unique to the eighteenth century, but does not mean that its solutions are convincing. And always these are solutions which do not only look paradoxical, but which on closer inspection are also contradicted by Rousseau himself without taking them back. Thus, that which could be called his "philosophy of education" consists – like music – of some basic themes, various variations, and also discords. Rousseau himself emphasized certain topics and topoi; he claimed a core for his theory, but this does not mean that questions of education are reflected systematically, free of irritation and without variations according to context.

Rousseau's thoughts are based on antique philosophy, on the history of Geneva, as well as on the close observation of the culture of France and its intellectuals. He discussed no other culture in a way to be compared to this; at most, he felt close to Italy due to its music, but not to Great Britain or Germany. Despite this Francophile focus, Rousseau was perceived by all European national cultures and in the course of this was quite differently connoted. In philosophy, the "German Rousseau" is strongly constructed via his great admirer Immanuel Kant, while the "French Rousseau" is still understood by his opposition to Voltaire and the *philosophes*.

One more difficulty results from reception. Often, Rousseau's statements on education have been taken much too literally without looking at their literary form. But almost always he articulates his theories by way of novels, operas, plays, letters, and essays, not as strict philosophical deductions. They are comments in their own way in each case, which, although containing empirical knowledge – Rousseau was a keen and good observer of his times – allow only limited application, at one's own risk, so to speak. Thus, they do not simply result in a "new practice" of education, as has often been assumed by educational criticism. What Rousseau says is literature, not experience, except that of the author.

It was a particular challenge to adjust this text to an English-speaking readership. For this, it was necessary to study English editions of Rousseau's works, that is to revise my previous French and German reading to a large extent. This was also connected to my attempt of approaching the "English Rousseau," who is in many respects different from the way in which "Jean-Jacques" was and still is perceived by French culture. Until today, in respect of evaluating Rousseau's topics, this cultural difference most of all influences current secondary literature. It is also conspicuous that educational topics appear rather subordinate, which might be due to the fact that the principal scholars are literary critics and philosophers.

For this volume the French quotations were revised to the English editions, or were translated especially for this volume. Most of the letters are only available in the original language. I used several editions of the letters, but most references are to R. A. Leigh's definitive edition, the internet version of which is still under construction. Many of Rousseau's works are meanwhile available by electronic editions on the internet, which I consulted but did not use for quotations. Given the state of the editions, it was not always possible to use English sources. The *Collected Writings of Rousseau* contains only a few letters, and there are translations of the main works which are of varying quality and must be compared with the original editions.

This book was completed in Hiroshima between February and June, 2006. I express my thanks to the President of the University of Hiroshima for appointing me as Visiting Professor at the Department of Learning Science, which offered me enough time to concentrate on this book. I express my special thanks to Professor Satoshi Higuchi and his team. I would also like to thank the Institute of Education of the University of Zürich for its support. Sonja Geiser organized research literature to be sent to me while in Japan and co-ordinated the development of the text. Karin Manz and Sylvia Bürkler harmonized the quotations from several of Rousseau's letter editions. Monika Wicki made various sources from the eighteenth century available. I have to thank Rita Casale and Philipp Gonon for inspiring emails and comments when writing the text. Mirko Wittwar translated most parts of the book before I made the final draft.

Jürgen Oelkers
Professor of Education, University of Zürich
Higashihiroshima, June 26th, 2006

Note

1. This thesis was supported, for example, by Gustave Lanson (1912); his influential contribution introduced the eighth year of the *Annales de la Société Jean-Jacques Rousseau*. The year 1912, Rousseau's 200th birthday, was dedicated to re-assessing his work.

Part 1

Intellectual Biography

1

Citoyen De Genève: Jean-Jacques Rousseau

Jean-Jacques Rousseau was born on June 28th, 1712 in Geneva and was also raised there.[1] Unlike today, the city of Geneva was not part of Switzerland but an independent republic. Since 1309 the citizens of Geneva owned the right to rule themselves after the city had become a center of local commerce in the preceding century. The city then was small, not much more than three thousand inhabitants, but powerful. Later in the fourteenth century it came under the influence of the Duchy of Savoy while some leading Geneva families remained in power. A military pact of 1525 between Geneva and the two Swiss cantons of Berne and Fribourg secured mutual interests, which prevented the Duke of Savoy from occupying the city.

In 1528 the Canton of Berne converted to Protestantism, followed five years later by the ruling class of Geneva. On August 27th, 1535 the Genevan *Grand Conseil* (Council of Two Hundred) ended five hundred years of power of the Roman Episcopal Church by suspending Catholic Mass and confiscating the Church's goods. The main person behind this conversion was the French preacher Guillaume Farel (1489–1565), who led the Reformation party in Geneva. One year later Farel, whose pseudonym was "Ursinus" from his voice when preaching, asked a young French theologian named Jean (John) Calvin (1509–1564) to come to Geneva and help to establish the new religion in which Rousseau was raised.

Calvin is the author of the *Edits civils*, which appeared in 1543 and constituted the Republic of Geneva. The city became finally independent after a battle called l'Escalade in December, 1602 when the besieging troops of the Duke of Savoy were beaten in one night. This still small but growing republic, which hosted many Protestant refugees from France and elsewhere in Europe, became the center of what was later called "Calvinism," perhaps the first educational religion ever established. Calvin, himself not a native Genevan, not only founded in 1559 the two institutions of Higher Education in Geneva[2] and wrote the catechism for Christian learning (*brève instruction chrétienne*), but also argued for a new type of teacher and a new relationship between believers.

Rousseau's life and work are, in some ways, a manner of dealing with Calvinism as it was understood in the middle of the eighteenth century. These, of course, were not the original views of the sixteenth century's religious reformers as Richard Muller (2000) reconstructed them. For Rousseau, Calvinism was more a habit of virtue than a religion. Due to this reason it was not Calvin's theology that interested Rousseau but rather his theory of morals and his role as a lawgiver. While Rousseau did not write formal treatises on Calvin, evidently he was occupied with the basic moral themes of Calvinism. He re-thought these themes and they can be seen clearly in each of his important works.

Calvinistic rigor fascinated Rousseau, along with ancient stoicism. Following the banning and public burning of his own books, Rousseau dispensed with the citizenship of the Republic of Geneva in 1763, but not, however, his membership of Calvin's church, which he had renewed in 1754. The first publication of John Calvin in 1532 was a commentary on Seneca's *De Clementia*, a key text of political stoicism written in AD 55 or 56 which argued for moderation and against self-interest. Only after this commentary, Calvin, a humanist by education who studied in Paris at the Collège de Montaigu and completed his doctorate in law, turned his attention to religious problems.

Calvin was thrown out of Geneva in April, 1538 because the City Council thought his teachings were too rigid. But he was called back by new officials in 1541, after he had started to comment on books of the Bible while living in Strasbourg. The City Council changed its mind and later ratified Calvin's *Ecclesiastical Ordinance of the Church of Geneva*, which formulated the basic principles of "Calvinism." One of their representatives was Rousseau's father, Isaac Rousseau (1655–1747), citizen of Geneva[3] and a master watchmaker. Rousseau grew up with these principles and the Calvinistic rules of life as they were exhibited within Genevan craftsmanship at the beginning of the eighteenth century.

At the time of Rousseau's birth, Geneva was still a comparatively small city with scarcely more than 20,000 inhabitants. The relevance of social size is a key to Rousseau's thinking. Big cities in France around 1720 were Lyon with more than 100,000 inhabitants and of course Paris with over half a million. The biggest city in Europe was London, which in 1760, when George III ascended the throne, had a population of over 750,000 inhabitants. In the mid-eighteenth century more than one-tenth of the British population resided in London, which became an economic and cultural capital[4] while at the same time remaining in some parts a medieval mud hole. The death rate in the City of London was twice its birth rate throughout the eighteenth century.

In his writings Rousseau called himself *Citoyen de Genève*, to express his feelings of loyalty toward the city of his birth and his youth. For him the ideal republic was always Geneva despite the Calvinistic theocracy that really ruled the city. But for Rousseau size is a function of social order. During his lifetime he came to know big cities like Lyon, Paris, and London, and for him they were not all the right size for a good society. Rousseau's assumptions about the limits of social progress have to do with his notions of social place and size. He was not alone in this view: many visitors coming to Geneva in the eighteenth century thought of the city as nothing short of an ideal republic.

Rousseau left Geneva in 1728 at the age of 16. As a young man he came back for occasional visits but then only once after he had left for Paris and become famous. Apart from that visit in 1754 he never saw Geneva again, although he always stayed in contact with the city's life and remained an active participant in Genevan politics. For all these reasons Rousseau is not a French but a Genevan thinker who looked at the culture and history of France from the point of view of his city, its traditions and modes of life (Rosenblatt 1997). His ideas are not simply part of French Enlightenment, as most commentaries still see it, but must be understood against the background of a Calvinist city that formed his views in more ways than one. Not coincidentally, he called himself "a foreigner living in France" (Rousseau 2000, p. 396).

Rousseau's dramatic life (Trousson 1988–1989; Cranston 1991, 1997; documents in: *Le CD-Rom Jean-Jacques Rousseau* 1999; latest English biographical study: Damrosch 2005) is characterized by an ascent outside the elite and by remaining an outsider for his whole life. He was an intelligent and creative stranger with a different outlook and the mental reserves of a man who never held any rank and had no power apart from his writings. His several patrons and more patronesses supported and even funded him but they did not make him servile. This life had its price. Rousseau's striving for independence was as much a burden for him as his rise to fame; he never settled down and always feared the loss of control over his life. Many contemporaries thought of him as "crazy," or "selfish," or at least "difficult," while he himself felt persecuted, the more so the longer he lived.[5]

Rousseau had attempted to gain control over his biography by writing his *Confessions*, which were published posthumously; indeed, these have largely determined his image ever since. Most biographers followed the trails Rousseau laid down and only recently have independent biographies appeared that do not use the data, metaphors, and interpretations Rousseau himself had chosen for his intellectual life after death. But still no interpreter can write about Rousseau without taking into account how he himself saw the drama of his life. In this respect he in fact controlled the interpretations of his life: "Since my name is certain to live on among men, I do not want the reputation it transmits to them to be a false one" (Rousseau 2000, p. 647).[6]

His fluctuating career[7] alternated between Geneva, Savoy, and Paris, northern Italy and Switzerland, later also England and rural France, ever independently and restlessly. Rousseau's way through life ended in solitude. Loneliness was not the plan but the result of Rousseau's intellectual and physical wanderings. His life was without aim but full of ambitions and sentiments; the form of this life was very unusual and his manners were peculiar in many ways. Yet Rousseau was the ultimate author of his time, who fascinated the public with radical ideas on religion, philosophy, education, and politics. Part of his success was his view as an outsider: he was not a member of the Establishment and remained an observer at the edge of society throughout his life. He lived and thought outside social conventions.

At the age of 13, young Rousseau began an apprenticeship as an engraver, and three years later he left his trade and his home town. Only a few hours from Geneva, he met by chance a French Catholic baroness called Françoise-Louise de Warens (1699–1768), the first woman to change his life. Madame de Warens had annulled her marriage in 1726 and lived a free life on an estate called Annecy near Chambéry in Savoy.[8] Rousseau met her on Palm Sunday, March 21st, 1728. Fifty years later he wrote: "This first moment determined my whole life and by an inevitable chain of events shaped the destiny of the rest of my days" (Rousseau 2000a, p. 89).

Some years later he became her lover and even converted to Catholicism for her.[9] Rousseau called Madame de Warens "ma très-chère-maman" (Correspondance t. I, p. 99), but in fact she was both his mother, his educator, and his mistress. He was not in her service, but lived near and with her for 12 years. In a sense she was his true teacher because she introduced him to music and culture and tried to guide his studies. Apart from antique philosophy, stoic morals, and botany, *music* became Rousseau's key intellectual profession. Some of the early biographers overlooked what music meant to Rousseau. He wrote operas and even developed a new system of musical notation. Also, we can say that the elegance and style of his writings came from music.

Rousseau had no formal education, and although he received some teaching first from his father and then from some occasional instructors, he was largely autodidactic. He mostly learned what he wanted to know without any experience of schools, with the exception of a short stay in an Italian seminary[10] and some months in the Séminaire des Lazaristes d'Annecy in 1729. His readings as a young man were led by both Madame de Warens and his own interests. His very unconventional intellectual biography was a main source for his radical critique of schooling and formal education, which made him famous.

In an early letter dated at the beginning of the year 1740 to Monsieur d'Eybens,[11] Rousseau commented on his education. He wrote that Madame de Warens tried her best to spur his enthusiasm for the liberal arts (les belles connoissances), but that the principles of his profession often led him to neglect the cultivation of his intellectual talents "in favor of those that come from the intuitions of his heart" (en faveur de celles de sentiment du Coeur) (*ibid.*, p. 116). And he had always been more encouraged to think than to know very much (*ibid.*). This letter is one of the first documents in which Rousseau values "heart" more than "knowledge."

Rousseau stayed at Chambéry with several intermissions until the spring of 1740. After some wanderings in 1730 he held various jobs; despite his lack of formal training he was able, for example, to teach music for some time in 1732. He also worked in a cadastral office when Madame de Warens moved from Annecy to Chambéry. This was the only time Rousseau experienced some kind of regular life. And it was also the time when he discovered his talents as a writer. In the summer of 1736, Rousseau accompanied Madame de Warens to a lovely valley called Les Charmettes. Here he started writing, surrounded by nature and often left alone by her. His poem "The Orchard of Madame de Warens" was privately printed in 1739 (Damrosch 2005, p. 146).

At the end of this period of low-level but regular activities, Rousseau, aged 28, took up a position as a private tutor in Lyon in 1740 and through *Mémoire à M. de Mably* wrote his first text on education. Here Rousseau described in a rather conventional way his experiences as a tutor of the two children in the house of Jean Bonnet de Mably (1709–1785), who served as General Provost of the province of Lyon. Rousseau was hired at a fixed salary and earned his first money. In eighteenth-century France, Mably was a famous political writer and a well-known deist. He is regarded as one of the influences for Rousseau's admiration of antique philosophy and literature (Aurenche 1934).

In 1741 Rousseau went to Paris for a second time,[12] working as a copyist and music teacher. His new system of notation in figures was read at the Académie des Sciences in Paris on August 22nd, 1742 but failed to attract attention. Although it was considered original in some respects, it seemed to be too complicated and practically worthless. It was published later under the title *Dissertation sur la musique moderne*, but again to no significant reaction. On the other hand, Rousseau seemed to be talented enough for the French ambassador in Venice to accept him as a secretary. Rousseau stayed in Venice for one year between September 1743 and August 1744. Venice was the other republican city he often referred to, although negatively, in his political writings.[13]

Back in Paris, Rousseau deepened his acquaintance with intellectual leaders like the multi-talented writer and editor Denis Diderot (1713–1784) and the German diplomat and music critic Friedrich Melchior Baron von Grimm (1723–1807), but he never became an intimate part of the Paris *salons*, where the key discussions of the Enlightenment's philosophy, politics, and esthetics took place. Rousseau was not good at conversation[14] and began to detest Parisian city and court life, which became the counter-example to his ideal republic. For him, Paris and Geneva represented the two basic models of society: the former stood for big size and corruption and the latter for small size and virtue.

In 1745 Rousseau met Marie-Thérèse (Thérèse) Lavasseur (1721–1801). In many biographies Thérèse Lavasseur has been depicted as an illiterate woman that Rousseau tried in vain to educate.[15] She was considered to be crude and awkward, not to say stupid. But their relationship remained intact until his death and it was the only lasting relationship he ever had. What he called his "friends" were often penfriends and with them he never shared experiences of day-to-day life. None of his affairs ever led to a lasting passion. Only Thérèse stayed at his side, and she was the sole support he trusted.

They first met in the hotel in Paris[16] where Rousseau lodged and she worked as a seamstress. Rousseau described his relationship with Thérèse in his *Confessions*, but despite his rather generous portrayal emphasizing her tender and honest heart[17] as well as her practical abilities, most of Rousseau's friends and admirers did not regard her to be the right woman at his side. Rumors that she had an affair with Scottish writer James Boswell (1740–1795)[18] did not enhance her reputation either. But she was not as "illiterate" as she is still judged today.[19] One source that is seldom taken into consideration is her numerous letters to Rousseau: here she demonstrated her wit and good judgment.

Thérèse influenced his opinions and views more than conventional biographies are willing to admit (see Guyot 1962). She was not simply a woman "in dreams and tears" (Wille 1937 and numerous others), but the woman at his side who looked after him, his *gouvernante* as he called her, and whom he finally married in August, 1768,[20] one year after they had fled from England.[21] Rousseau described the relationship in his later letters as "my wife and I" (ma femme et moi) (Correspondance t. XXXVIII, p. 234).[22] And what Rousseau (2000, p. 346) called her "simplicity of mind" proved to be indispensable for the course of his life.

In 1749 Rousseau wrote the articles on music for Diderot's *Encyclopédie*, and his first major literary success came one year later with the *Discours sur les sciences et les arts*, which was awarded a prize by the Academy of Dijon. In 1752 his opera *The Cunning Man of the Village*[23] was staged in Paris in the presence of the king of France and became Rousseau's only success as a composer. What earned his renown in the intellectual world early in his career were not his contributions to music but the two political discourses he published in 1750 and 1755. For many readers he offered new solutions, the choice of his topics were unusual and his writings seemed to be very promising.

The first, *Discourse on the Sciences and the Arts* (Rousseau 1992a), is concerned with the decadent role of modern science and culture and its relationship to moral behavior; the second, *Discourse on the Origins of Inequality* (Rousseau 1992), questions the emergence of inequality among men since the beginning of society. Modern science, according to Rousseau, does not make the world better because progress in science cannot be equated with progress in morals. This Calvinistic theme made Rousseau famous overnight. He argued against the mainstream of the French Enlightenment while at the same did not support the position of the Catholic Church. He was banned by the Church because he did not underline the theory of original sin, which was the Catholic Church's cornerstone against the Enlightenment and the idea of human progress.

But not everybody agreed with his thesis. Voltaire,[24] for example, reacts with hostility against the idea that modern science did not change the moral situation of society. He also regarded Rousseau's concept of the noble savage to be quite ridiculous. Only progress will protect man from retreating to the time of the barbarians that Voltaire described in his magistral *Essai sur les moers*, which first appeared as a book in 1756. Voltaire rejected the idea that savages living in tribes (des sauvages) could be the role model for the future of mankind, and he also rejected Rousseau's claim that a "natural man" existed who was innocent and good by origin. Rather, Voltaire held, the nature of man is always the same and only society, knowledge, and culture may change. And the nature of man is social, not individual, thus society cannot be the derivate of nature (Voltaire: *Essai*, Introduction, Chapter VII).[25]

Rousseau retreated from the intellectual circles of Paris. On April 9th, 1756, half a year after his return from Geneva, he moved together with Thérèse and her mother to a small house on an estate called La Chevrette near Montmorency, north of Paris.[26] This house, offered to him by Madame d'Epinay,[27] became famous under the name of Ermitage, one of Rousseau's in years to come. Two years later, after the break with Madame d'Epinay and Denis Diderot, Rousseau and Thérèse moved to a house he named Petit Château (Little Castle). This house on their estate, also at Montmorency, was offered by the Duke and Duchess of Luxembourg. Rousseau thus had enough political protection for his work.

In these retreats he concentrated on his three major works. The Ermitage and the Little Castle were the two major places where he wrote the *Nouvelle Héloise* (1761), throughout Europe a very successful and widely read novel, the *Contrat Social* (1762), Rousseau's theory of society, and *Emile ou de l'éducation* (1762), the theory of "new education." *Emile* and the *Contrat Social* were banned directly after publication. *Emile* was publicly burned in Paris and Geneva almost simultaneously; both books were burned in Geneva.

After this, Rousseau was on the run, a "restless genius," as Leo Damrosch (2005) called him. Rousseau was granted asylum by the Prussian governor in Neuchâtel soon after his flight from Paris and settled at a place called Môtiers. He lived in this exile for almost two years, admired by many readers of his books. During his stay in the Prussian asylum Rousseau became the idol of the generation of *Sturm und Drang*,[28] young *literati* from throughout Europe who discussed Rousseau and made him famous. Many of his followers visited him at Môtiers even though he did not remember the visitors very well (Rousseau 2000, pp. 597–8). At the same time he became subject to public attacks by such differing authors as the General Procurator of Geneva, Jean-Robert Tronchin (1710–1793), and Rousseau's arch-enemy, Voltaire,[29] who lived in the Estate of Ferney near Geneva.

At Môtiers Rousseau started working on his confessions in 1765. On December 18th the *Letters Written from the Mountain*, a discussion of criticism of his theological positions, had arrived in Geneva; after this Rousseau decided to write his *Confessions*. On January 22nd, 1765 his *Letters* were publicly burned in Paris, and in September Rousseau had to leave Môtiers after having been threatened and ill-treated. Originally, his situation in exile had been rather comfortable: he and Thérèse were friendly with and accepted by the community, although they were not married. This changed after *Emile* had been banned in Neuchâtel.

The parish priest of Môtiers, Frédéric-Guillaume de Montmollin (1709–1783), had originally been a friend and correspondent of Rousseau. Under pressure from the Neuchâtel clergy, he turned against Rousseau and preached against him in public. Rousseau was accused of being godless, his writings were condemned, and the community was stirred up against him. On September 6th, 1765 Rousseau's house was targeted by an enraged mob and stones were thrown at it.[30] According to contemporary sources, he was even in danger of being stoned by the village children (Guyot 1958, pp. 104–5). In the face of an untenable situation he fled to the lonely St Peter's Island in lac de Bienne, but following an order from the Berne government he had to leave the island on October 26th, 1765 and after this traveled restlessly throughout Europe.

In January, 1766 the fugitive Rousseau made for England following an invitation by David Hume (1711–1776). Both had mistaken hopes and expectations of each other and soon their friendship was to fragment. This story is revealing. Hume, one of the most sensitive writers of the eighteenth century, served as a private secretary to Lord Hertford in Paris for two years from 1763. He and Rousseau had not met in person before, but Hume's letters to Rousseau[31] showed admiration, the same with Rousseau's correspondence to Hume, and it was not that unusual to make friends by way of exchanging letters. But this friendship broke up and ended in hostility. One of the witnesses to the quarrel was the English writer and politician Horatio (Horace) Walpole, 4th Earl of Oxford (1717–1797), who was in Paris and London at the time when events occurred.

On December 16th, 1765 Rousseau had secretly arrived in Paris, but moved openly throughout the city and aroused great attention. A few weeks earlier, a letter by Hume from October 22nd had reached him in French Strasbourg, convincing him to go to Britain to stay with Hume to evade the danger of further prosecution. Rousseau decided in favor of this invitation but wanted a stay in Paris first. On January 4th, 1766 Hume, Rousseau, and their traveling companion Jean-Jacques de Luze[32] went to Calais from Paris and reached Dover on January 11th. Thérèse Lavasseur arrived some weeks later, accompanied by James Boswell.

On the way to Calais a strange event occurred. Rousseau, who shared a room with Hume, heard Hume say during his sleep "I hold Jean-Jacques Rousseau!"[33] During the crossing Hume noticed that Rousseau, despite constantly fretting about his bad health, spent the stormy and ice-cold night on the deck of the ship and seemed to be in good shape. On January 13th Hume and Rousseau arrived in London; the next day the British newspapers reported on Rousseau being prosecuted on the Continent.[34] On February 4th the *London Chronicle* published a portrait of the French – not Genevan – author, as he was regarded. Rousseau, an author famous throughout Europe, was warmly welcomed in Britain, but his reaction to this was paradoxical, condemning favor and rejecting respect.

The whole stay on the island was a public one, as was the fierce argument between Rousseau and Hume, which started a few weeks after the arrival. Together with Thérèse, Rousseau visited Hume in London on March 18th, 1766; during the dinner party a quarrel started which soon escalated, although the reason was trivial.[35] Rousseau did not understand English[36] and anyway tended to interpret even minor signs as disasters. After the evening in Lisle Street he developed the suspicion that Hume was not his friend but was rather playing nothing less than a double game with him (Edmonds and Eidinow 2006, pp. 149ff.).

Some days after the quarrel had started, the British press published a letter by the Prussian King Frederick II against Rousseau.[37] Because he appreciated him and his work, the king had granted Rousseau asylum[38] but had never personally written to him or answered his letters.[39] Thus, Rousseau considered the letter published by the British press a forgery, as it indeed it was. The letter (Cottret and Cottret 2005, pp. 416ff.) was a satire written by Horace Walpole and had circulated in Paris since December, 1765. Rousseau felt confronted with a conspiracy and drew a clear line between himself and his "enemies," which was accompanied by blunt letters.

His conflict with David Hume escalated and was discussed throughout Europe, by no means all unsympathetic to Rousseau. Hume had constructed his own conspiracy theory which proved more harmful to himself than to Rousseau, who knew how to present himself skillfully as the victim (Edmonds and Eidinow 2006, pp. 215ff.). In the eyes of his followers just the fact that he even rejected a pension by the British king, which had been offered to him thanks to Hume's negotiations, spoke for him rather than against him. However, Rousseau's letter from May 12th, 1766, by which he rejected the pension, is more cryptic than clear,[40] as after all he was close to receiving the pension.[41]

Rousseau believed Hume to be the head of the conspiracy against him. He claimed to have been lured to Britain on a pretext and that now he had to fear for his life. That was exactly what was written in the forged letter from the Prussian king, which obviously had been written with Hume's collaboration. Nevertheless, Hume was shocked by these accusations and already in 1766 published his own account of the facts (*Exposé* 1766).[42] The reason was to protect his own reputation in the face of the rumors about Rousseau's *Confessions*. The friendship of these two men had come to an end long before, if it had ever existed at all. Hume at first sight considered Rousseau a "nice little man," but he was never able to meet his complex personality let alone to share emotions with him (Mossner 1980, pp. 511ff.).

On July 10th, 1766 Rousseau wrote a long letter to Hume, explaining the situation, as it had developed, from his point of view. There it says as an introduction: "I do not see anything in the world; I ignore that which happens; I do not have any companion, no ally, no intrigues; I am not told anything; I know only that which I feel; but I know very well how I am made to feel" (Correspondance t. XXX, p. 29). On this basis Rousseau answers Hume's question of who, after all, had accused him, that is Hume. For this, says Rousseau, there was only one person in question, that is Hume himself (*ibid.*).

He, says Rousseau, had left Switzerland due to barbarous treatment and had followed the invitation to Britain with great expectations, most of all to be able to renew and increase his friendship with Hume (*ibid.*, p. 30). Indeed, at first this had been the case, but then their relationship had darkened because of Hume's machinations, and now all of Rousseau's enemies were Hume's friends (*ibid.*, p. 41). And public prosecution by the press was much worse in London than in Paris (*ibid.*, p. 43). Hume, having great influence in London but having failed to use it in Rousseau's favor, was to be blamed for the brusque change of public opinion (*ibid.*, pp. 43–4).

After this passage Rousseau constructs and names the conspiracy against him. Not without good reason he believes Walpole to be one of the conspirators (*ibid.*, p. 39). Walpole (1797)[43] himself notes that it was Rousseau who wrote incomprehensible, ridiculous, and often even impudent letters in Britain, which were to set everybody against him.[44] He was not the only one to see matters this way. "Il hasarde son salut et sa réputation" Voltaire (1961, p. 690) wrote to Hume on October 24th, 1766 and added: "Just imagine, this poor man had never to get along with a teacher [maître] and had never to maintain any friendship, so it is no wonder that he thinks it to be beneath his dignity to be taught by anyone and that for him friendship is a kind of weakness which natural man [un sage] must resist" (*ibid.*, p. 691).

Rousseau, on the other hand, wrote to his close friend Pierre-Alexandre DuPeyrou on January 8th, 1767 that only Hume was to be blamed for everything that happened. He – Hume – had misinterpreted and publicly exploited his – Rousseau's – letters without taking their intimate nature into consideration (Correspondance t. XXXII, pp. 27ff.). Rousseau suspected even DuPeyrou to have changed sides and to have joined the ranks of those who wrongly blamed him for something for which Hume was to be blamed. And he even offers an explanation: "Malice exists in the intention to cause harm" (*ibid.*, p. 28).

At the beginning of May, 1767 Rousseau and Thérèse left England hurriedly. On April 30th Rousseau in a letter had thanked his loyal host, Richard Davenport,[45] for all he had done for him. In face of the situation, Rousseau wrote, he had no option but to leave England immediately. "I have no choice than to bravely end a career. It is easy to suppress me but difficult to degrade me" (Correspondance t. V, p. 146). On May 12th, 1767 the *London Chronicle* made an angry comment on Rousseau's flight from Britain, pointing out the irrational behavior of the great "French" author.

But "rationality" was what challenged Rousseau if this meant the unambiguous clarity of other people's behavior. For Rousseau, the world was full of obstacles, that is it was not at all "transparent" or "enlightened" (Starobinski 1980). To meet the obstacles he should act as a moralist, but nobody was able to meet his moral demands, which only made him demand them even more intensely. Also the motif of *solitude* intensified after his stay in Britain and became the dominating topic of Rousseau's later writings, which, except for his publications on botany, dealt almost exclusively with himself.

At the end of his confessions, Rousseau reports that he had originally intended to go to Berlin from Strasbourg but then had been persuaded by others to accept Hume's invitation (Rousseau 2000, p. 642). Hume's invitation[46] is described in the *Confessions* (*ibid.*, p. 616); Rousseau also makes statements on Hume's character and on his own expectations (*ibid.*, p. 617) but not on the quarrel and their separation.[47] Instead, Rousseau speaks of the "storm" (orage) which had been incited against him (*ibid.*, p. 622), of public abuse, of those having disappointed him the most to whom he had been particularly kind (*ibid.*, pp. 617–18), and finally of sermons in the course of which he had been called "Antichrist" (*ibid.*, p. 621).

After his return to France, Rousseau worked, in increasing ill-health, on his autobiography, which can also be seen as an attempt at self-therapy. Not everybody judged him like Walpole:[48] Rousseau still had enough friends who assisted him during the last years of his life. With Thérèse Lavasseur he lived in several places, mostly on the run, sometimes from himself, but always working on the *Confessions*. They were finished when at last he was allowed to come back to Paris under his own name, after having lived under the pseudonym of "Jean-Joseph Renou." In 1771 the police banned Rousseau's further readings from the manuscript of the *Confessions* in private sessions because there was the fear of disclosure of moral scandal and public shaming.

The manuscripts circulated in secret and were never printed in Rousseau's lifetime. During the last eight years of his life, from 1770 to 1778, he hardly published anything, continued to live from copying, and at the end of his life concentrated intensively on botany. This may also be considered a symbol of his life, which led into carefully classifying nature, accompanied by endless reflections on his work and the quality of his principles. He was trying, as written in his last work, the *Reveries of the Solitary Walker*, to record everything that came into his mind when wandering around, both his own preoccupations and others' ideas (Rousseau 2000a, p. 7).[49]

Concentrating on himself in the *Confessions* was a carefully planned exercise. As in the case of only a few authors, Rousseau's theories can be closely related, if not equated, to his life. His work is of an autobiographical nature through and through, something which becomes clear by his repeated attempts to come to terms with both himself and his life. *Mon Portrait*, for example, is the title of a compilation of fragments from the years 1761–2, which remained unpublished.[50] This was followed by the four *Lettres à M. De Malherbes*, written between January 4th and 28th, 1762, being a kind of interim evaluation of his life. Then in 1764 there followed an *Introduction* to his life which was also not published.

Rousseau's intellectual disciplines are always attempts to understand himself. Even shortly before his death he tries a "new understanding" of himself (*ibid.*). The attempt to understand is entitled "Confessions," that is confessions of a life which Rousseau in every respect understood to be unique and exemplary. The *Confessions* are Rousseau's masterpiece. He alone summed up his life and put a price tag on it. What came out of this is a previously unknown fusion of philosophy, literature, and personal confession which analyzes but does not justify. As it clearly says, it is "a confession, not a justification" (Rousseau 2000, p. 349).

All this was done under the constant threat of prosecution and during many flights. With Rousseau's life there came unreliable income, a dependency on other people's favors, and an illness which he clearly perceived (Damrosch 2005, pp. 440–1) and against which he had to write for a living. Not without reason he occasionally signed letters "pauvre Jean-Jacques."[51] In the end, he found a place to rest. His precarious financial situation improved suddenly in May, 1778 when Rousseau and Thérèse Lavasseur moved to Ermenonville into an estate owned by the Marquis de Girardin, Rousseau's last benefactor. His sudden death on July 2nd, 1778 ended a very unlikely literary and philosophical career which was lived *à rebour* – contrary to convention.

In one of his last letters, to the Comte Duprat on February 3rd, 1778, Rousseau summed up the situation at the end of his life as follows: "All the care, all the hardships I suffered from, the tiredness I must bear drive away my apathy, all the things I need would need to come as one; my vitality is not sufficient anymore to look for them; exactly in this state of destruction, closed off from every help and support, from those around me, I have nothing to believe in than myself" (Correspondance t. XL, pp. 194ff.).

Notes

1. The data of Rousseau's life are comprehensively collected in Courtois (1923) and Trousson and Eigeldinger (1998). Most of the names connected to Rousseau are available in Trousson and Eigeldinger (2001).
2. The College and the Academy of Geneva.
3. The Rousseau family originated from Montlhéry near Paris. Being Protestants, they fled to Geneva in 1549 and became citizens in 1555.
4. "Cette capitale" Rousseau called London in a letter to David Hume on February 19th, 1763 (Correspondance t. XV, p. 200).
5. Rousseau's "paranoia" has been the subject of major speculation up to Möbius's diagnosis that all of Rousseau's theories were nothing more than the work of a madman. Paul Julius Möbius (1853–1907) was a German psychiatrist who in 1889 published *J. J. Rousseaus Krankheitsgeschichte* (enlarged edition 1903). Many of these psycho-pathologies appeared

between 1880 and 1950. The history of the varying diagnoses can be read in Jean Starobinski's essay "On Rousseau's Illness" (Starobinski 1980). For a broader account see Farrell (2006).

6. Preface to the Neuchâtel edition of the *Confessions*.
7. Rousseau himself spoke of his "career" in his later works (Rousseau 1990, p. 152).
8. The town of Chambéry is located half an hour from Grenoble in the French Alps, near the castle of the Dukes of Savoy.
9. In fact, Françoise-Louise de Warens received a pension from the Church for propagating the Catholic faith to youngsters like Rousseau especially if they came from Geneva, the historical foundation of the Reformation.
10. The *Spirito Sancto* in Turin, a hospice of the catechumens. Here Rousseau was prepared for his baptism, which took place on April 23rd, 1728. After that, Rousseau, who was 16 years old, stayed more than a year in Turin, working in service.
11. His wife, Madame d'Eybens, was a friend of Françoise-Louise de Warens in Grenoble.
12. He first visited Paris in September, 1731 for a few days and was very disillusioned.
13. "It is a mistake to regard the government of Venice as a genuine aristocracy. For while the Venetian people has no part in the government, the Venetian nobility is itself a people" (Rousseau 2004a, p. 130). See also Voltaire, *Idées républicaines* XXXV.
14. "I almost found him ponderous in his thinking, clumsy in his speech, always exhausting himself in search of the right word which never came to him, and tangling up ideas that were already unclear by his poor manner of expressing them" (Rousseau 1990, pp. 108–9).
15. Rousseau (2000, p. 322) himself describes the futile attempt to provide her with some education. He says that she was "limited" but had proven to be an excellent advisor throughout all difficult situations in his life (*ibid.*, p. 323).
16. Hotel Saint-Quentin, no. 57 Rue des Petits-Champs in Paris. For details of her life see Hastier (1965).
17. *Confessions*, Book VII. Rousseau wrote about their mutual affections: "She believed she had found in me a man of honour; she was not mistaken; I believed I had found in her a sensitive, simple, and unaffected girl; I was not mistaken either" (Rousseau 2000, p. 321).
18. Boswell visited Rousseau in December, 1764 in Môtiers. He later went to Corsica and returned to London in February, 1766 accompanied by Thérèse Lavasseur. The affair happened on their way from Paris to London (Damrosch 2005, pp. 409ff.).

19. An "intellectually disadvantaged creature" (Edmonds and Eidinow 2006, p. 111).
20. They were married on August 29th in a civil ceremony that took place at the Auberge de la Fontaine d'Or in Bourgoin near Lyon. This form of marriage had no legal standing.
21. Thérèse Lavasseur outlived Rousseau by more than twenty years and was sole heir to all his writings, manuscripts, and other author's rights. After his death she lived in the town of Plessis-Belleville near Ermenonville without marrying again.
22. Letter to Pierre-Alexandre DuPeyrou dated July 2nd, 1771.
23. Original title: *Le devin du village*; first performance at Fontainebleau, October 18th, 1752.
24. Documents of Voltaire's readings on Rousseau can be found in Havens (1933).
25. The latest and best work on Voltaire and his views on Rousseau is Pearson (2005).
26. Rousseau describes moving to La Chevrette in his *Confessions* (2000, pp. 393ff.).
27. Louise Tardieu d'Esclavelle de la Live, Madame d'Epinay (1726–1783), led a *salon* of liberal discussion on her estate at Montmorency near Paris. After 1770 the *salon* moved to Paris, remaining a center of intellectual discourse. She first met Rousseau in 1747. The relationship broke up because of Rousseau's passion for Sophie d'Houdetot (1730–1813), Louise d'Epinay's cousin. Rousseau's passion remained unrequited, as can be read in Book IX of his *Confessions*.
28. Literature of *Storm and Stress*.
29. For example, one of Voltaire's polemical texts against Rousseau is called "sentiments des citoyens" (Voltaire 1961, pp. 715–18). It was written and published in late 1764.
30. The scene is described in the *Confessions* in a very dramatic way: Rousseau 2000, pp. 621ff.
31. *The Letters of David Hume* (1932).
32. Jean-Jacques de Luze was the owner of the estate of Bied and a famous factory owner in Prussian Neuenburg.
33. "Je tiens Jean-Jacques Rousseau."
34. *London Chronicle*, January 16th, 1766. Also the January edition of the *Monthly Review* reported on Rousseau, as well as the *London Magazine* in its February edition (Courtois 1923, p. 182).
35. As Hume understood it, it was about a perk which was not as such communicated to Rousseau, so that the latter felt he was being treated like a child (Edmonds and Eidinow 2006, p. 151). As Rousseau

understood it, there was an indiscretion by Hume, who wanted to read one of Rousseau's letters (*ibid.*, p. 174).

36. On March 29th, 1766 Rousseau wrote to Hume that indeed he was accommodated according to his taste but that he was annoyed by being spoken to in English, a language which he understood as little as the culture of the country (Correspondance t. XXIX, pp. 66–7). However, Rousseau was able to read English correspondence.

37. *St. James's Chronicle*, April 3rd, 1766. Rousseau answered by public statement on April 7th, 1766, which was published in the *Chronicle* edition of April 8th–10th.

38. In a letter to Frederick II on November 1st, 1762 he rejected every personal perk and gave up on subsidies. Instead, he told the Prussian king to look after his people, whose father he wanted to be after all (Correspondance t. XIV, p. 1).

39. Immediately before, on March 30th, 1766, Rousseau had sent a short note to the king, telling him how much he was in need of his proctection while in exile (Correspondance t. XIV, p. 76).

40. Letter to Henry Seymour Conway (1721–1795). At this time Field Marshal Conway was Head of the Northern Department of the British government. He had arranged the pension by the king.

41. This story shows some irony. In the end only Thérèse received a state pension, not by the British king, however, but by the French Revolution.

42. The French edition, organized by Paris friends of Hume, was published in October, 1766; the English version, which was partly different from it, was published in London one month later.

43. Walpole's report on the argument dates from September 13th, 1767.

44. A key situation from the year 1766 is described by Walpole as follows: "Rousseau, quitting his Armenian masquerade, crossed the country with his *gouvernante* and arrived at Boston in Lincolnshire. There a gentleman who admired his writings waited on him, offered him assistance in money, and called him *the great Rousseau*. He replied with warmth, 'No sir, no, I am not *the great Rousseau*, I am the poor neglected Rousseau, of whom nobody takes any notice'" (Walpole 1797, p. 254).

45. Lord Richard Davenport (1706/1707–1807) was Rousseau's host on the estate of Wootton Hall from March 22nd, 1766 to May 1st, 1767. Davenport tried to educate his grandson according to the principles of *Emile*.

46. This was not the first invitation. In a letter from February 19th, 1763 Rousseau regrets not having accepted an earlier invitation to London and thus having missed the opportunity to philosophize together with Hume (Correspondance t. XV, pp. 198–9).

47. Both, however, make up a large part of the correspondence (Correspondance t. XXIV, pp. 7ff.).
48. "The brightest parts, the most established fame, could not satisfy him, unless he was the perpetual object of admiration and discourse; and to keep this attention, he descended at all the little tricks of a mountebank" (Walpole 1797, p. 254).
49. What was published was *Rêveries du promeneur solitaire* 1782.
50. The majority of the 37 different fragments were published at different places in the nineteenth century. The integral text was published in 1905 in the first volume of *Annales de la Société Jean-Jacques Rousseau*.
51. For example, the letter to Jacqueline Danel from July 22nd, 1761.

Part 2

Critical Exposition of Rousseau's Work

2

Basic Ideas of Philosophy

In several respects it is not really possible to speak of a "philosophy" as presented by Rousseau. Neither did he present a system of philosophy nor did he write scholarly historical studies nor found new sub-disciplines of philosophy, as in the eighteenth century David Hume did for the theory of knowledge or Georges-Louis Leclerc de Buffon for the theory of nature. Rousseau was not a *philosophe* like Voltaire, Grimm, or Diderot, that is he was not a man of public speech and Enlightenment. Rousseau was a writer, a composer, an essayist; he wrote in an elegant style and a very musical way, and his way of thinking was in opposition to the doctrines of his time. Arguably, his passion was for music and botany, not for public speech.

His thoughts, however, show sharp contours: they are "philosophical" in the sense of an unmistakable way of asking questions and solving problems. Fundamental to Rousseau's philosophy is his attitude toward religion, which does not give up on the idea of a Supreme Being (être suprème) or of God without speaking in favor of the doctrines of the Christian Churches. If God can be recognized, not by Himself but by creation, that is nature. Thus, nature is more fundamental than society. Man is a part of nature; social community of men is a state which is following this and artificial, its relationship to nature necessarily being precarious.

From combining these three elements – creation, nature, and society – there results a key question on Rousseau's philosophy of education: how could man be prepared for society if this weakens him and does not allow his nature to develop? Or in other words and less paradoxically: how is a kind of education possible which refers to man's nature and makes him self-confident and steadfast in himself, autarchic in this sense, so that he will survive in society and still be himself? Thus, the goal of education would be to maintain man's natural strength, which is understood by Rousseau to be a commodity of God's creation.

Both questions were new: nobody dealing with education theory before Rousseau had so precariously related "nature" and "society" to each other without giving priority to *society* or its institutions, that is following the quintessential Aristotelian vision of society as preceding the individual. And nobody before had considered society to be changeable in favour of *man*, provided the latter is able to keep his nature and develop himself by help of education. This way, society is put in a critical position toward man's nature. Only if the nature of man can be developed by itself, and according to its own guidelines, will society find legitimacy. Society, Rousseau claimed, is not an end in itself.

This question can be explained by Rousseau's marginal position in society and his fragile self. His theory of man comes from the outsider's sharpened awareness. Man's nature must develop, but how can education contribute to making man able to live congruent with his nature without being dependent on other people's judgment? Constant comparison with others weakens man; he can be part of society – that is always a sort of comparison – only after having become "sovereign". This question is the key to *Emile* and thus to the concept of so often misunderstood and only superficially interpreted "natural education."

Rousseau was not afraid of thinking paradoxically; on the contrary, he enjoyed his paradoxes. After all, his philosophy does not offer clear solutions: contradictions remain unresolved and it absolutely invites objection. Not coincidently, the motto of this philosophy is found in the second book of *Emile*. After having introduced his most debated conceived idea, that is bringing children up in a natural way in a moratorium away from society, Rousseau notes on his way of thinking: "I hope that every-day readers will excuse my paradoxes; you cannot avoid paradox if you think for yourself, and whatever you may say I would rather fall into paradox than into prejudice" (Rousseau 1993, S. 67).

He was not a *philosophe*, Rousseau writes to Charles-Hubert Méreau (1725–1795) on March 1st, 1763. Méreau, who worked at the court of Saxe-Gotha, was a French dance master and a pupil of the famous François-Robert Marcel. Rousseau told him that one should beware of philosophers because they make everything difficult and demand special teaching everywhere, even where none is necessary (Correspondance t. XV, p. 249). He himself, Rousseau says, echoing Socrates, had never wanted to be a philosopher and had no ambition ever to be one (*ibid.*). After all, "philosopher" is only a title and not a name of value or merits, and then one has to ask: "Can you force a man to merit a title despite himself, one he does not want to bear?" (Rousseau 1937, p. 260)

To this question Rousseau adds a distinction which is fundamental to his work: "I know it is permitted only to philosophers to give out Philosophy, but every man may talk about philosophy and I have done nothing more than this" (*ibid.*). Not everybody is able to talk *of* philosophy, as this requires knowledge of them, but everybody is allowed to speak *about* philosophy, and he, Rousseau claims, had done nothing other than that. And this is not about a new system of philosophy and thus about a discourse among experts but about concrete problems visible to everyone. Philosophy, he concludes, is *not* what philosophers claim.

Rousseau declares himself an enemy of philosophical abstractions which he constantly discusses, however, and not only to refute them. But his attitude was against "philosophers." Farmers, he wrote to his long-term correspondent Malherbes[1] on January 28th, 1762, are by far more useful members of society than those sitting around in academies and doing nothing really. Farmers act for themselves and their subsistence, they do not depend on other people's opinions and in this sense they are independent. This conclusion is connected to another essential topic of Rousseau's thoughts: "It is necessary to warn the people of the madness of opinions which will make them unhappy" (Correspondance t. X, p. 64).

He defines the sovereign way of life as being independent of others. Freedom means not having to obey anybody, especially in respect of intellect. At the same time, Rousseau demands high morals from himself, which in a letter to the Genevan watchmaker Christophe Beauchâteau (1729–1803) from February 26th, 1763 he describes thus: "I only wanted to know how to write to learn how to love the good ones and how to hate the bad ones" (Correspondance t. XV, p. 239). And in another letter from March 21st, 1763 he says about the addressee of the books: "My ideas are a suggestion to those working with young people; but I do not know how to write for young people" (Correspondance t. XV, pp. 309–10).

Natural Religion

Rousseau was not a "materialist" like other philosophers of the Paris Enlightenment, who in the mid-eighteenth century presented radical theories of negating every idea of God and any kind of religion at all. Rousseau did not do so. Although he criticized theological dogmas and the hierarchy of the Churches, even rejecting doctrines of a personal and punishing God, he did not deduce materialist conclusions from this. The third way was a philosophical theory which had developed in Britain during the seventeenth century and which one century later was shared by many intellectuals in Europe and America, that is the theory of *deism* (Oelkers 2006). According to this theory, God is not a single although distant *person* to which human expectations could be connected. The object of belief is a deity whom the founder of British deism, Edward Herbert of Cherbury (1583–1649), called *supreme deity*. Believing in this deity is not tied to denominations or doctrines and it requires only one attitude, that is "virtue combined with pity."[2] This superior being or deity cannot be proven by supernatural insights or miracles. If this deity appears, it is in creation and not as a person toward which one may turn ritually or mystically. Thus, there can also be no revelation which is connected to an unexplainable act of mercy.

John Toland (1670–1722) postulated in 1696[3] that Christianity was not mysterious but compatible with the human intellect. This means that practical morals do not need a religious dogma but may rely on reason; the same is true for religion. It is reasonable to believe in a superior being without needing a mystery for this. Such a rational approach to belief allowed the deists historically to criticize the text of the Bible and thus to move away from literally interpreting the Old and New Testaments.[4] In the eighteenth century Newton's physics were also connected to this theory, which assumes that God must be understood to be the "first mover," who, although having started the world's motion, does not interfere with it.

Many intellectuals and contemporaries of Rousseau, like Denis Diderot, drew the skeptical conclusion from this that neither the Christian God nor the "deity" of the deists were open to human experience and that human knowledge was thus to stay free from transcendental speculation. Knowledge and understanding start out from sensual experience, with the last referring man to himself and not to a mystical form of belief. Certainly, man is a part of nature, but nature does not know any higher principle than itself. Thus, it is not creation but a physical fact. A "superior being" is as unnecessary for the laws of nature as for man's business.[5]

The most important document on this concept is the *Encyclopédie ou dictionnaire raisonnée des sciences, des arts et des métiers*, published between 1751 and 1776, with Diderot substantially contributing to it, and reaching a total of 28 volumes. The *Encyclopédie* assumes the world to be rationally controllable, which besides sciences, arts, and professions does not know or need any transcendence. Religions are reduced to personal belief without being able to grasp outside nature and the empirical world. Typical for the *Encyclopédie* was the didactic principle of seeking the greatest transparency for the way of explaining nature and for communicating the facts (Bürchler 2004). Any remaining mysticism became a private affair.

Rousseau, although contributing to the *Encyclopédie*, did not follow this idea. For him, man has access to the superior being or to the deity because man is part of God's creation. Access to God is described by a theory of sentiment, which is fundamental for Rousseau's natural religion. God is too big for human intellect, but that does not mean that man has no connection to the Divine. It is only that this access cannot be sought by way of intellect but from the heart. The heart feels God where reason might hold doubt. And imagining God is not a question of knowledge.

To a certain extent Rousseau was a sensualist, like all deists after John Locke (1632–1704), that is he assumed that in the mind there cannot be anything which has not been experienced by the senses beforehand. Locke renewed this doctrine from antiquity in 1689[6] and turned it toward psychology. The structure of the unfolding mind is understood from the child's process of learning. Life begins with simple ideas which become more complex and are habitualized in the course of growing up. Rousseau followed Locke's sensualism as far as the structure of cognition was concerned. For Rousseau, like Locke, there are no innate ideas and no impersonal soul independent of learning processes; however, for Rousseau intelligence cannot be derived from the senses, and this brought him into conflict with Lockean sensualism.

Intellect is not everything. Besides it, there exists a world of intuition, which is described by the metaphor of the "heart" and which goes beyond the world of intellect. God or the deity is to be felt with one's heart. The basis of belief is not intellect, like in Toland or the other British deists, but the French *sentiment*. Voltaire had taught that only cultivated intellect could lead to a non-dogmatic belief; Rousseau, in contrast, starts out from the unadulterated, natural feeling of the heart. True belief does not require education but a natural religion and hence as natural an upbringing as possible.

This changes also the question about true Christianity. In a letter to Daniel de Pury, the Procureur of Neuchâtel, Rousseau wrote on December 30th, 1763: "True Christianity is nothing other than natural religion, explained in a better way" (Correspondance t. XIV, p. 234). All human knowledge, the letter continues, is confronted with objections, and many face unsolvable difficulties. No philosophy is able to answer the essential questions. This is true also for Christianity and its doctrines. Whatever one may call the believers, "friends of truth," "men of belief," or "true Christians," they are not able to solve the fundamental difficulties of knowledge, even if they constantly claim to be able (*ibid.*). Different from them are those who do not assume any access through intellect but believe with their hearts.

The dualism of "heart" and "intellect" was founded by Blaise Pascal (1623–1662) in his *Pensées*,[7] to which Rousseau referred on occasion. The theology of the heart was indeed a spiritual movement which at the end of the seventeenth and the beginning of the eighteenth centuries had a strong influence on the idea and organization of piety. One of these circles was the monastery (and important educational institute) of Port Royal near Paris, where Pascal wrote down his *Pensées*. Here, the theory of mercy of the Dutch bishop Cornelius Jansen (1585–1638) was taught and spread, according to which man's redemption is dependent completely and only on God's will. God's will cannot be influenced by anyone or anything, that is not even by the rules and regulations of the Church. Thus, what is left for man is only humility of the heart.

The doctrines of the "Jansenists" were banned by the Pope in 1719, ten years before the monastery of Port Royal had been destroyed by order of the French King Louis XIV. The mystical theory of the heart was considered a threat to the believers' loyalty to the doctrines of the Church. The Jansenists, who throughout the entire eighteenth century were able to maintain their spiritual influence, were opposed by the Jesuits, who above all contested the anti-intellectual aspect of Jansen's doctrines.[8] The Jesuits were banned in France in 1764 after their schools of higher education (collèges) had been disbanded one year before, due not least to the influence of the Jansenists.

There are good reasons for understanding the doctrines of the Jansenists to be one of the points of reference for Rousseau's thoughts (Osterwalder 1995, 2002) although they were not accepted unconditionally – Rousseau (2000, pp. 558ff.) felt persecuted by the Paris Jansenists[9] – but as a leitmotif of his reflection. Here, relativizing reason during the age of Enlightenment finds one of its origins. In the face of nature's greatness and grandeur, Rousseau did not believe in the superiority of the human mind, which despite all education will never be able to solve the contradictions of the world and to become finally perfect. Thus, knowledge requires humility. At the same time the Jansenists strengthened the concept of education because it is the only way to guide the nature of man toward humility.

To criticism, Rousseau answers[10] that true belief (religion essentielle) results in an attitude which he says to be "simple et ignorant" and thus able to serve God by the simplicity of the heart without getting lost in theological speculation (Correspondance t. XVI, pp. 261–2). This, he says, is not meant against Christian religion but would just lead the latter back to its core (Correspondance t. XV, p. 309).[11] This core is a moral attitude and not a dogmatic conviction. This attitude is the precondition of acting, and it has nothing to do with achievement and merit, as taught by the Calvinists. Natural religion does not need any kind of dogma but reduces belief to intuition.

The intellectual focus of Rousseau's *Emile* is formed by a confession, the "creed of a Savoyard priest."[12] This is most unusual for a theory of education and can hardly be explained if one has only the interpretations of those educationalists in mind who suppose Rousseau to be the founder of "natural education" and connect him to the child-centered education of the twentieth century. Rousseau is considered their first author, and in fact there are in particular many passages in *Emile*, as mentioned above, in the first three books which may be connected to postulations of child-centered education. It is very easy to make these connections but it is not what Rousseau intended.

Rousseau does not have a concept of child in mind to be defined psychologically. Rather, he discusses a theological problem, that is under which conditions the child could be thought to be free from original sin and what would be the consequences of this step for education. Thus, essentially Rousseau argues for a post-Augustinean theory of education which does not start out from original sin but focuses on good nature. This aims against the Augustine-based Christian doctrine of sinful nature and the countless theories connected to it on how education might be possible under the precondition of sin. Rousseau's *Emile* is the anticlimax of these theories.

Rousseau asks what nature must be like to be considered God's creation on the one hand, but reverses the Christian myth of creation at a decisive point on the other hand, that is the consequences of the expulsion from Paradise. Augustine had taught that sin was both precondition and result of expulsion, which was to be passed on until the end of the world. Rousseau wanted to show that in nature there could be no sin at all and that the primordial state is not a paradise from which men could be expelled. If at all, they are only able to expel themselves, and not from Paradise but from the primordial state. This, however, requires a different idea of God than that which is referred to by Augustine.

As in the case of the Jansenists, Rousseau's view of humility and simplicity of the heart assumes an unrecognizable God, who exists but evades human intellect. For Rousseau, God is infinite and represents superior intelligence, a doctrine which he adopts in part from the English philosopher Samuel Clarke (1675–1729). Clarke also coined the expression *natural religion*,[13] which Rousseau, however, used in his own way, that is following his very special theology of the heart which does not play any role in Clarke. Clarke's attack was meant against materialist philosophy, which understands nature to be without intelligence, moving in accordance to mechanical laws, and to require neither creation nor intelligent further development.

Rousseau adopts the doctrine of superior intelligence, but adds that in the face of infinite God man is not alone because he may rely on nature within and around himself. This requires a non-corrupt, "pure" access to nature that only children and believers can possess. For Rousseau, nature is not Milton's *Paradise Lost* but the only experience from which it is possible to deduce God or the Divine. Compared with Calvinism, Rousseau argues that man is not close to mercy through the sum of his deeds, but reaches God through feeling, as far as the original purity of the heart can be maintained. God manifests himself by his deeds and "he reveals himself to enlightened people in the spectacle of nature" (Rousseau 2001, p. 41).

During his exile at Môtiers (1762–1765) Rousseau had to cope with accusations of "deism"[14] and of denying the Christian faith. His *Letters Written from the Mountain* (1764) must be understood as a justification for his two banned books from 1762.[15] The history of this ban, whose consequences he had never anticipated, initiated Rousseau's *Letters*. In April, 1762 the *Contrat Social* had been published in Amsterdam; in May, 1762, simulataneously in Amsterdam and Paris, *Emile*, which was instantly banned by the Parliament or High Court of Paris. The reasons for this ban were given in a *mandement* by the Archbishop of Paris, written especially for the case, which considered the child's innocence and thus education of pure nature to be incompatible with the doctrine of original sin and the educational demands of the Church.

In the eyes of the Church the children of God must be those who in the Augustinean sense accept the world's original sinfulness (peccatum originale) and thus that of their own nature. Who denies this must be dangerous. Rousseau repeatedly made statements against original sin in his letters, but he denied that this could be dangerous. On April 25th, 1762, from Montmorency, he wrote to his close friend Paul-Claude Moultou (1731–1797)[16] in Geneva that the accusation could not be true, simply because the people had a positive religion based on historical authorities and not endangered by books like his. Also, the people in Geneva in particular would not simply give up on their own religion, which was not, incidentally, dependent on miracles. Whoever considers the people only from the point of view of their belief in miracles does not take them at all seriously regarding their belief (Correspondance t. X, pp. 209–10).

But that did not help much. Rousseau, 40 years of age, had to leave his *petit château* on June 9th, 1762 under dramatic circumstances[17] and at first intended to flee to Geneva, but had soon recognized how hopeless that was. He traveled on to the city of Yverdon at the southern end of Lake Neuchâtel, where his friend Daniel Roguin (1691–1771) lived, but stayed there only a short time and then moved to his exile at Môtiers. Here he observed the events in Geneva, which challenged him to give reasons to his attitude toward Christian faith again and to publicly defend it. It was about nothing less than to prove that only natural religion was an appropriate expression of the message of Christian faith.

On June 19th, 1762 the Geneva Small Council (*Petit Conseil*) condemned both the *Contrat Social* and *Emile*; copies which had already been delivered to Geneva were publicly torn apart and burned. Rousseau was banned from entering his home town, while having a premonition that this ban would be permanent. When Rousseau received the news he wrote to Paul-Claude Moultou on June 22nd, 1762 that this ban was hard to believe: "What! A writ against one without being heard! And where is the violation? Where are the proofs of it? Oh man of Geneva, if this is your liberty, I find it little to be regretted" (Rousseau 1937, p. 242).

After his return to the Calvinist Church in 1754 Rousseau became a citizen of the city again. He had to be prepared for his books to be banned, but he felt the ban on entering the city to be unconstitutional, as he believed that he could not be thrown out as a citizen. After having been granted asylum in the Prussian enclave of Neuenburg[18] he decided on a radical solution. In a letter from May 12th, 1763 he gave back his citizenship, which triggered off a long argument on constitution. The letter renouncing his citizenship was addressed to Jacob Favre, *Premier syndic*[19] de la République de Genève. Essentially, Rousseau's dramatic letter concerned the question of which rights the citizens of Geneva had against the patricians who ruled the city. In this sense Rousseau's letter initiated a republican debate the like of which had never before been held in Geneva.

The Geneva Prokurator General, Jean-Robert Tronchin,[20] interfered in this quarrel[21] by writing a polemic entitled *Lettres écrites de la campagne* (*Letters written from the country*). It was printed outside Geneva, which was to be understood symbolically. Rousseau took this title and turned to irony; he resided some seven hundred meters above Lake Neuenburg and thus wrote his answering letters "down from the mountain." Rousseau thus seized the opportunity to defend his ideas. The public, being mainly concerned with theology, was more interested in this defense than in the original writings and thus in Rousseau's theories.

Rousseau commented on the Geneva constitutional problem only in the last three out of nine letters. His main interest was to make clear the theological core of the problem, and it is not a coincidence that in the course of this he spoke principally on the question of the reality of miracles. Belief in supernatural, physically unexplainable "miracles" was a widespread phenomenon in the eighteenth century throughout all classes. Since the deists, the attitude of the Churches, especially the Catholic Church, toward miracles had been an essential criterion, so it was no coincidence that Rousseau's defense started here.

In his *Letters Written from the Mountain* Rousseau commented on two essential passages of his theory, the *religion civile* at the end of *Contrat Social* and most of all the confession of the Savoyard vicar in the fourth book of *Emile*.[22] Both passages are anti-Church and show a basic deist conviction, although Rousseau, as did Clarke, rejected deist rationalism. By his natural religion of God, Rousseau represents ideas which were indeed suitable for challenging the Christian denominations and for making bans plausible. Rousseau knew this and in his apology concentrated on his enemies' weak spots.

God's revelation, as Rousseau writes in the third letter, does not need any miracles for evidence (O.C. III, p. 733). That which is called "miracles" by doctrinaire theology are allegories and parables (*ibid.*); if there is proof then it is in Jesus's words, that is in moral preaching and not in miracles (*ibid.*, p. 734). Jesus did not want to astonish people but to produce virtue. In this sense he is an educator and not a magician. The core of Christian religion is the example of Jesus, which speaks for itself and does not need to be communicated by churches and doctrines.

If "miracle" is understood to be an immediately visible act by the divine power which changes natural order and is a true exception from the laws of nature,[23] two questions must be asked: is God *able* and is He *willing* to do miracles? The first question is answered by itself: God is infinite, which also means that His power is indefinite; "God is able to make miracles happen," but this is not the subject of human thoughts. Thus, whoever negates the question if God is *able to do* miracles is "absurd," but this question can only be negated if asked, something which has to be ruled out (*ibid.*, p. 737).

The second question – is God *willing* to do miracles? – has very often led to religious dispute, but it is as unnecessary, the reason given in an argument by Pascal: we do not know anything of God except His immeasurability (immensité) (*ibid.*). If we used miracles as evidence of belief, we would need witnesses and signs, but then we would have to deliver immeasurability to *human* hands, something which again has to be ruled out (*ibid.*, pp. 737–8). Nobody can guarantee God's immeasurability, as this would at once doubt omnipotence and thus would be nothing more than arrogation.

It must be added that, for Rousseau, miracles cannot be distinguished from superstition.[24] Superstition is an instrument of political power and requires absence of knowledge. The authority of miracles is based on the ignorance of those for whom they are performed (*ibid.*, p. 742). Their evidence is evidence for simple people (les simples), who perceive the natural laws only in their closest vicinity. But the spheres of knowledge will be extended the more the people will be taught, and only then will they feel how much knowledge they are still lacking and thus what remains to be learned (*ibid.*, pp. 742–3).[25]

Rousseau is thus far a philosopher of Enlightenment and these thoughts somewhat contradict his First Discourse. He defends physical knowledge against the unreasonable demands of religious doctrines (*ibid.*, p. 741). Belief in miracles is the decisive provocation for this; miracles contradict the knowledge of the laws of nature, which are constantly improving without coming to an end. To be true, miracles would have to transcend the laws of nature, which in the eyes of learned people is an impossible demand. No knowing person (sage) is thus able to tell if a miracle is a miracle, as "miracles" happen beyond the boundaries of knowledge (*ibid.*, p. 744). And even if there were true miracles, of what use would they be if they could not be distinguished from the false ones? (*ibid.*) For evidence, there would only ever be *symbols*, but symbols by themselves do not prove anything;[26] one can only interpret symbols and do so endlessly (*ibid.*, p. 745).

The symbols of the "whole" are never the whole itself; conclusion from imagination on reality is not possible, otherwise nature – essential for Rousseau – could not be understood to be an entity independent from man. Occult "entireties" contradict reason, something which Rousseau assumes. Reason depends on observation, modern science does not describe the symbols of nature but *nature itself*, and it is not possible either to conclude from sheer symbols on the hidden nature of things, or, even less, to expect miracles from nature which might overcome its laws. Nature's reactions cannot be influenced by magic circles and other esoteric calculations, as claimed as a matter of course in the mid-eighteenth century by countless occult writings.

On the other hand, Rousseau wants to avoid materialist conclusions. By chance, his deist confession is in *Emile*, in the philosophy of "pure" or "natural" education. This *profession de foi*, which was his own,[27] is commented on in his letter, already mentioned, from March 21st, 1763 to Jean Burnand, saying that there was nothing in it to deny religion (Correspondance t. XV, p. 309). However, this confession does also not contain anything which could be used for Christian doctrines. The truth which he loved, as Rousseau wrote in another letter from December, 1763 to an unknown recipient, had nothing to do with metaphysics but only with morals (*ibid.*, p. 269). And even if he loved any metaphysical truth, it would not come from books (*ibid.*).

Rousseau is not interested in doctrinaire truths, and this is not about taking the position of a heretic who denies certain dogmas of the Church in favor of his own. Much more the basic principle of faith, the reason why there shall be faith *at all* shall be made clear. For this, no denominational doctrines are needed, nor holy texts, but only humility and simplicity of the heart. The confession of the Savoyard vicar, in other words, could also have been written by Pascal in respect of its essential statements. That kind of truth which is useful for us is *next to* us, writes Rousseau;[28] one must know how to take it up and use it directly, it does not require scientific teaching and it is not based on books (Correspondance t. III, p. 269).

This can only be imagined if we have Rousseau's concept of nature in mind. To understand "next to us" there is only nature, which can always and directly be experienced without teaching. The Savoyard vicar confesses that he had found peace for his soul only after having experienced himself to be in accordance with nature. This had become possible by giving up on all spiritual comparisons and only reading in the book of nature (O.C. IV, pp. 624–5). Knowledge, and in particular knowledge of "philosophie moderne" (*ibid.*, pp. 595–6) was essential but contemplation or intuition of the heart. A key sentence of the confession is thus "We can be man without being educated" ("Nous pouvons être hommes sans être savans") (*ibid.*, p. 601).[29]

The letter from the end of December, 1763 comments on this sentence as follows: "I believe, but I do not know it; I do not even know if the science which I am lacking would be a good thing for me even if I had it; and then it is perhaps not necessary that I say: *Alto quoevisit coelo lucem, ingemuitque reperta*" (Correspondance t. III, p. 270). God is served best by simplicity of the heart, and then the dogmas and cults of single religions are no longer important, only intuition. For this there stands the metaphor of the "heart" which opens up the access to the book of nature. Another key sentence in the confession of the Savoyard vicar is: "The essential cult is that of the heart" ("Le culte essenciel est celui du coeur") (O.C. IV, p. 627).

In British contemporary literature, the "language of the heart" was an often chosen metaphor to characterize people who were supposed to appear as good or simple people, sometimes leaving open how this attribution was meant. One example is found in Alexander Pope's *Epistle to Dr Arbruthnot*[30] from 1734. The "good man"[31] travels through life innocuously, never experiences accusation, nor has to swear oaths, nor needs to risk a lie. He does not know temptation because he speaks the language of the heart and not that of education.

> Un-unlearn'd, he knew no Schoolmans' subtle Art,
> No Language, but the Language of the Heart.
> By Nature honest, by Experience wise,
> Healthy by Temp'rance and by Exercise:
> His Life, tho' long, to sickness past unknown,
> His Death was instant, and without a groan   (Pope 1961, p. 126)

Rousseau gives utmost dignity to the language of the heart. It is not only a random characterization, which could also be understood satirically, but the only reliable articulation of faith. It does not – as in Pope's example – require formal education but is meant as a general principle, not as the specific feature of an individual. The "cult of the heart" must be understood as criticism of contemporary materialist philosophy which does not deal anymore with religious questions but ignores them resolutely.

For Rousseau, God or the superior being is the *prima causa* of the universe. The cause of material movements is not itself a material one; divine will moves the universe and animates (animer) nature (O.C. IV, p. 576). God is active without a cause (cet Etre actif par lui-même), but this is only the human idea of God, not an insight. God evades both senses and intellect; He exists without our being able to know *how* or *why* (*ibid.*, p. 581). What

God does and whether He "acts" at all is obscure to man. God is only the first cause; every other form of causality is inappropriate.

Only nature – creation, not the creator – can be experienced, and from nature there comes how man must live, according to that which he knows to read from *its* book. Rousseau renews this early Christian topos[32] in his own way. Instead of seeing God's book, in other words the Bible, and the book of nature as contiguous and referring to each other, one shall mistrust the text and its interpretation and shall only rely on the book of nature. Only one who is able to do so will experience a reliable guideline for his life: "Take away our fatal progress, take away our faults and our vices, take away man's handiwork, and all is well" (Rousseau 1993, p. 293). And to be more precise: "Where all is well, there is no such thing as injustice. Justice and goodness are inseparable" (*ibid.*).

The "Book of Nature" is not, as in the Christian Middle Ages,[33] a true description of nature, something which would require distance. Much more, nature is *immediately* felt and experienced, only this way is it a reliable guideline for action. In this sense Rousseau has indeed a natural religion in mind, which is seen as a release from the evils of society. On December 6th, 1760, in the midst of working on *Emile*, Rousseau writes in a letter that he could hardly imagine somebody to take religion more seriously than him. But he despised those who by way of it had brought barbarious, unjust, and harmful states into society (Correspondance t. II, p. 133).

True belief requires criticism of practiced religion. A little less than two years before, on February 18th, 1758, he writes to his Geneva compatriot Jacob Vernes (1729–1791)[34] that he, Rousseau, definitely had a religion despite all suspicions. Only, he did not believe in that which everywhere around him was claimed and practiced as "religion." Also, he had not relied on philosophy which with its naïve belief in reason had only increased uncertainty and which lacked the most simple sufficient answers. "So I have abandoned reason to its fate, and consulted nature, that is to say, the internal sentiment which directs my belief independently of my reason" (Rousseau 1937, p. 147).

But why does natural religion refer to *good* nature? Whoever reads in the book of nature objectively might come to the conclusion that nature has also an evil side if, for example, it *destroys* those "handiworks" of man (ouvrages de l'homme: O.C. IV, p. 388) which are useful in God's eyes or which can serve the idea of the good. Rousseau's answer again refers to the God of creation: nature is good because God can only be wanting the good: God is not the God of the dead but of the living. He could not be destructive or evil without doing harm to himself. He who can do all can only will what is good: "The omnipotent can only will what is good" (Rousseau 1993, p. 293).

From this concludes self-knowledge: the more I turn my gaze inward, the more I read myself, and the more I read these words written in my soul: "Be just and you will be happy" (*ibid.*). The opposite is not true. Who is happy cannot be just because he is "happy." It is much more that whoever wants to be happy must be just. Justice means accordance with moral principles, something which must be found by way of the heart, even if this demands the price of happiness and company. No price is too high for virtue, and its organ is the heart, not education, which accordingly can only be negative.

Pursuit of happiness is not the primary objective of man, as that requires pretense and distance from the simple truths of natural religion. Happiness is tied to society and not to humility. The latter can only be caused by belief, as far as it does not come along with lectures and does not require teaching by the Church. In December, 1763 Rousseau wrote to an unknown Madame de B. who wanted to ask him about true religion while referring to Voltaire of all people: "You have a religion which is free from every kind of examination; follow it by the simplicity of the heart. This is the best piece of advice I could offer you, and I myself follow it as well as I can" (Correspondance t. XVIII, p. 186).

Before this, on August 1st, 1763, in a letter to Paul-Claude Moultou, he had commented on the accusation of being a materialist, with which he had been confronted by Jacob Vernes, for example. Rousseau, Vernes said, used the "jargon of metaphysics," and only in this way was he able to support a "religion naturelle" apart from Christian teaching. This criticism refers to the materialist Claude-Adrien Helvétius (1715–1771) and his book *De l'esprit*, which had been published in 1758. The essential principle of this book is *juger est sentir* – judging is feeling, but Rousseau says he did not share this opinion. Thus, Vernes accused him of that which had been claimed by Helvétius and misunderstood that, and how Rousseau had refuted materialism in *Professions de foi* (Correspondance t. XVII, pp. 114–15).

Indeed, for Rousseau "to judge" and "to feel" are two different faculties which cannot be referred to each other. This is the basis of his refutation of materialism. "To perceive is to feel, to compare is to judge, to judge and to feel are not the same" (Rousseau 1993, p. 279). "Mind" is not simply a more complex kind of sensation, as Helvétius had assumed. Judgment requires intelligence, but intelligence cannot be explained by referring to sensual perception. From perceptions alone never comes intelligent judgment which compares different impressions and thus must be more than these impressions themselves or their association.

In more detail, this is said as follows: "Through sensation objects present themselves to me separately and singly as they are in nature; by comparing them I rearrange them, I shift them so to speak, I place one upon another to decide whether they are alike or different, or more generally to find out their relations" (*ibid.*). The intelligent power, which compares and judges, must be more than classification:

> To my mind, the distinctive faculty of an active or intelligent being is the power of understanding this word "is". I seek in vain in the merely sensitive entity that intelligent force which compares and judges; I can find no trace of it in its nature. This passive entity will be aware of each object separately, it will even be aware of the whole formed by the two together, but having no power to place them side by side it can never compare them, it can never form a judgment with regard to them. (*ibid.*)

This power of mind, which brings sensual perceptions together and compares them, can be named differently, "attention, meditation, reflection, or what you will." The decisive aspect is that it is *in me* and not in things or in objects; reflection is not simply mirroring of material objects or events. Reflection is a creation and it can be created only by myself, although this is only possible if I have an impression of things. But things alone and impressions do not reveal anything if they are not examined and intelligently connected. "Though I am compelled to feel or not to feel, I am free to examine more or less what I feel" (*ibid.*, p. 280).

This way I can become "sure of myself," says Rousseau (*ibid.*). What I reflect is more than the reflection of things, and only because of this am I able to look beyond myself and to recognize the limitations of my knowledge. A mirror would never be astonished, something I am able to be when looking at the universe and comparing myself to it (*ibid.*). Everything I can perceive by my senses is matter (*ibid.*). But this does not explain how matter was made and why it is "diffused and dead" on the one hand and why it moves on the other hand (*ibid.*, p. 281).

> This same universe is in motion, and in its movements, ordered, uniform, and subject to fixed laws, it has none of that freedom which appears in the spontaneous movements of men and animals. So the world is not some huge animal which moves of its own accord; its movements are therefore due to some external cause, a cause which I cannot perceive, but the inner voice makes this cause so apparent to me that I cannot watch the course of the sun without imagining a force which drives it, and when the earth revolves I think I see the hand that sets it in motion. (*ibid.*, pp. 281–2)

The first reasons for the movement of the universe cannot be found in matter. Matter receives and transforms movement but does not initiate it. The first cause is not matter but God, and this, the Savoyard vicar says, is the first principle or the central dogma of his confession:

The more I observe the action and reaction of the forces of nature playing on one another, the more I see that we must always go back from one effect to another, till we arrive at a first cause in some will; for to assume an infinite succession of causes is to assume that there is no first cause. In a word, no motion which is not caused by another motion can take place, except by a spontaneous, voluntary action; inanimate bodies have no action but motion, and there is no real action without will. (*ibid.*, p. 282)

This doctrine is "obscure" in many respects, but "there is nothing in it repugnant to reason or experience" (*ibid.*, p. 283). To say more is impossible for the human mind, as then it must get lost in abstraction and will only be able to cultivate its errors. This way, Rousseau's dislike of philosophy is put in a nutshell:

The chief source of human error is to be found in general and abstract ideas; the jargon of metaphysics has never led to the discovery of any single truth, and it has filled philosophy with absurdities of which we are ashamed as soon as we strip them of their long words. (*ibid.*)

I judge on the order of the world although I do not know anything about its purpose. I do not know why the universe exists but I see how it constantly changes. I constantly perceive how its parts fit together to make the existing whole, but this whole I do not understand. "I am like a man who sees the works of a watch for the first time; he is never weary of admiring the mechanism, though he does not know the use of the instrument and has never seen its face" (*ibid.*, p. 284).

But what is more, it is not only that the materialist does not understand why the universe exists and what its essential structure is; neither does he find the way to feel astonishment at creation and thus at himself. For him, not only is the use of a watch unclear but, together with time, neither is the beauty of existence. It cannot be explained as a blind mechanism or a "work of chance" (*ibid.*, p. 285) but requires a creator or a highest form of intelligence. Otherwise there would only be the force of attraction and of repulsion but not the harmony of the universe which every sensitive being must assume: "What absurd assumptions are required to deduce all this harmony from the blind mechanism of matter set in motion by chance!" (*ibid.*, p. 286).

Not physics but nature is the measure of man, who must be understood to be a part of creation and who only due to this deserves dignity. Nature is referred to its creator; it does not happen coincidently, just as the universe cannot be imagined as a blind mechanism. This is contradicted by the natural harmony of the universe, which does not know anything evil. Consequently, also man's nature must be good. And this is because a Supreme Intelligence or God is acting upon it.

In the Age of Enlightenment no one gave a better picture of the good God than Rousseau:

> God is intelligent, but how? Man is intelligent when he reasons, but the Supreme Intelligence does not need to reason; there is neither premise nor conclusion for him, there is not even a proposition. The Supreme Intelligence is wholly intuitive, it sees what is and what shall be; all truths are one for it, as all places are but one point and all time but one moment. Man's power makes use of means, the divine power is self-active. God can because he wills; his will is his power. God is good, this is certain; but man finds his happiness in the welfare of his kind. (*ibid.*, p. 297)

Nature as the Measure for Man

On July 20th, 1763 James Boswell in his *London Journal* noted a statement by Samuel Johnson (1709–1784).[35] It was on Rousseau. Boswell reported on a discussion between Johnson, George Dempster,[36] and himself; the subject of the discussion had been man's natural goodness. Johnson doubted that there was a good natural state; after all, children were as cruel as savages. Boswell found this statement shocking, as he was proud of his children and was of the opinion that by their birth they had all of man's necessary virtues (*Boswell's London Journal* 1950, p. 312).

Dempster, the republican, pointed out Rousseau's teachings to the circle, "that the goods of fortune and advantages of rank were nothing to a wise man, who ought only to value internal merit" (*ibid.*, p. 313). To this Johnson remarked: "If man were a savage, living in the woods by himself, this might be true. But in civilized society we all depend upon each other, and our happiness is very much owing to the good opinions of others. Now, Sir, in civilized society, external advantages make us more respected by individuals. A man who has a good coat upon his back meets a better reception than he who has a bad one" (*ibid.*).[37]

Dempster was horrified and Boswell seemed indecisive. Johnson went on: to a civilized society money mattered, not internal goodness: "Sir, you make the experiment. Go to the street and give one man a lecture of morals and another a shilling, and you will see who will respect you the most" (*ibid.*). To this, Dempster said "that internal merit *ought* to make the only distinction amongst mankind" (*ibid.*, p. 314). But Johnson could not be convinced, he doubted the basis of the argument. Referring to man's nature does not matter; mankind knows "from experience" that internal goodness is of no relevance for life. And: "How shall we determine the proportion of internal merit?" (*ibid.*)

Although the situation seems to be clear, it is not easy to decide whether Rousseau was perceived correctly a few years before his visit to England. Similar to Voltaire, Johnson does not take him seriously. Whoever wanted merely to support nature would need, according to a suggestion by William Petty, nothing more than three pounds a year.[38] As times had changed since, today one could just as well say six pounds, Johnson said. "This will fill your belly, shelter you from the weather, and even get you a strong lasting coat, supposing it made of good bull's hide" (*ibid.*). Everything beyond was "artificial taste, and is desired in order to obtain a greater degree of respect from our fellow creatures" (*ibid.*).[39]

On the one hand, Rousseau did indeed oppose equation of value and wealth (*ibid.*, p. 315);[40] on the other hand, his argument is not as simple and absurd as Johnson imputed. But above all there is more than *one* argument. Often, Rousseau used the two terms "nature" and "society" in strict opposition, but never in the way of Johnson's polemic, which assumes that referring to nature would result in society not being able to punish crime anymore, as every thief would be entitled to plead his "nature" (*ibid.*). For Rousseau "nature" is not at all the same as pleading it, and his concept does not result in somebody's "internal merit."

It is not easy to deduce what Rousseau meant by "nature." Nowhere did he define his concept of nature, and it is not as if there were a hidden term which could be reconstructed later, simply because Rousseau meant very different things by "nature" and used the expression according to each context of his arguments. At one point "nature" is identical with a "natural" way of life, that is a simple life without luxury; at another the expression refers to a romantic landscape; then it means God's creation, man's internal quality, or the origins of society.

In respect of education, the terms "nature" or "natural" are also used as polemic counter-terms against the educational institutions of society. In this respect, school and teaching were "unnatural" while on the other hand the development of the child's nature does not depend on teaching, at least up to a certain age. True education is able to adjust to the child's nature, while school and teaching are not, even if they tried. In this sense, at school there cannot be anything like *natural education*, as has been claimed by countless authors after Rousseau. School as an institution of society is opposed to man's nature.

Notwithstanding all the variance and flexibility of the term "nature," Rousseau constantly and fundamentally distinguishes *societal* from *natural state*. However, he uses this distinction from the natural law of the seventeenth century in a different way than legal theories, that is in the sense of a historical sequence. Historically earlier and original is the natural state; societal state comes after it and comes along with a massive restriction of the natural state. Originally, man lived in accordance with his natural powers. This accordance is lost when societies develop, which man did not need in his natural state.

In this sense, not simply "nature" but nature as the *origins* are the criteria for future development. In the Second Discourse on the development of inequality Rousseau clearly says that there cannot be a "back to nature," as the societal state as such is not a matter of debate. "Society," once established, cannot be ended anymore, it can only be changed. It is possible, however, to consider the natural state as a kind of regulative idea and to use it as a criterion for criticism. This way, the question of how man's nature could be maintained and at the same time socialized becomes the main problem of education.

This seems to be paradoxical, for how could anything be maintained which at the same time must be given up? Man's nature changes *in* and *by* the state of society, there is nothing left of the original state, man is not a savage anymore, but maybe the process of man's socialization could be repeated and in the course of this done *differently*. That is precisely Rousseau's idea. By every birth life starts again and thus also the socialization of nature. Whoever interferes with this process and rearranges it has the chance to do justice to man's nature more than previous society does and at the same time has the chance to renew society.

If the beginning of education is newly chosen and the process determined in a different way, it will be possible at the same time to break the alleged chain of original sin. For this, only one *first child* is necessary, which is assumed to be free of sin. If it is possible to break the chain in one place, maybe only in theory, it is possible everywhere, provided the paradigm of education is convincing. This is the case if reason-giving arguments include something which for Rousseau cannot be doubted, and that is nature and its goodness. It is renewed by and in every child; whoever denied this would have to attack the fundamentals of life.

The two books from the year 1762 were supposed to explain this idea in detail. The *Contrat Social* describes how society could be founded again by a constitutive act and a contract; *Emile* suggests what a kind of education looks like which comes close to man's original nature or is even appropriate for it. Rousseau indicated the combination of the two concepts but never really thought this through and completed it. But it is clearly a basic idea: education assumes that man's original state, that of *homme sauvage*, is repeated by every child. Whoever is able to maintain this state maintains his natural strength and is thus able to prepare for society in a way different from conventional education, which wastes natural strength.

This creates a number of problems: the fundamental problem results from the question of how far the premise is true. Rousseau's theory assumes that societal state is preceded by a state of nature which is not only "original" but also "good." On the one hand, nature must be assumed to be free of sin; on the other hand it must be free of evil effects. Only in this way can nature appear as the measure for education, which also means that nature no longer needs to be restricted or cut, as in all Augustinian educational theories up to Freud's impulse theory.

An early test of the theory of good nature was the Lisbon earthquake, which brought Rousseau into a very fundamental opposition to Voltaire. On November 1st, 1755, All Saints' Day, the ground beneath the city of Lisbon shook, with the epicenter out to sea; later the quake was determined to have had a strength of 8.5 on the Richter scale. The shaking extended from northern Africa to Scandinavia, the first seismic shock immediately followed by two more, but worst of all a tsunami arose which inundated an enormous quantity of water from the ocean into the mouth of the Tejo, flooding the lower parts of the city.

The 30 churches of the city collapsed and buried worshipers, who had been gathering for mass on All Saints' Day, under the debris. Immediately after the first seismic shock, fires broke out which, in addition to earthquake and flood, completely destroyed Lisbon. Between 20,000 and 60,000 people are estimated to have died and probably many more than 30,000, the number of victims of a natural disaster considered a warning against the optimism of Enlightenment.

In March, 1756 Voltaire published his famous poem on the Lisbon earthquake. His contemporaries understood this poem to be a rejection of "belief in progress"; Voltaire, however, never understood it as a naïve expectation of perfectibility (*perfectibilité*). For him nature works always as a limitation of human aspiration, not least by disasters. To Voltaire, "progress" was never a counter-balance to nature or life in accordance with its goodness, but only the mastering of some of its forces, not least intellectual power, that is knowledge, insight, and criticism.

Nature itself cannot be mastered. After the Lisbon earthquake Voltaire, like other observers, felt the concept of living in the "best of all worlds" to be dubious. Leibniz's or Pope's philosophy, as it says in the introduction to the poem, is incompatible with the catastrophic power of nature, otherwise one would have to assume that the victims of Lisbon confirmed the good power. But if such a disaster cannot be a sign of goodness, a whole philosophical world collapses, which in no way confirms that nature can be dangerous for man.

In 1710[41] the German philosopher Gottfried Wilhelm Leibniz (1646–1716) had tried to prove that God created a world for man which among all imaginable worlds was the best possible one. The reason for this is that only man is free to release himself from certain evils, something which can also be considered "progress", that is the constant improvement of the conditions of human life. Later, the English poet Alexander Pope (1688–1744)[42] used the argument of the best of all worlds to explain man as the center of the universe. This universe is God's creation and thus perfect; evils are man-made, but man can also "improve" his nature provided that there is a "universal good" (Pope 1993, p. 82).

According to Pope, the axiom of this philosophy is *all is good* (tout est bien). Given the disaster of Lisbon, however, this looked strange, Voltaire wrote (1756a, p. 3). According to this experience, we are obviously not living in the best of all worlds and we also are not able to enter one, as each of our worlds can be shaken by natural disasters which nobody can predict or ban. The best of all worlds requires *perfectibilité*, constant improvement of man and nature, but this idea demands what is impossible, that is controlling the evil that comes from nature (*ibid.*, pp. 6–7).

Thus, says Voltaire, one must admit that the good and the evil are and will be co-existing. And from this one had also to admit that the miseries of man's life will endure and that all his enlightenment will not abolish his weakness (*ibid.*, p. 7). It is not possible, as the poem says, to deduce nature's goodness from its necessity, that is to put creation itself under man's control. And even if nature is God's creation, disasters like that of Lisbon show how high-handed nature is and to what little extent one succeeds in putting it under man's control (*ibid.*, pp. 9–10).

The world can never be made free from error; it is a theater of passion and of misery, which will never have a happy ending. That which we call "good," man's *plaisir*, is cursory and untenable, and the moment of positive experience must not blind us to the fatality of life.[43] Thus, life cannot be "good," as it is fleeting and void, and nobody can resolve man's suffering from himself (*ibid.*, pp. 16, 18). One might, as Voltaire says at the end of the poem, well add hope to this conclusion (*ibid.*, p. 17) but given nature's violence this remains a vague concept.

Although some of his own motifs were mentioned, Rousseau reacted most vehemently to the poem *Sur le désastre de Lisbonne*,[44] as Voltaire doubted nature's goodness, the later premise for natural education, according to which only society is able to corrupt man. Rousseau did not want to and could not admit that nature is able or even willing to do harm to man, as the general optimism of education could not then be defended. Without nature's goodness, as Rousseau already knew at that time, there was no real alternative to society.

That is why in his letter to Voltaire on providence (August 18th, 1756) Rousseau shifts the problem. For Rousseau there are two sorts of evil: "particular evil," whose existence no philosopher has ever denied and, "general evil," which the optimist denies: "It is not a question of knowing whether each one of us suffers or not; but whether it be good that the universe exists, and whether our ills be inevitable in the constitution of the universe" (Rousseau 1992, p. 115). Adding an article would define the theorem[45] more clearly, and instead of saying *Everything is good* it would be better to say: *The whole is good*, or *Everything is good for the whole*. "Then it is quite evident that no man would know how to give direct proof either for or against; for these proofs depend on a perfect knowledge of the constitution of the world and of the purpose of its Author, and this knowledge is incontestably above human intelligence" (*ibid.*).

From that follows: "The true principles of optimism can be drawn neither from the properties of matter, nor from the mechanics of the universe, but only by inference from the perfections of God who presides over everything" (*ibid.*). Thus not human intellect but providence was to take action (*ibid.*, pp. 115–16).[46] One could only *believe* in nature's goodness because there is no physical evidence for it. But should we give up on believing in good nature only because of this? On the contrary, because optimism is a matter of providence, it is easy to defend (*ibid.*, p. 118). And there is another reason: Voltaire's skeptical intellect is without use for the people. Whoever understands the "good" and the "bad" simply in relation which in the face of the experience of nature and society cannot be decided in favor of the *good* does not contribute at all to the happiness of people.

> It is that there is inhumanity in troubling peaceful souls, and in afflicting men to no purpose, when what one wishes to teach them is neither certain nor useful. I think, in a word, that by your example, the superstition which troubles society cannot be attacked too strongly nor the Religion that sustains it too much respected. (*ibid.*, pp. 118–19)

Optimism must be certain and useful at the same time, something which is only possible with nature or the universe is its basis. One can only *believe* that "the whole" is good, and it is only providence that will make this belief certain. This belief is useful for life, but it must be kept independent from experience if the theorem of nature's goodness is supposed to be convincing. Applied to experience, too many counter-examples will be immediately at hand to be able to maintain the naivity of believing optimism for long. Disasters prove the contingency of the world and nature's unpredictability, while belief is supposed to assume that everything – world and man – is perfect by itself and by its nature.

Criticism of Voltaire is summarized in Rousseau's *Confessions* by a much clearer statement: "Voltaire, while always appearing to believe in God, has only ever really believed in the devil, since his so-called God is nothing but a malevolent being who, according to him, takes pleasure only in doing harm" (Rousseau 2000, p. 419). This cannot or must not be true, since the whole construction of "good nature" will then collapse. The causes of evil must not be looked for in nature or even in God, which is why Voltaire must refer to the devil when considering the Lisbon earthquake a disaster of nature and of optimism.

On September 10th, 1755 Rousseau had written to Voltaire:

The taste for Letters and the Arts in a People is born from an internal vice which it enlarges. And if it is true that all human progress is pernicious to the species, the progress of the mind and of knowledge that enlarges our pride and multiplies our errors soon hastens our misfortunes. But a time comes when the evil is such that the very causes that gave birth to it are necessary to prevent it from becoming larger. It is the sword that must be left in the wound for fear that the wounded person will die when it is removed. (Rousseau 1992, p. 106)

This letter was Rousseau's answer after his Second Discourse had been heavily criticized by Voltaire. Here, Rousseau presented his theorem of *perfectibilité* for the first time, which is introduced as the principle of nature. Each being must perfect itself, and thus also man, but even man is free to stand up to this principle. Freedom of choice or of decision according to his own will is what makes man different from all other beings, "and in the sentiment of this power are found only purely spiritual acts about which the Laws of Mechanics explain nothing" (*ibid.*, p. 26).

But how does man use his possibilities of self-improvement? Rousseau speaks of the "faculty of self-perfection," that is striving for improvement, which he says to be typical for man but which constantly results in the opposite of the intended purpose. With the aid of circumstances man tries to improve constantly, but everything that the faculty of self-perfection makes and has been achieved in the name of progress, in the end falls back lower than the Beast itself. The Beast has nothing to lose because it has acquired nothing (*ibid.*). Man will lose because he is driven to be perfect.

It would be sad for us to be forced to agree that this distinctive and almost unlimited faculty is the source of all man's misfortunes; that it is this faculty which, by the dint of time, draws him out of that original condition in which he would pass tranquil and innocent days; that it is this faculty which, bringing to flower over the centuries his enlightenment and his errors, his vices and virtues, in the long run makes him the tyrant of himself and of Nature. (*ibid.*)

The good multiplies the evil, as far as the causes of evil still exist. The assumption of progress is naïve because it does not take into account that every improvement may change to the contrary. Man becomes his own tyrant and that of nature if he does not find a substitute for the origins. This cannot be the sheer state of society, as from it have come the evils which originally did not exist at all. The instincts of savage man have not found a substitute in society (*ibid.*, p. 27) and instead have been corrupted by fantasies of perfectibility.

Passions are fundamental for man. In the natural state needs and passions are interlocking, and no natural man would come to think of being able or even of having to improve himself because philosophy wants him to do so. "His desires do not exceed his Physical needs, the only goods he knows in the Universe are nourishment, female, and repose; and the only evils he fears are pain and hunger" (*ibid.*). This animal condition is overcome by the knowledge of being mortal and by the image of horror created by this knowledge. The progress of mind that follows has been "in proportion to the needs that Peoples had received from Nature or to those to which circumstances had subjected them, and consequently to the passions which inclined them to provide for those needs" (*ibid.*). This has more and more led away the passions from the original balance.

From this historical description there concludes the contrast between good nature and man living in a society. Not coincidentally, in the confession of the Savoyard vicar this contrast is described by musical metaphors: there is "a secret voice of nature" which is much stronger than the voice of the Gods (Rousseau 1993, p. 312). While nature is in harmony, man is in disarray;[47] "chaos" is social dissonance which prevents living together from an order which is suitable for man's nature. Originally, an organized way of living together was unnecessary, as people were self-sufficient and had to be so.[48]

This is not an idea which Rousseau could claim to be exclusively his own. His "savage man" is an often-met literary figure in the first half of the eighteenth century, which Rousseau simply linked to a particular philosophy of origin. Descriptions of the life of the "savage people," particularly in travel literature from America, were popular reading matter and the subject of many discussions in the mid-eighteenth century. Often, by referring to the *homme sauvage* the positive distance of the age of Enlightenment from the "barbarians" was supposed to be shown, but there were also attempts in the other direction. Thus, the "noble savage" is not an invention by Rousseau but an often-used topos of contemporary literature. It is therefore a little bit exaggerated to call Rousseau the "father of anthropology" (Lévi-Strauss 1963).

The term "noble savage" probably emerged for the first time in British literature in John Dryden's (1631–1700) heroic drama *The Conquest of Granada*[49] and was then used frequently in the first half of the eighteenth century, although not in Dryden's sense. Several works were about holding up the mirror of its better origins to society. Natural man is described as being free from the evils of society, independent of luxurious needs, being not in need of vanities, and noble in respect of his attitudes. Even Voltaire in *L'Ingénu* (1767)[50] tried out this topic. To quote Rousseau (1993, p. 200), "Every one knows that the learned societies of Europe are mere schools of falsehood, and there is assuredly more mistaken notions in the Academy of Sciences than in a whole tribe of American Indians."

An early example of this much-read literature in Britain and France is Joseph François Latifau's (1681–1740) *Moers des sauvages américains* (1724), an English translation of which was published that same year.[51] Latifau, who had been living as a Jesuit missionary in America and presented detailed descriptions of the ways of life of tribal cultures, wanted to prove that the Native Americans were not "primitive" because they also believed in God. Thus, their customs were not "wild" but civilized and good. This had also been claimed by Nicolas Guedeville (1654–1721) as early as in 1704,[52] and in this literature we also find indications of perceiving the Divine with the heart if doctrines are lacking. God, as it says in the English translation of Latifau's book on the customs of the Native Americans, engraved the sentiment in the heart of all man (Latifau 1974, Vol. II, ch. IV).

Sometimes the concept of "natural history" (histoire naturelle) is used in these early ethnological descriptions (e.g. Labat 1722), as is the ancient topos of the "Golden Age."[53] By this topos it becomes possible to assume ideal origins of the present state, corrupt society being the successor of the former. The history of society thus has to be seen as removal from the good origins. This topos of history as decline is used long before Rousseau[54] and is a common theme in several passages of contemporary literature. This is also true for appreciating rural life, which many eighteenth-century authors presented as a role model[55] and distinguished from the decadent experience of the city. And finally, already Alexander Pope in the poem *Essay on Man* had written that the "State of Nature" is the state of social innocence:

Nor think, in Nature's state they blindly trod;
The State of Nature was the reign of God:
Self-love and Social at her birth began,
Union was the bond of all things, and of Man.

Pride then was not; nor arts, that pride to aid;
Man walk'd with beast, joint tenant of the shade;
The same his table, and the same his bed;
No murder cloath'd him, and no murder fed. (Pope 1993, p. 64)

Rousseau (1992, p. 25) explicitly refers to the "reports of Travelers." In the context of this literature he constructs a special variant which assumes that the *homme sauvage* must be understood to be unique. As a human, he lived on his own and free from belonging to a social group or a tribe. Being in the natural state, man has neither moral relationships nor particular duties and thus can be neither good nor bad but only innocent. He does not know about virtues or vice. "Thus one could say that Savages are not evil precisely because they do not know what it is to be good" (*ibid.*, p. 35).[56] Neither increasing enlightenment nor the power of law but only freedom of passions and ignorance of vice prevented them from doing harm (*ibid.*, pp. 35–6).

In this sense, ignorance creates strength, and only the moral sentiment of compassion made the robust savage a weak child, as a famous metaphor says. This metaphor is aimed at Thomas Hobbes (1588–1679), and it is instructive in respect of Rousseau's construction of education. According to Rousseau, Hobbes says that the evil man is a robust child (*ibid.*, p. 35). But this, Rousseau says, does justice neither to human nature nor to children. The evil is not a part of the natural state because the *homme sauvage* has no moral knowledge and thus cannot distinguish "good" from "bad." Children are brought up innocent like the *homme sauvage*, but not as strong as him. The longer one lets them stay in the natural state, the more robust they will be able to become, provided they do not have any contact to the distinction between the good and the bad.

Thus, education would assume a moral moratorium, a state of innocence which is kept away from society as far as possible. This is not a Paradise from which one is expelled but a second natural state. In the Second Discourse Rousseau describes a social *juste milieu* where it was possible to maintain "a golden mean between the indolence of the primitive state and the petulant activity of our amour-propre" (*ibid.*, p. 48). The "new state" of society, he says, was characterized by "a simple and solitary life," "very limited needs," and the use of new, useful tools (*ibid.*, p. 46). This age had been the happiest and most stable in the history of human society (*ibid.*, p. 48) but it was irrevocably over.

The problem is, what is supposed to be replaced by this *juste milieu*? The answer Rousseau suggests refers to the theories of society and of education at the same time. The originator of evil, it says in the confession of the Savoyard vicar, is nobody other than man himself (Rousseau 1993, p. 293).

There is no evil, with the exception of that which has been created by man. The general evil is the general disorder, which can be undone if man's works are *not* significant any longer. For all sorrows and thus all pain man himself is responsible; they do not exist by nature. Only he who consults reflection excessively, that is constantly compares himself to others and designs himself for society, experiences pain to be painful.

Whoever – like young children – knows neither memory nor prediction cannot be really affected by any pain, as between himself and feeling pain he does not need to perceive anything else. "Pain has little power over those who, having thought little, look neither before nor after. Take away our fatal progress, take away our faults and vices, take away man's handiwork, and all is well" (*ibid.*). Then, "society" was simply an association without social evil, which develops only as far as nature is *not* considered for man's work. For criticism of education there concludes from this: "Man is weak when he is dependent, and he is emancipated before he is robust" (Rousseau 1992, p. 35).

If nature was the measure, no degeneration of morals could happen, the cause of which Rousseau already links to constant reflection in his early fragment "On Taste": "Never is taste or virtue so much talked about as in times in which it is the least possessed" (Rousseau 2005, p. 17). Everything beautiful and every kind of taste are only based on imitation, and "all the true models of taste are in nature" (*ibid.*). The more one gets away from "master" nature, the less one will find a suitable form of life. Thus, societal life is artificial and experience is degenerated. They imitate imitations.

One essential evil of modern civilization is trust in the reliable increase of knowledge, which assumes that errors will disappear. Rousseau was an understanding reader of Seneca's theories. From him he takes over the ancient doctrine of *ataraxia*, of internal resoluteness or unshakeability, which must be part of the way of life but does not demand knowledge. Whoever wants to live virtuously must evade the temptations of society. Wisdom is not knowledge; although the ignorant is a fool (*stulti*), wisdom and virtuous life do not come from simply increasing knowledge. Also, for the active side Rousseau is indebted to a stoic concept, namely the theory of *oikeiosis* or self-awareness that is manifested in "self-preserving instincts" (Martin 2006, p. 25).

In the third book of *Emile* this stoic motif is expressed thus: "The more we know, the more mistakes we make; therefore ignorance is the only way to escape error" (Rousseau 1993, p. 200). Earlier, in the critical letter to Voltaire from September 7th, 1755, Rousseau says: "But let us first question the interest in our private matters and the truth of our writings. Although philosophers, historians, scholars are necessary for enlightening the world and guiding its blind inhabitants, – if I was correctly reported by wise Menon, I do not know anything to be as foolish as a people of wise men"

(Correspondance t. III, p. 165). And at the end of a letter to the Marquise de Verdelin from March 12th, 1760 Rousseau writes: "Glory of philosophy! The century of philosophers is the century of madmen, of cowards, and of rascals. It is said that all these people fight my maxims. They are wrong; they are constantly working on proving them" (Correspondance t. VII, p. 58).

Philosophy is in contrast to nature. The philosophical systems argue about best knowledge, but they all are misleading, Rousseau writes to Pierre-Alexandre DuPeyrou[57] on March 21st, 1769, as they are so contradictory that everything could be concluded from them and nothing becomes clear. Only nature shows the reliable way (Correspondance t. VI, p. 63); it is thus the criterion for society and for education. And nature's maxim is as simple as one could imagine. It demands to begin and end with oneself (*ibid.*, p. 64). Theories are not reliable, but it is just a theory of society that Rousseau expounded.

Theory and Criticism of Society

For Rousseau, society is not the "society" of late-ninetenth-century sociology, that is, not an internally differentiated, greater social unit on a certain territory, which is called a "people" or a "nation." When Rousseau speaks of a *contrat social*, he has an association of individuals in mind which does not know any stratification and must be of a suitable size. Only a small society of equals can be a good one. Therefore society is a kind of unity of will, not a historical entity like the national state of the nineteenth century. To the latter, man belongs due to language or territorial existence but does not decide for or against it.

On the other hand, Rousseau asks how society could be more than a sheer or "conventional" union of its members. Social exchange is inevitable. "There can be no society without exchange, no exchange without a common standard of measurement, no common standard of measurement without equality" (Rousseau 1993, p. 182). When individuals meet, this is not enough for building a society, as Rousseau (1992, p. 40) showed in the Second Discourse. In the natural state encounters happen, but there is no social solidarity, whereas the societal state provided a unification which more and more turned against nature. Savage man has become a social being while at the same time is unequal and unfree; embodiment into society assigns a place to him which he has neither decided for nor created. Man himself became a social standard. Original equality was lost in favor of a hierarchical structure which determines differences according to income and property.

The mechanism of social assignment is comparison. Individuals who are united in one and the same society are treated most differently, as they are forced to compare themselves to others in order to determine differences about which they find out by way of living together. As Samuel Johnson said: "In general wealth, nobility or rank, Power, and personal merit being the principal distinctions by which one is measured in Society" (*ibid.*, p. 63). Existing society does not appreciate virtue but reputation, which is built on doubtful foundations and forces man to be outside himself (*ibid.*):

> I would point out how much that universal desire for reputation, honors, and preferences, which devours us all, trains and compares talents and strengths; how much it stimulates and multiplies passions; and making all men competitors, rivals, or rather enemies, how many reverses, successes, and catastrophes of all kind it causes daily by making so many Contenders race the same course. (*ibid.*)

As mentioned above, distinguishing the societal from the natural state goes back to the natural law of the seventeenth century and was also used earlier for the constitutional law of absolutism. Here, it was fundamental that even in a borderline case both states cannot coincide or be identical. Rousseau takes up this difference, making both a sequence of historical states from it and a relationship of mutual reflection. He asks what nature means for society and vice versa. Like Hobbes, Rousseau uses this relationship to criticize the state of society, not to justify it.

Rousseau assumes that there cannot be *one* state of society but different ones, both better and worse. The intention to improve a given state of society is not enough, as Rousseau explained by his criticism of the *faculté de perfectionner*. Whoever wants to improve a bad state increases the level of the bad and not of the good: at any time, improvement of knowledge may turn into a state of morals and virtues which is even worse than it is already. But why is it that society has become worse and worse, if nature is definitely good?

One reason for assuming social degradation is for personal reasons. Rousseau equates bad "society" with the city, to be precise, with Paris. On January 4th, 1762 he writes to Malherbes: "You think I am unhappy and consumed with melancholy. Oh, Sir, how very mistaken you are! At Paris I was so; it was at Paris a black bile corroded my heart; and the bitterness of it is only too evident in all the writing I published while there" (Rousseau 1937, p. 204). This is no exaggeration; the negative criterion of "Paris" indeed runs through his work and his letters. The opacity of the French capital is also one of the main sources for his constant complaints of being prosecuted and in the midst of enemies.

The negative backdrop of "Paris" dominates many of Rousseau's judgments on "society." On July 15th, 1763 he explains to Leonhard Usteri

$(1741-1789)^{58}$ in Zürich that the situation in Switzerland could not be compared to that in Paris. The problem of society, however, was dominated by developments in cities like Paris, and plans made in Zürich would not stop anything. A rigorous Christian republic, as Usteri had in mind, would not change anything. Even Christians live in society, and even they cannot replace that which lacks society. And why should good Christians be virtuous? Only because they are "good Christians"?

It was definitely true, as Rousseau goes on, that the "ideal society" (grande société) was based on universal goodwill (bienfaisance) and that humanity was its foundation, to which Christian faith had decisively contributed. But that which confronts us is not "ideal" but "particular societies" consisting of individuals only, that is they are not tied together by goodwill. Selfishness dominates social life, not religion, whichever it may be, and belief was nothing other than personal image which had taken over a certain function for society (Correspondance t. XVII, pp. 62–3).

Vice can be hidden behind virtues (*ibid.*, p. 63); merely claiming a certain belief for oneself does not guarantee a virtuous way of life. You cannot be naïve; equating reality and appearance contradicts every experience. Disguise is easy in the city, in particular, the more one touches the heart and lets discourse become sentimental. A good observer can achieve gains especially with the rich and the most corrupt people without needing to be virtuous. Appearance, not moral intentions, is essential (*ibid.*, pp. 63–4). Ambitious people are two-faced, not unjust; if they are successful they may throw off their masks (masques), having been so concerned with their reputation. "Cromwell was unmasked as a tyrant after having been able for fifteen years to act the keeper of laws and defender of faith" (*ibid.*, p. 64).

Behind these observations is a far-reaching theory which Rousseau developed in one of his writings for his defense. The first of these writings is the answer to the condemnation of his book on education by the Archbishop of Paris, Christophe de Beaumont $(1703-1781).^{59}$ The latter's pastoral letter mentioned all the doctrinaire reasons why it was against Christian faith to bring up children according to their nature. Children are not good by nature but are subject to the ban of sin which nobody can evade (Mandement 1762).^{60} Reasons for the doctrine of original sin are given by the consequences of the expulsion from Paradise, which would be undone only by revelation at the end of time. Rousseau had an easy job of this argument, as he sharply distinguished the natural state from the "Paradise" of the Old Testament.

Rousseau's *Letter to Beaumont* was written between October and December, 1762, then printed, and circulating more or less exclusively among Rousseau's friends, and distributed until September, 1763. Rousseau's publisher, Marc-Michel Rey in Amsterdam,[61] was able to publish five editions in quick succession until the end of that year. There was immense interest in Rousseau's first extended justification, even before the printing of the circulating copies. The reason for this is simple enough: Rousseau, the "citizen of Geneva," recently driven out of Paris and having struggled to find a place of exile, picked an argument with the most powerful institution of Christian faith and stood up against it in regard to an essential question.

On June 5th, 1763, Rousseau wrote to one of his critics and expanded on the letter to Beaumont. The letter was based on three simple statements:

1. Christianity is nothing other than the explication and application of Jewish faith. The apostles have no doctrines other than those of the Jews, so except for Moses, they are not original lawmakers.
2. There are cults where true religion (religion essentielle) is found and there are those where this is not the case. Only the former[62] are good; all the others, however, are bad. Nobody is obliged to follow the particular religion of a state if it contradicts true religion.
3. In any case, God's Law is superior to that of man, and God's Law may result in giving up on man's law.

Christian catechism claims to give the predication of the gospels.The people, however, must be obedient only when it is God who speaks to them, that is not when hearing simple doctrines or having to learn answers to questions which they have not asked and cannot connect with God (Correspondance t. XVI, p. 262).

This is the reason behind Rousseau's strategy in his letter to Beaumont, which essentially is dedicated to refuting original sin. According to the premise that nature is good and anyway nothing contradicts the belief in nature's goodness, Rousseau doubts the foundation of the Augustinean doctrine.[63] Expulsion from Paradise is a story from the Jewish Old Testament, which of all apostles only Paul[64] took up with determination. Augustine refers to Paul, but the apostles are no lawmakers, thus their doctrines cannot have the value of a dogma, which has been repeatedly tried among Christian denominations.

If, however, the evils of the world cannot be explained by the first sinful deed having been inherited and if at the same time it is assumed that nature is originally good, why is it that the state of society is not perfect but, on the contrary, full of evil? Rousseau's answer is far-reaching. He writes to the Bishop of Paris that the evils of the world could not come from man's nature but must be of other origins. "If man is good by nature, as I believe to have demonstrated, it follows that he remains so as long as nothing foreign to himself spoils him. And if men are wicked, as they have gone to the trouble of teaching me, it follows that their wickedness comes from elsewhere" (Rousseau 2001, p. 35).

This "elsewhere" is defined in more detail. Rousseau rejects the idea that there might be "absolute evil" (*ibid.*, p. 43). Only God is absolute. The evils of the world are caused by society, where they happen, and thus it must be held responsible for them. Being and appearing are distant from each other, the actions of the people have nothing to do with what they say, and whoever asks for the reason to why virtue is only appearance and evil is unchallenged reality receives an unequivocal answer: "I found it in our social order which – at every point contrary to nature, which nothing destroys – tyrannizes over nature constantly and constantly makes nature demand its rights" (*ibid.*, p. 52).

The doctrine of original sin is nothing other than a projection which is supposed to distract the people from the state society is in. Actually, only society is able to create vice and produce evils. Thus, man is not sinful but only the society he lives in (*ibid.*). Whoever wants to avoid sin must change society and not punish the people. To this, natural education must essentially contribute, whose task is radically distinguished from all "Christian education" which Beaumont had brought up (*ibid.*, p. 37). In its shortest version the task is as follows: "Close the entrance to vice . . . and the human heart will always be good" (*ibid.*, p. 35).

Shifting sin toward society is not a fundamentally new thought. While discussing the doctrine of original sin, the British author Richard Steele (1672–1729)[65] had already pointed out the idea that not the mythical fall but wrong education might be blamed for corrupt society. In his famous story of "Inkle and Yarico"[66] Steele explains why nature is innocent and only society provides vice and evils. This story, based on Richard Ligon's book *A True and Exact History of the Island of Barbados* (1673), counts among the most influential motifs of British literature and was even staged as an opera in London in 1787.

Thus, Rousseau's topics are ready-made. He discovers and adapts them to his own course, which above all concerns how definitive society may be if it is experienced as corrupt, unjust, and bigoted. Rousseau does not believe in another Golden Age; good nature by itself is not a guarantor of the future, which cannot return. After all, society must be newly invented, no more and no less. More than this, it must be invented how man could adjust to society and still be himself. Thus, Rousseau does *not*, like many writers of his time, start out from a social utopia which, if at all, is a far-away country[67] but shifts the problem toward the midst of society.

In the *Contrat Social* from 1762 Rousseau asks how natural freedom could be translated without loss into social order. In the first book of the *Social Contract* he says: men reach a point where the obstacles to human preservation have become greater than each individual can cope with by his own strength. This primitive state cannot endure. Men cannot create new forces but only combine and control those that exist. An adequate combination of forces must be the result of men coming together. Such a sum of powers can be produced only by the union of separate men. Still, each man's power and freedom are his main means of self-preservation. How could he put them under the control of others without damaging himself?

> This difficulty . . . might be expressed in these words: "How to find a form of association which will defend the person and goods of each member with the collective force of all, and under which each individual while uniting himself with others, obeys no one but himself and remains as free as before." This is the fundamental problem to which the social contract holds the solution. (Rousseau 2004a, p. 14)

The topic of the constitution of society had already been dealt with by David Hume. A comparison is worth making, as Hume draws a completely different conclusion because he does not assume what is fundamental for Rousseau's political philosophy, that is a theory of man's estrangement from his own nature. For Rousseau, man joins society so that he may also express reservations, something which Hume declares impossible. For the latter, it is not necessary to decide for society by way of an act of foundation but society has always existed without being only a state of estrangement. Thus, Rousseau's view from outside society was not possible at all.

For Hume, social relationships are processes of mutual exchange, that is they are more than contracts. Exchange among humans is provided through two media of communication: "public praise and blame." Both media are fundamental for the politics of civil society. In his essays from 1741,[68] Hume writes that governments really needed nothing more for their support than public opinion. Whoever asks himself why *the many* let *a few* govern them is referred to opinion. Otherwise, the miracle of "implicit submission," through which humans make their own emotions and passions subject to those of their rulers, could not be explained.

> It is therefore, on opinion *only* that government is founded; and this maxim extends to the most despotic and most military governments, as well as to the most free and most popular. (Hume 1994, p. 16; italics J.O.)

Humans do not voluntarily allow others to rule them, but on the other hand they do not simply make contracts, as in Hobbes's version of civil society which gives reason to government by monopolizing power. But how are humans supposed to transfer their inherited rights to the state and to give up on sovereignty?

To answer this question Hume points to a dimension which is seldom considered in theories of social contract: that of *opinion*; in more detail, that of *public* opinion. The term "opinion" is described in more detail by two categories: interest-related and rights-related opinions. Opinion of rights, again, has two categories: right to power and right to property. In all three respects, governments are not autarchic; these respects thus cannot be arbitrarily neglected without the government suffering disadvantages. Government is not simply the execution of power but giving evidence to legitimacy, which happens publicly. Thus, for Hume the opinion on the government is as important as the government itself, the latter needing to prove itself acceptable, whether it likes this or not.

On the first field of acceptance Hume notes:

By opinion of interest, I chiefly understand the sense of the general advantage which is reaped from government; together with the persuasion, that the particular government, which is established, is equally advantageous with any other that could easily be settled. When this opinion prevails among the generality of a state, or among those who have the force in their hands, it gives great security to any government. (*ibid.*, p. 16)

Thus, "acceptance" means perceiving general progress due to the government's work as well as being convinced of having the comparably best government in office, provided it is easy to install new governments. If both convictions determine the people and the power elites, the government is provided with optimal security, something which at the same time means that this security is endangered when opinion changes. Thus, in the long run no government is safe from public interest, which is its starting point. This is also true in respect of estimating the legitimacy of power as well as for being of the opinion that the government protects the rights of property or opens it up to infringements.

Upon these three opinions, therefore, of public *interest*, of *right to power*, and of *right to property*, are all governments founded, and all authority of the few over the many. (*ibid.*, p. 17)

Every government must pay attention to how public opinion develops and must try to influence it, without in the long run being able to act purely manipulatively. A government without acceptance can become despotic, but terror will increase the crisis and will accelerate what Hume calls "unavoidable" "political death" (*ibid.*, p. 31). Skeptical as Hume was, he assumed all governments to be mortal; however, certain ways of dying are preferable to others (*ibid.*, pp. 31–2). An absolute and violent government has the shortest life expectancy because it is least able to be a civil one (*ibid.*, p. 32).

It results in constant convulsion and violates public expectations without service in return.

One precondition for this is that not simply "interests" stabilize rule, as is often assumed, but that all interests on every human matter are controlled by *opinion* (*ibid.*, p. 30). There are not interests as such; interests must be articulated as and by opinions, something for which public resonance is needed. For this, *education* plays a decisive role, as Hume states when looking at the progress of his century. Education, he says, has overcome superstition, and that was irreversible. "Now, there has been a sudden and sensible change in the opinions of men within the last fifty years, by the progress of learning and of liberty" (*ibid.*).

Nobody who has some education, Hume continues, still believes in the magic of names or in the superstition through which earlier authorities had secured themselves. The clergy has become a joke in respect of its doctrines and ambitions, religion has lost its predominant place in the world, and the great titles of rule do not make any impression anymore. It is no longer possible to astound mankind because occult powers have lost their power, and this is true in respect of both religion and politics. Neither is it possible for the king or for the Pope to be God's deputy as there is no evidence of descent (king) or mercy (Pope). Both ways of reason-giving can be seen through and unmasked without being able to be successfully renewed (*ibid.*, pp. 30–1).

The reason for this is progress of education and freedom, which both have irreversible consequences. Morals and criticism, Hume says, have become public, referring to general opinion and not to book scholarship, which is the only criterion upon which controversies on morals or criticism can be decided (*ibid.*, p. 200). Whoever wants to contribute to the formation of opinion must be provided with education and freedom at the same time. These are related to each other and cannot be separated, as Rousseau wanted to do. For Hume, "natural freedom" is unimaginable and absurd.

Even if there were only a few who cultivated sciences and arts to achieve astonishing success, Hume writes, the spread of these still has consequences. The masses cannot stay stupid when the spirit of sciences and arts is diffused and overcomes the context of traditional scholarship (*ibid.*, p. 60). It is not possible, however, to spread the spirit of sciences and arts if the people are not blessed with a "free government" (*ibid.*, p. 61). In this context, "free" means above all public judgment on the performance of the government, which must abandon censorship and must be open to criticism.

This refers to both educational and legal conditions: experience and education must refine judgment (*ibid.*). A legal state is assumed. Only law creates social security, and only security makes curiosity possible, and only curiosity stimulates knowledge. Thus, a republic without law will neither last nor support sciences and arts (*ibid.*, p. 63). But a constitution is not enough. The people must be able to live together; "society" must thus be built on *sociability*, without which there will be no social exchange.

This condition is often overlooked. Civility does not simply mean government but a way of life which must be self-regulating. Scholarship is not enough for this; public opinion must be provided with a social basis transcending class or caste. By using a famous formula, Hume calls this the "intercourse of minds" (*ibid.*, p. 73), without which a civil society would not last. It exists in the form of a good-natured interaction which can only be realized through agreement and consent, that is it must control the execution of power. For this, free exchange and good manners are necessary, not a contract (*ibid.*).

Goodwill and *justice* are the principles of public morals, Hume wrote in 1751,[69] and man's nature has learned how to adjust *to this*. It is neither completely selfish nor exclusively tied to interests, provided a society makes goodwill as well as justice the maxims of acting and thus also of education. Rousseau's questions are completely different and he also draws completely different conclusions on educational theory. For Hume, there is no "nature" besides society; man by his emotions and opinions is interested in society, but that exactly is the subject of Rousseau's criticism.

Social man is not simply the continuation of natural man; society has its price which in the Second Discourse is expressed as follows: "The Savage lives within himself; the sociable man, always outside of himself, knows how to live only in the opinions of others; and it is, so to speak, from their judgments alone that he draws the sentiment of his own existence" (Rousseau 1992, p. 66). That which Hume called "public praise and blame" means in reality to surrender man to public opinion, behind which man's nature disappears, as communication requires pretense and trust is not rewarded.

In today's "civil" society, Rousseau continues, all life is reduced to manifestations: nature is nothing more than its depiction, and never before has there been so much artificiality together with sublime morals and public philosophy in society. Due to this, the origins have been forgotten, man in society estranged from his own nature. The thesis of the alienation of man is expressed as follows: we have nothing to show for ourselves but a frivolous and deceitful appearance, "honour without virtue, reason without wisdom, and pleasure without happiness" (*ibid.*, pp. 66–7). The answer to this theory of estrangement is given in the *Contrat Social*.

Here, Rousseau discusses Hume's topic of public opinion; however, he doubts its power to determine the political will. At best, that which is behind public opinion is the will of the majority, which includes the will of the minority but does not express it. The *volonté de tous* is thus a purely arithmetical relation which may be most changeable without its general validity being guaranteed. Due to this, Rousseau introduces a second, higher authority which he calls *volonté générale* (general will). Politics must obey laws; by them as by all political decisions the *volonté générale* must be expressed, that is not simply public opinion and the will of the majority which is influenced by it. Sovereignty is nothing other than the "exercise of the general will" (Rousseau 2004a, p. 26).

An essential role for Rousseau's theory of social contract is the "liberté conventionelle" or civil freedom, which in *Emile* becomes a fundamental category. Each of its members must surrender to society his natural freedom and for this gets an egalitarian order or a common "corps politique" (O.C. III, p. 363). This political body is virtuous and collective at the same time. It is based on a contract which is voluntarily made by individuals. This way, a state develops which is itself a moral person (personne morale) (*ibid.*). If ever the social pact is violated, "every man regains his original rights and, recovering his natural freedom, loses that civil freedom for which he exchanged it" (Rousseau 2004a, p. 15).

The state is not simply the rational administration of power but a moral person. To the latter, and *only to the latter*, the citizens are obliged. This, however, comes along with one condition, which Rousseau names clearly: if the social contract is supposed to be more than an empty formula, it is tacitly implied in the commitment "that whoever refuses to obey the general will shall be constrained to do so by the whole body, which means nothing other that he shall *be forced to be free*" (*ibid.*, p.19; italics J.O.).

For this is the necessary condition which, by giving each citizen to the nation,[70] secures him against all personal dependence, it is the condition which shapes both the design and the working of the political machine, and which alone bestows justice on civil contracts – without it, such contracts would be absurd, tyrannical and liable to the grossest abuse. (*ibid.*, pp. 19–20)

One could add that this condition in certain respects also counts for the pedagogical machine. The child, too, is not free but bound to the general will of education. All liberties are well regulated, there is a sovereign and contract, but Emile is led by a person and not by a body politic, and the child cannot decide upon the contract.

At the end of the *Contrat Social* Rousseau sketched the *religion civile*, the *civil religion* which was supposed to be the opposite of the Christian "religion of humanity."[71] That is the real reason for his dispute with Leonhard Usteri. The latter's draft of a Christian republic (république chrétienne) had no basis, Rousseau writes on July 18th, 1763. If "simple love of conversation" was supposed to be the foundation of social community, then "à la bonne heure"; this kind of love is felt by everybody and does not oblige anyone to anything. What is lacking is the "love of duties" and an answer to the question of toward where the passions of the people should be orientated. Great things require great passions, not simply conversation (Correspondance t. XVII, pp. 62–5).

In the *Contrat Social* Rousseau had given reasons as to why a Christian republic which many contemporary authors dreamed of was definitely impossible. Christianity "preaches only servitude and submission," and its spirit is too much in favor of political tyranny which at all times had derived benefit from it (Rousseau 2004a, p. 164). Considered in connection with societies generally, there are three types of religion, which all have "defects": the "religion of man" is to be distinguished from the "religion of the citizen" and the "religion of priests." The first is "pure and simple religion of the Gospel"; the second is the religion "established in one country"; and the third gives men two orders, one for society and one for religion, and "prevents their being at the same both churchman and citizen" (*ibid.*, p. 160). This religion divides the political body while the other two are either too close or too distant to it (*ibid.*, pp. 161–2).

In respect of politics, not only Christian but all religions would have to be replaced by a purely civilian confession. It is not based on dogmas but on emotions, the "sentimens de sociabilité" (O.C. III, p. 468). Without these "expressions of social conscience" it is impossible "to be either a good citizen or a loyal subject" (*ibid.*, p. 166). His social emotions tie the loyal citizen to society and they teach him how to respect and to love at the same time the contract with this society. Whoever is not able to do so must be considered asocial (insociable). He can or must be exiled, not because he lacks faith but because he is incapable of seriously loving the laws (aimer les loix), striving for justice, and, if necessary, sacrificing his life for civil duty.

This does not happen due to insight but to emotional obligation, which is supposed to be the foundation of society. The dogmas of civil religion are in accordance with this obligation as they do not serve the Church but natural God and society, under the precondition of a final threat. "If anyone, after having publicly acknowledged these ... dogmas, behaves as if he did not believe in them, then let him be put to death, for he has committed the greatest crime, that of lying before the law" (*ibid.*).

The dogmas of civil religion serve for being loyal to society. Rousseau, critic of Church doctrine, definitely not without thinking, speaks of "dogmas," that is codifications of the obligation of faith. Originally, the Greek word *dogma* translates as "opinion" and "instruction" or "doctrine" without attaching a final meaning to this. Only the Church councils of ancient Christianity formulated dogmas in today's sense, that is doctrines which are not allowed to be doubted.[72]

In this sense Rousseau understands dogmas to be the foundation of civil religion, that is the precondition of the cohesion of society, which does not come by itself. Other than in Hume, there are no media of communication through which praise or rejection are publicly expressed; more so that social cohesion must be doubtlessly secured. "Public praise or blame" would provide a loose obligation which could be broken up according to every change of public opinion. Society would not be a constant but a changing and even unpredictable entity. It would depend on the formation of public opinion and definitely would not be a holy tie. But just that it would have to be if it was supposed to replace the natural state without loss. Due to this, there must be a civil religion and thus new dogmas:

> The dogmas of civil religion must be simple and few of number, expressed precisely and without explanations or commentaries. The existence of an omnipotent, intelligent, benevolent divinity that foresees and provides; the life to come; the happiness of the just; the punishment of sinners; the sanctity of the social contract and the law – these are the positive dogmas. As for the negative dogmas I would limit them to a single one: no intolerance. Intolerance is something which belongs to the religions we have rejected. (*ibid.*)

"Civil religion" is clearly a substitute, a religion where really there cannot be any. But also in respect of sociology no materialist conclusions shall be drawn. Even the civil religion needs the idea of a deity, otherwise there could be no talk of creation and there would indeed be the need to argue materialistically. Man's accordance with nature would not be possible, not even indirectly through natural education.

Thus, at the end of the *Contrat Social* Rousseau no longer argues by way of legal theory but by starting out from the problem of what must replace the Church if a civil society is supposed to be constituted. Religion must be taken away from the sovereignty of interpretation by the denominations without opening up possibilities to retreat to them. There is only one way to achieve this: shifting the holy toward society and putting all other social obligations last. The social contract must be considered a kind of second creation if it is supposed to come close to first nature.

The social contract, Rousseau says in the *Letters Written from the Mountain*, is a pact of a special kind, "by which each engages himself toward all, from which follows the reciprocal engagement of all toward each, which is the immediate object of the union" (Rousseau 2001, p. 231). This commitment is absolute, that is without any condition or reserve, and it can neither be unjust nor be in danger of being abused, as it forms a political body and this body will not hurt itself "as long as the whole wills only for all" (*ibid.*, pp. 231–2).

But by his life Rousseau himself showed most of all one thing: the significance of *being different*. The counter-model of his theory of the sovereign and of the political body is found in his own way of life, which was focused on himself and his own ambitions. If friendship is a social contract based on mutuality, then during his life Rousseau rarely kept one contract without ever accepting any other "sovereign" than himself. He lived against the grain and was not subject to any kind of civil life. "Society" was fought for or idealized by Rousseau but never accepted, and not at all in the form of public blame or praise.

In *Nouvelle Héloise* there is a contrast which is telling in this respect. "Worldly honour," St Preux writes to Julie in the second part of the novel, may increase wealth but does not reach the soul and does not influence true happiness. The very essence of happiness is "genuine honour," that is inner appreciation which is independent of public opinion. "Only in it can that permanent sentiment of inner satisfaction be found which alone can make a thinking being happy" (Rousseau 1997, p. 69). Rousseau's different accounts of his life always concern the question of whether this equation of happiness and honor has ever been true for him.

Life as a Confession

Since St Augustine, "confessions" have been a repeatedly employed genre of occidental literature. Rousseau does not choose this reference coincidentally but prudently. The *Confessiones*, Augustine's "confessions," were written between AD 397 and 401.[73] They count among the most widely read books in the Christian world because they express an individual search and a common ground of each experience of faith. The thirteen books of the *Confessions* are a manifest of the inner world or a history of heart (Brown 2000, ch. 16). The "burden of the world" (St Augustine 1998, p. 141) is combined with man's looking at himself or "profound self-examination" in the "sight of [his] heart" (*ibid.*, p. 152), and the search for God is explained as a conversion of life (*ibid.*, pp. 163ff.).

By his own example Augustine tells how out of the misery of the world man can learn to be close to God. False life must be given up and a new life must be searched for. God is called the "inward teacher" in the "school of heart" (*ibid.*, p. 170). The metaphor *schola pectoris* (Augustinus 1987, p. 460) is probably used for the first time in Christian literature. Whoever follows his heart guided by God is close to Christian humility, which cannot be achieved in the world because the latter is determined by vanity and luxury. Thus, Augustine described a rejection of the society of the courts toward Christian life, which alone is dedicated to virtue by faith. What has to be found is called *Deus cordis mei* (*ibid.*, p. 478) or "God of my heart" (Saint Augustine 1998, p. 177).

Rousseau's *Confessions*, written for himself and meant to be published after his death,[74] are not only by their title adapted from Augustine's confessions. However, they are not a confession of faith but of life. In this sense, Rousseau's *Confessions* are not an "answer" to Augustine, as has occasionally been stated (Hartle 1983). But Rousseau followed Augustine in respect of a very fundamental question: how can one tell the truth and how can others know about it when no one "knows what is going on in a person except the human spirit which is within"? (*ibid.*, p. 180) This was also the key question in St Paul's First Letter to the Corinthians.[75] The confessions of a person form the literary genre to cope with this question.

That which Augustine calls his "internal doctor" (*medicus meus intime*) (Augustinus 1987, *ibid.*),[76] that is God who guides the confession, becomes for Rousseau a profoundly explored self-research at the end of his life. But there is a similar aspiration in both confessions. Augustine asked how his readers can be sure that he is telling the truth when confessing his life and sins:

> So as I make my confessions, they wish to learn about my inner self, where they cannot penetrate with eye or ear or mind. Yet although they wish to do that and are ready to believe me, they cannot really have certain knowledge. The love which makes them good people tells them that *I am not lying in confessing about myself*, and the love in them believes me. (St Augustine 1998, p. 181; italics J.O.)

Rousseau claims just this veracity. He wants to recount his life just as it really was, without lies or omissions. What he presents is neither a radical conversion nor a declaration of believing in God, but the confessions of a life, a "self" which is without disguise and therefore truly accessible. Thus, Rousseau is responsible to no other sovereign than himself.

In this respect, Augustine's "confessions" were meant not to be reached but to be surpassed in a new way. In his preface of the *Confessions* Rousseau sketches what awaits the reader. The first sentence of the book says: "This is the only portrait of a man, painted exactly according to nature and in all its truth that exists and will probably ever exist" (Rousseau 2000, p. 3). Nothing else, it says, was depicted in the *Confessions* than his own life, according to what nature had told him, and this was done by unrestrained sincerity for which there was no historical example. It was the "only sure monument" of his character which had not already been disfigured by his enemies (*ibid.*).

Augustine does not know such a demand, and here lies the difference. Rousseau does not look for God, who is certain, but for himself and for the course of his life. Augustine is able to refer to divine mercy, no matter how far away it may be; in this sense Augustine speaks of himself as God's newborn "child" (St Augustine 1998, p.182); Rousseau is only able to refer to and rely on himself. But also he wants to show – like Augustine – as the result of his confessions not "what I was but *what I am now*" (*ibid.*, p. 181; italics J.O.). Thus, the confession of life tells not only about the course of life but also about the making of inner self.

This way, Rousseau (2000, p. 270) writes the "history of his soul" and not that of his faith. "The particular object of my confessions is to make known my inner self, exactly as it was in every circumstances of my life" (*ibid.*). This history is confronted with a rigorous demand: in every respect, at every time and to everybody he wanted to be "truthful and just" (*ibid.*, p. 390) even if other people do not like it. Due to this demand the memoirs of his life stood alone, "a work that would be unique for a veracity for which there was no model, so that for once at least a man might be seen from the inside and exactly as he was" (*ibid.*, p. 505), without needing to pretend and without depending on other people's opinions.

The first six books of the *Confessions*[77] were published in 1781, three years after Rousseau's death, the last six as late as 1788, one year before the French Revolution. Both publications were done by friends of Rousseau, and the volumes published in Geneva, not in Paris.[78] Rousseau's confessions aroused great attention, due in part to the much-feared disclosures on those whom Rousseau considered his enemies. In his letters he had indicated the development and purpose of this work, and right from the beginning many rumors circulated on his *Confessions*.

Why should he write about himself, Rousseau had asked at the beginning of the year 1762.[79] If he looked at his life, it was marked by unease regarding the matters of the world and the kind of society where he did not find a place. "For a long time I myself was deceived as to the cause of that unconquerable distaste I always experienced for intercourse with people. I attributed it to the chagrin at not having presence of mind enough to show in conversation what little wit I do have, and consequently to take the place in the world I thought I deserved" (Rousseau 1937, p. 204). But what was the reason for this experience? "It is none other than that unconquerable spirit of liberty which nothing has been able to put down, and before which honours, fortune, and reputation itself are as nothing" (*ibid.*).

Freedom from the world and from the ordinary business of men was what Rousseau demanded for himself. The image of this life is a counter-portrait which is supposed to show by the example of at least one person – himself – what a free life is and the price of leaving society for it. He was born for loneliness, Rousseau says,[80] and writing down his life should be a confession of his own path, self-confession alone being the appropriate form to judge on a life. Only he could understand himself; nobody else could judge on his life, which belonged only to himself: "No one can write a man's life except himself" (Rousseau 2000, p. 644).

The way one looks at oneself and remembers life is the way one is. There is no other authentic picture of a person and there cannot be another one. In this sense, Rousseau writes to Malherbes:

> I am unburdening my heart to you in writing this, and I cannot take any other course. I will paint myself without deception and without modesty; I will reveal myself to you as I see myself and as I am, for since I spend my life alone, I ought to know myself, and I see by the way those who think they know me interpret my actions and conduct that they know nothing about it: no one in the world knows me but myself – you will say so too, when I have told you all. (Rousseau 1937, p. 206)

Rousseau himself read from the manuscript of the *Confessions* to private audiences during the last months of 1770 and the first of 1771. In the course of hour-long sessions, which sometimes lasted half a day or longer, curious listeners were informed of details, most of all from Books VI to IX, which deal with experiences of life in Paris and also give events and names clearly. These readings were banned and the ban goes back to an intervention by Madame d'Epinay at the police in Paris. Rousseau's former patron was enraged upon hearing about the readings and the rumors on their content.[81]

But that is a contemporary side-note. The *Confessions* are no investigative novel about revenge. What Rousseau presents is indeed a confession which tries to make the freedom of his way of life with all its contradictions understandable. "Few men have done worse things than I, and no man has ever said of himself what I have to say about myself" (Rousseau 2000, p. 647). Doing this, Rousseau handles the demand of showing himself "by the complete truth of his nature" (Lecercle 1976) in such a superior way that behind this confession his own nature threatens to disappear.[82] He himself is the confession. And that is not done without methodological reflection.

Rousseau frequently relates his method. In the preface of *Narcisse* from 1753 he says: "To do so I will follow, according to my customary practice, the simple and easy method that suits the truth. I will establish the state of the question anew, I will set out my sentiment anew, and I will wait to be shown how, based on that exposition, my actions belie my discourses" (Rousseau 1992a, p.189). This is also the method of the *Confessions*, only the topic has shifted. This is now the question of which way should one describe one's own life, that is *all* actions and discourses which were of importance? Nobody has recorded them, and the author never knows what was added later when remembering his own past.

In the first book (2000, p. 17) Rousseau speaks of the "dark and miry labyrinth," which he says to have felt during his confessions. The reason is given as follows: "It is not what is criminal that is hardest to reveal, but what is laughable or shameful." The *Confessions* start with a scene of feeling ashamed of some erotic fantasy. Only after this, as Rousseau says, he had found his role of a confessor and had been able to write down what his sentiment suggested to him (*ibid.*). In the confessions he presented the *être sensible* (sentimental being) which he was right from the first traces of his life, without knowing how the single elements fitted together.

> I find elements in myself which, while they may seen incompatible, have nevertheless united to produce a uniform and simple effect, while I find others which, although they appear to be the same, have, thanks to the conjunction of circumstances, entered into such different combinations that one cannot imagine how there could ever have been any connection between them. (*ibid.*)

In this sense, he researches his inner universe and hides neither his astonishment nor his fear. His confessions do show the projects of his life but not the expected or claimed successes. Experience consists of occasions which may change every direction of life; only emotion is reliable and thus the lessons of the heart. "I am left with only *one faithful guide* upon which I can rely: and that is *the chain of feelings* that have marked the successive stages of my being and, through them, of the events that were their cause or effect" (*ibid.*, p. 270; italics J.O.).

In his confessions Rousseau describes the whim of emotion and company, of being lifted up, and of rejection, the etiquette of flattery, of favor, the advantages of false life, education by women who make him forget about everything that in theory he found so convincing. It is not *vertu* that guides life, but, if anything, the *attitude* of virtue behind which the passions hide whose fulfillment is only increased by loneliness in the end. One must draw attention to oneself, services by other people await repayment, and appreciation by those who are in the position to judge others must always be regained (Rousseau 2000, p. 298). No society or relationship can overcome this state; one would only be "alone together" (Todorov 1996).

One must be careful about good luck, every success makes enemies, failures are constantly increasing, often great events are the path to misery, the next day is uncertain, but still one must be ready for it. What one is striving for is not what one gets. Expectations of pleasure are predictions of pain, and "true pleasure cannot be described" (Rousseau 2000, p. 345). By attempting this one will punish oneself without being able to really recognize oneself. The moment cannot be grasped because time changes everything and may change every form of life once found. And it is not only true for his always precarious health when Rousseau notes: "Everything that brings relief to others . . . only increased my suffering" (*ibid.*, p. 345).

In *Reveries of the Solitary Walker* the dissipating happiness of life becomes an even stronger topic: "As for happiness which lasts, I doubt that it is known here. In our most intense enjoyments, there is hardly an instant when the heart can genuinely say to us: *I would like this instant to last forever*. And how can we call happiness a fleeting state which leaves our heart still worried and empty, which makes us long for something beforehand or desire something else afterward?" (Rousseau 2000a, p. 46) Only nature offers the chance of experiencing a truly happy moment which has got nothing to do "with an imperfect, poor, and relative happiness such as one finds in the pleasures of life" (*ibid.*).

However, even the most intense confession of life cannot always be honest. At least, it is also playing with exaggeration or with hiding true motivations, particularly when honesty is supposed to be demonstrated. It is not only a confession but also a projection when Rousseau discusses his role as the father of children and then says: "Never for a single moment in his life could Jean-Jacques have been without sentiment, without pity, an unnatural father. I may have deceived myself, but I could never have hardened my heart" (Rousseau 2000, p. 347). Here there is that which was supposed to be avoided, that is justification. Rousseau knew that the decision to give his children to orphanages (enfants-trouvés) after their birth cannot be understood to be anything other than "hardening."

Early on he looked for confidantes and used them for justification. On April 20th, 1751 Rousseau wrote to Madame de Francueil that he had given away his children (Correspondance t. II, pp. 142–4).[83] If he considered his situation, this was a misery but not a crime. Besides, he had to pay for the support of the children, and at the orphanage they were doing better than with him. "You, Madame, know about my situation; I find it laboriously enough to earn my bread from day to day. How should I additionally support a family? And if I was forced to reach back to writing, how could I in my dive, with domestic worries and the noise of children, keep the quietness of spirit which is necessary for gainful work?"

Responsible for his situation, he says further, were the rich, that is the class to which she, Madame de Francueil, belonged. But at the same time this offered the advantage that he had not to give his children away to this class. At the orphanages they are educated in a better way than with the rich. The orphanages have simple and strict rules, she could easily see for herself. "I know that the children are not brought up tenderly; the better for them, they will be stronger this way; they are not given more than necessary but they have what they need. They are not made fine lords but farmers or craftsmen. I do not see anything about this way of bringing up than what I would not choose myself for my children."

This doubtful confession is also found in a letter to the Duchess of Luxembourg,[84] dated June 12th, 1761 (Correspondance t. IX, pp. 14–17). Rousseau reports on having to shorten his confession and to reveal his ultimate secret to the Duchess's heart. Circumstances had brought him and the mother of his children to give their five children to orphanages, and given such a small chance of ever seeing his children again he had not even remembered their dates of birth. Later he had regretted his decision but had not been able to make amends for this deed. He had tried to find out the whereabouts of one of the children, something which would have made their mother happy, but his action was in vain.

As if trying to raise his own status, Rousseau then writes that his experiences had been included in the book which he was currently writing: "My mistakes as a father inspired my mind while writing my *Treatise on Education*. You will find there in the first book one passage that clearly indicates this disposition."[85] This statement is also written in the *Confessions* (Rousseau 2000, p. 581), where Rousseau works further on his justification which runs also through these two letters. It was an error, he writes in the eighth book of the *Confessions*, to give his children to the orphanage; he had not acted as a "true citizen and father" but as if he had been "a member of Plato's republic" (*ibid.*, p. 348).

On the other hand, he had saved the children from their father's fate and also from being educated by him (*ibid.*). And if he had given them to Madame d'Epinay or to the Duchess of Luxembourg, who had offered to do this for some unknown reason, even worse would have happened to them, that is the fate of the rich: "I am sure that they would have been taught to hate and perhaps betray their parents; it is a hundred times better that they should never have known them" (*ibid.*). It had been a "mistake," it says finally, but "committed through error." He had neglected his duties, but he had never felt the wish to hurt anybody, and after all a father's emotions toward his children could not be very strong if he had never seen them (*ibid.*, p. 349).

The reality of orphanages does not have any bearing over these thoughts. Rousseau mentions neither the high mortality rate among babies given away, nor the rigorous practices of surveillance, nor the cruelties, the hunger, the poverty (Bocquentin 2003). The word "responsibility" is never used by Rousseau; this is about his honor, not his guilt. Giving away his children had been the only way of keeping his honor, he writes to French officer and author Louis Anglancier de Saint-Germain (1738–1773) on February 26th, 1770, in another lengthy letter of justification which would hardly have been necessary had the thesis been true that he had never been an "unnatural father" (Correspondance t. XXXVII, pp. 272–95). He appeared exactly as one.

However, historically it has been debated whether his story about the orphanages was true at all or whether the babies, as was much more common practice because of costs, were simply abandoned anonymously. After all, it is also unclear whether they were really his children or Thérèse's. All contemporary sources are Rousseau's own (Damrosch 2005, p. 194); they are part of a confession which assumes the facts but offers no evidence. Through them, Rousseau defended himself against slander which Voltaire (1961, pp. 715–18) in his *Sentiments des citoyens* from 1764 was able to present in a virtuoso manner.

"Emotion" and "heart" are ciphers for a personal cult, not for a confession to overcome the barriers of the self. This does not happen simply due to reasons of self-protection. In a letter[86] written after the *Confessions* had been completed Rousseau speaks of the "obscure labyrinth of the hearts" with which one is confronted who opens up his heart to others as clearly as a crystal. Whoever does this will never find real encounters; thus it is better to hide oneself and one's intentions. For the true self there is no place in this world (Correspondance t. XXXVIII, pp. 181–2).

In the middle of his *Confessions* Rousseau wrote about the person who had been developed through his life and who had not been allowed to follow his nature but still had to become himself: "I renounced forever any thought of fortune or preferment. Determined to spend the little time that remained to me in independence and poverty, I concentrated all my inner strength on breaking free of the shackles of public opinion and in doing so courageously, and without troubling myself about the judgement of others, whatever seemed to me to be right" (Rousseau 2000, p. 352).

Freedom in this sense of being independent of the judgment of others is one, if not *the*, leitmotif of Rousseau's philosophy. No luxury and no ambition were supposed to affect freedom which takes into account that sociability will fall by the wayside. Only one's own way of life can be the right one, and it is worth every effort to understand it. "The obstacles I was confronted with and the efforts I made to triumph over them are beyond belief. I succeeded as well as it was possible to do, and better than I had myself hoped. If only I had been able to shake off the yoke of friendship as easily as that of public opinion, I would have accomplished in full my objective, which was the grandest or at least the most consistent with virtue that any mortal has ever conceived" (*ibid.*, pp. 353–4).

Here, "virtue" is not a form of social interaction but truthfulness toward oneself, which must be pushed through against the whole world. At any rate, personal honesty and the struggle for one's own truths must be distinguished from that which is called "public opinion." Here, Rousseau's conflict with David Hume has a more rational dimension. Rousseau mistrusted that which Hume in his political philosophy assumed as being fundamental for civil society: the power and rationality of the political public, which he – Rousseau – had found neither in Paris nor in London.

In contrast, Rousseau refers to his own experience rather than an overarching rational foundation: "While trampling underfoot the mindless judgments of the vulgar crowd of the so-called great and the so-called good, I let myself be subdued and ruled like a child by my so-called friends, who, jealous at seeing me tread alone an untrodden path, and while appearing concerned only to make me happy, were in fact concerned only to make me look ridiculous, and began by working to demean me so that they might at length dishonour me. What attracted their jealousy was not so much my literary fame as my personal reform" (*ibid.*, p. 353). Trust nobody, not even your closest friends, and most of all beware of public opinion.

Montaigne in the Third Book of *Essais* had assumed a kind of law of nature of public exchange, according to which errors cumulate. By it, the nature of rumor or hearsay is described:

> The private error first creates the public error, and afterward in turn the public error creates the private error. Thus this whole structure goes on building itself up and shaping itself from hand to hand; so that the remotest witness is better instructed than the nearest, and the last informed more convinced than the first. It is a natural progression. For whoever believes anything esteems that it is a work of charity to persuade another of it, and in order to do so does not fear to add out of his own invention as much as he sees to be necessary in his story to take care of the resistance and the defect he thinks is in the other person's comprehension. (Montaigne 1958, p. 786)

Far from seeing matters in such a prosaic way, Rousseau, who often referred to Montaigne, in a letter from November 23rd, 1770 feels to be in the midst of a plot[87] for which he has no explanation but which must still clearly exist. For, again and again in the "gazettes," news about him was published against which he was unable to defend himself and which darkened all his life (Correspondance t. XXXVIII, pp. 137–8). The "age of decrees" against him is supposed to spoil his reputation, and not only his enemies, like Hume or Walpole, work against him in public, but also his friends turn away from him: "Step by step everything around me is changing," and not to the better but to the worse (*ibid.*, p. 138).

Gone is the "security of innocence" and thus his trust in friendship (*ibid.*, p. 139). The way of talking has changed, the "tune" of patrons has changed, some secret hate toward him was obvious: those who had been friendly toward him were now treating him with contempt, and those to whom he had entrusted his manuscripts had embezzled them and betrayed him (*ibid.*, pp. 139–40). Letters are answered with silence and inquiries only increase uncertainty (*ibid.*, p. 140). "The completed project of driving me into insanity could not have been carried out better" (*ibid.*, p. 141).

The *Reveries*, Rousseau writes in 1778, were laid out "as appendix to my *Confessions*." But these days he would not choose this title again because it does not mention anything which could be to his credit. "What would I still have to confess now that all my earthly affections have been torn from it? I have no more reason to praise than to blame myself: I am henceforward nothing among men, and that is all I can be, no longer having any real relations of genuine society with them. No longer able to do any good which does not turn evil, no longer able to act without harming another or myself, to abstain has become my sole duty and I fulfil it as much as it is in me to do so" (Rousseau 1992, p. 7).

In the above-quoted letter to DuPeyrou from March 31st, 1769 Rousseau had asked, why not do it like the children and the drunkards? They suffer neither broken arms nor legs when falling because they do not know about being careful and do not assume to fall. This, he says, leads back to the great maxim behind his work: if we let things happen and do not interfere, we will not make any mistakes; and: let us never act (regimber) against the necessities of nature to which we must bow (Correspondance t. XXXVII, p. 75).

Rousseau's *Confessions* also demonstrate that life and the theory of education are two different entities. It is definitely not "la route de la nature" which controls experience, there is no *amour de soi* to calm down the passions of comparison, control of society and sex by fixed ways of internalization is not possible, as truth requires error, virtues require vice, and no intention is free of the chance to fail. One will always be the victim of other people's judgments and thus will never be really independent. All power will be possible only gradually. In this sense, through his *Confessions* Rousseau also contests his own theories, and ultimately this ensures his greatness.

3

Theory of Education

Rousseau's interest in educational topics is explained not only by his life but also by the political premises of his question; that what he takes into account as being "natural education" is purpose-bound. When at the beginning of *Emile* he says that it is only possible to educate the man (l'homme) *or* the citizen (le citoyen) but never both of them (Rousseau 1993, p. 7), this means a sequence, not a relation of exclusion, as many Rousseau interpreters have assumed. As a child, man must be educated according to nature so that he will have the strength to be himself as a citizen and to join a social contract.

Rousseau's theory of education developed gradually, and it is neither free of contradictions nor a wide-ranging concept (Terrasse 1992). More precisely, one must say that Rousseau did not present *one* theory of education but several, which differ according to his method of argument. In *Nouvelle Héloise* (1761) "education" has a different meaning than in the *Considérations sur le gouvernement de Pologne et sur sa reformation projétée* (1770–1). And Rousseau's numerous comments on questions of education in his letters represent another different approach, as he is confronted with concrete questions which cannot be answered simply by referring to *Emile*.

In *Nouvelle Héloise* Rousseau stresses emphatically the significance of the mother in educating younger children, a topic which is not found at all in *Emile* one year later. In the *Considérations sur le gouvernement de Pologne* he considers the development of society as a factor which categorically excludes the theory of education found in *Emile*, that is national school education and lessons for all children. In the essay on political economy from 1755 he speaks in favor of a Spartan version of education toward patriotism, while in *Contrat Social* he conspicuously avoids any indication of education.

To judge Rousseau's theoretical achievements, the contexts of the contemporary debate must be considered. Rousseau was neither the first nor the only author of the eighteenth century to consider "natural education." The predominant significance of his theory in particular was developed later and refers only to *Emile*. Inconsistencies within Rousseau's educational theory have rarely been noticed by the critics. Thus, something may often appear comprehensive and unique which is in fact contradictory and leaves loose ends.

Why Rousseau dealt with questions of education to such an extent, something which would not have occurred to either Voltaire, Diderot, or Grimm, cannot be answered by simply referring to the increasing quantity of literature from the mid-1830s. Authors like LaMettrie or Helvétius have dealt with the topic of education to such an extent that Rousseau could even have decided against writing *Emile*. In addition, he probably would not have wanted to be one author among many. In the preface to *Emile*, which has often been ignored, Rousseau tells of his motivation to write on education after all, which he barely commented on in his letters.

The first sentence of *Emile* is as follows: "This collection of scattered thoughts and observations has little order or continuity; it was begun to give pleasure to a good mother who thinks for herself" (Rousseau 1993, p. 1). The addressee of the book is not simply the reading public but the "good mother"[88] whose genuine work of education is to be supported. Such a mother, however, is not found at all in *Emile*. The perspective is imaginary; Rousseau writes for a "thinking mother" who is mentioned only in the first sentence of the foreword. The exposé and the reason for this book go much further and are not restricted to the educational instincts of a mother who probably has only limited space for paradoxes. The boy, Emile, is considered to be an orphan for educational reasons. He left his father and mother to be guided by nature (*ibid.*, p. 23).

Originally, Rousseau continues in the preface, he had intended to write merely a short memoir; this had now developed into a kind of tract which was too long for what that entailed and too short for the subject matter. Although it was not perfect he had allowed the tract to be printed, as the topic of education deserved great public attention. He was not going to say much on the value of good education, or to prove that common education was bad. A thousand other authors had already done this, and he was not going to fill his book with common knowledge.

His demand is completely different, introduced thus: since the beginnings of history there has been a repeated outcry against established practice, be it of society or education, without saying how things could be handled better:

> The literature and science of our day tend rather to destroy than to build up. We find fault after the manner of a master; to suggest, we must adopt another style, a style less in accordance with the pride of a philosopher. In spite of all those books, whose only aim, so they say, is public utility, the

most useful of all arts, the art of training men,[89] is still neglected. Even after Locke's book was written the subject remained almost untouched, and I fear that my book leaves it pretty much as it found it. (*ibid.*, p. 1)

The demand is thus not to simply claim the use of his theory but to give evidence for practical education. But were there not hundreds of tracts precisely for this purpose? Literature on education has always been "practical," for around 1750 hundreds of writings can be evidenced for France alone, which show what Rousseau presents as his own and "completely new" topic. They must all have been wrong if Rousseau is to have been right. What made him so sure? Why did he believe that he had written the first real tract on education and thus the re-foundation of the field even after Locke?

The answer is as simple as it is clever: Rousseau introduces himself as the first author who designs education from the nature of childhood. Thus, the perspective is not that of the thinking mother but of the child, and for this Rousseau claims authenticity:

We know nothing of childhood; and with our mistaken notions the further we advance the further we go astray. The wisest writers devote themselves to what a man ought to know, without asking what a child is capable of learning. They are always looking for the man in the child, without considering what he is before he becomes a man. It is to this study that I have chiefly devoted myself, so that if my method is fanciful and unsound, my observations may still be of service. (*ibid.*, p. 2)

The key role of learning for educational theory had, however, already been discussed by Locke, without contrasting "knowledge" with "learning." But Rousseau wants to re-found *childhood*, not simply "learning." For this, he says later in the foreword, the systematic part of the book had been developed, which is on nothing less than the "course of nature." This makes Rousseau indeed different from Locke and all the sensualists, and due only to this is he able to understand knowledge and learning to be in contrast. He does not ask how learning could be influenced to improve knowledge but how education could adjust to the natural learning of the child.

Rousseau knew – and said so – that this systematic part would meet the severest criticism, which would condemn him. The theory itself and not the practicability of his suggestions would determine the reception. It speaks well for Rousseau that he is able to anticipate the reaction of many of his readers to the theoretical core of his book and that also he finds clear words for this: "It is here that the reader will probably go wrong, and no doubt I shall be attacked on this side, and perhaps my critics may be right. You will tell me, 'this is not so much a treatise on education but the visions of a dreamer with regards to education'" (*ibid.*).

Development of the Theory

Rousseau's first educational writing, a product of his short spell as a private tutor in Lyon,[90] recognizes two extreme positions of educational theory, pedagogical and paternal. The *educators*, that is the private tutors, want – in this order – to educate the heart, the faculty of judgment, and the mind; the *fathers*, that is the principals of the tutors, want future doctors to develop (O.C. IV, p. 7). It is a moderate kind of education, as Rousseau says, not to neglect the sciences, but also not to exaggerate studies and to lay the necessary emphasis on education toward morality, as it is not useful for the child to know about the sciences but at the same time – and due to this – to have his heart spoiled (*ibid.*).

In a letter from April, 1740, that is immediately before his own time as a tutor, Rousseau thinks about his future job and his chances as an educator. His master, Gabriel Bonnet de Mably, had asked about the conditions under which twenty-eight-year-old Rousseau would be ready to enter his service. He himself, Rousseau writes, was barely sensitive in respect of his interests, but much more so of the respect shown toward him. Only an honorable man was able to educate, and only somebody whose heart was free of misery and who had not to bear heavy burdens was able to get along with children (Correspondance t. I, pp. 119–20). Thus, it had to be in the fathers' interest that tutors were not in such a subordinate position, and only then could they expect children to show respect toward tutors (*ibid.*, p. 120).[91]

The compromise between the interests of fathers and those of tutors is formulated in the official report to Mably. In the *Confessions* (2000, p. 261) Rousseau describes how his work as tutor failed because of Mably's two sons. The older one had been open-minded, intelligent, and very lively; the younger one "appeared almost stupid, and certainly idle, stubborn as a mule and incapable of learning anything" (*ibid.*). Together, they proved to be bad and uneducable. Anyway, he was the wrong educator for them: "I studied my pupils' minds, I understood them thoroughly, and I do not think that I was ever once taken in by their ruses: but what good did it do me to recognize the ill, when I was incapable of applying the remedy? I may have understood everything, but I avoided nothing, I achieved nothing, and everything I did was precisely what I ought not to have done" (*ibid.*).

Ten years later, in the above-mentioned letter to Madame de Francueil from April 20th, 1751, Rousseau sketches a "robust education" (éducation rustique) which is distinguished from that which the children of the rich experience as bad education:

> If I had the power, I would not by softening prepare them. Labor and fresh air cause illnesses for those who are not used to this. In my education they would neither learn how to dance nor how to ride, but they would be provided with good, tireless legs. I would neither make them to be authors nor public officials: I would not teach them to handle the quill but the plough, the file, and the sword, instruments which enable to live a healthy, laborious, innocent life, which are never abused for doing evil and do not make enemies for the righteous. This is their destination; due to the robust education they are given they will be happier than their father. (Correspondance t. II, pp. 143–4)

In the sense of this passage the thesis is true that Rousseau's experience as a father influenced the development of his thoughts on education. The letter concerns the fate of his children, but the occasion of justification is used for sketching a counter-portrait of the conventional practice, a *rustic* or *robust* type of education which keeps distance from all kinds of pampering. Rousseau does not want a child to be coddled. Nature alone is supposed to be essential for education, to prepare children for a healthy, laborious, and virtuous life which has not been spoiled by social class.

In the Second Discourse from 1755 Rousseau connected nature's "robust" education to a suitable historical example. His concept of education is to be considered not just a theory but an experience of the past:

> Children, bringing into the world the excellent constitution of their Fathers and fortifying it with the same training that produced it, thus acquire all the vigour of which the human species is capable. Nature treats them precisely as the Law of Sparta treated the Children of Citizens: it renders strong and robust those who are well constituted and makes all the others perish, thereby differing from our societies, in which the state, by making Children burdensome to their fathers, kills them indiscriminately before their birth. (Rousseau 1992, p. 21)

In the fall of 1758 Rousseau started work on *Emile*[92] and tried to tie his scattered thoughts on education together. Three years before only the basic question was clear. The education of the natural state, when children leave their mothers as soon as they are strong enough to support themselves (*ibid.*, p. 30), did not know social ties but only functions, and it demanded more from the children than from their parents (*ibid.*). Savage man from his childhood onward was "alone, idle, and always near danger" (*ibid.*, p. 25).

The question is what natural education may be under the preconditions of a developed society, where danger appears to be different than in nature.

To answer this question, Rousseau moves away from the argument in the report to Mably. This way of arguing could not be sustained; both tutors and fathers are not right and misunderstand the child's nature. A robust education is orientated neither toward the expectations of fathers nor toward those of schools. Rousseau is no longer interested in the traditional relation of educating the heart on the one hand and teaching and knowledge on the other; his theory is by no means about formal teaching and training but about development and the moratorium of nature, which is put in a strict contrast to society and thus to educational institutions. This becomes ever clearer in the later stages of *Emile*.

Rousseau's first attempts at theory were under the influence of Charles Rollin's *Traité des études*, the authoritative compendium of French tutors until 1750 and one of the few educational writings which can be authenticated for Rousseau's own reading.[93] Rollin founded new principles of scholarly lessons: on the one hand, in respect of the significance of studying national history; and on the other hand, in respect of the use of French instead of Latin textbooks. How does Rousseau end up from a many-volumned work of didactics on reforming scholarly teaching with the concept of "natural education," which speaks out against any kind of learning in the course of which children are taught by help of books?

The development of the theory has, not least, to do with Rousseau's reading of contemporary literature on pediatrics (e.g. Brouzet 1754).[94] Since their beginnings in the fifteenth century, pediatrics' textbooks allowed a view of education which was independent of "teachers" and "fathers."[95] In the relevant works of children's medicine the *nature* of the child is described, what could be done for his healthy development, and how one should react to children's illnesses. In this sense, these textbooks are manuals where the natural ways of education are introduced and proven by the analysis of concrete cases.[96]

Not only childhood illnesses but also concepts of "children" are part of the professional knowledge of general medicine (James 1747, pp. 541–74).[97] This empirical knowledge has decisively influenced the standards of domestic education.[98] The natural "management of children" in British literature of the mid-eighteenth century (Cadogan 1748) refers to care, diet,[99] and sympathetic ways of handling, not to studies and lessons. Learning by books either plays no role for this literature or it was said to affect health.

"Natural" meant education in respect of strengthening natural resistance, as was shown, for example, by cures against fevers (Falconet 1723). Like passions, illnesses were supposed to be understood as a part of the natural history of man (histoire naturelle de l'homme) (Moreau de Saint Elier 1738), which had to start with correct diet and the careful nursing of newborn children (Bermingham 1750). Additionally, children's orthopedics supposed that nature was "correctable" in the case of congenital malformation (e.g. Andry 1741). In this sense, there exists a *medical* natural state of children which can be shaped by doctors and parents. It is the precondition of every kind of education.

Thus, it is one-sided and somewhat misleading to refer the development of Rousseau's concept only to the *educational* discourse, for example to Abbé de Morelly's *Principles of Natural Education*.[100] Also, contemporary writings on morals (for example Toussaint 1748) were not decisive for Rousseau's concept. If Rousseau in the *Confessions* speaks of his "historical study of morality" (Rousseau 2000, p. 395), this means the political theories of antiquity, not contemporary literature on morals. The latter plays a role rather for demarcation. Emile shall be educated according to nature and not to morals.

The unconventional construction of *Emile* is explained by moving away both from concepts of education toward morality and from teaching at school. Rousseau's incentive was not the concept of "natural education" itself, which had already been discussed in the courtly literature of the seventeenth century (Mercier 1961) and which was widespread in France by the mid-eighteenth century. Both the different ideas on health education and the means of communication between parents and their children were considered to be natural. An entire literary genre, for example, suggested that mothers breast-feed their children themselves rather than leave this to wet nurses. Finally, children's talents were also considered to be "natural," as documented by the numerous literature of the *enfants prodiges*.

The concept of nature as "moral authority" goes back to Greek Antiquity (Daston and Vidal 2004) and was revived in the eighteenth century. It has been linked to education not only through pediatrics but also through various kinds of manuals. Rousseau is different in that he equated nature with education. Many authors referred to "nature" as the basis of education but no one said that nature is the only locus where education should take place without any connections to society. Rousseau used the cultural metaphor of a "hermit" to construct the basic scene of his version of natural education, which is more than just stoic; it implies a retreat from society.

The development of Rousseau's theories of education is based on various negations, not only those of the didactics and textbooks of the tutors. One important step is rejecting the concepts of public education. On September 27th, 1758 Rousseau answers a letter by the Geneva jurist Robert Tronchin, who was to attack him later. Tronchin had previously suggested – in Rousseau's eyes – a "very judicial" distinction of how the ancient republic might be distinguished from theirs, that is Geneva. The difference, as Tronchin said, was in "public education," (instruction publique) which was known to the ancient republics but not to the modern ones. If the modern republics were supposed to develop further, they would have to develop a modern kind of public education, as it was indeed discussed by various parts of Swiss republicanism in the eighteenth century.

Rousseau objects that it was not at all certain that a republic like Geneva really needed public education. As an example for this thesis there are the craftsmen (artisans) of Geneva, who are trained by their trade and not by schools. A watchmaker from Geneva must know everything about his trade; a watchmaker from Paris needs only to be able to talk convincingly about watches. The former makes; the latter sells. From this Rousseau draws the conclusion "The education of a worker tends to develop his fingers, nothing more. The citizen, however, still remains; whether for good or evil his head and his heart develop – they always find some time for that – and there you have the things for which our system of education ought to provide" (Rousseau 1937, p. 160).

Thus, if one looks at them in detail, the "general observations" on public education are of little value (*ibid.*). They are abstractions of theory, which cannot present any experience. If thought over thoroughly, equal education for everybody will only result in having the bottom drop out of one's world and in not learning anything sufficiently. Craftsmen will never turn into artificial citoyens, a state which cannot be achieved by school. That which "public education" will only support in the end is corruption of society, and it would be highly unjust to make the craftsmen with their proven way of life a victim of "public corruption" (*ibid.*).

Craftsmen are trained by their trade and not by abstract lessons. Only trade guarantees a solid position in the corrupt world, which starts with the rich while the poor follow it. "This is precisely the average education which is convenient for us, an education between the public education of the Greek and the domestic education of the monarchies, where the subjects remain isolated and have nothing in common but obedience" (*ibid.*). At the end of *Emile* Rousseau will return to this idea; public and equal education for everybody, organized by the state in schools, is out of the question – at least as far as the argument of *Emile* reaches for Rousseau.

However, the provocative nature of Rousseau's theory does not come only from rejecting general school education. It has most of all to do with its literary construction or with that which one might call the "setting" of *Emile*. It contradicts everything which up to then had been considered "education." In Rousseau's setting of childhood there are only two persons, the child and the educator.[101] Absent are all institutions of education such as schools and families, but absent also are all informal influencing entities, like the rows of siblings and children's peer groups. Finally, all signs of particular games and communication cultures of children are lacking. Thus, the setting starts out from a historical *tabula rasa* of education which is supposed to be considered in a completely new way, and that is the course of nature.

The child is a boy named Emile, probably after Plutarch.[102] The boy undergoes a course of treatment, as became common in eighteenth-century medicine. Specifically, Rousseau goes through a fictitious case of education in a setting which requires the remoteness and concentration of a health cure without sharing the latter's special kind of sociability (Essner and Fuchs 2003). The objective is to strengthen the child's nature and to prevent the occurrence of any kind of weaknesses. The child is supposed to become robust and thus to discard every kind of weakness. At the "age of nature" *nothing else* is supposed to count other than the experience of nature.

Rousseau's *Emile*, which is usually called a novel, happens *à la campagne* (O.C. IV, p. 326), that is in a landscape or a natural idyll far away from urban decadence.[103] This motif is found early in Rousseau's letters, thus it was not specially invented for *Emile*. Around 1739 he writes to an unknown addressee on the "tumulte de villes" (hustle and bustle of the cities) and the "fracas du grande monde" (rumble of the wide world) from which one had to escape. "There, one cannot enjoy remoteness and quietness. Let us flee to the country, let us look there for recreation and satisfaction which we could not find near meetings and amusements. Let us try this new way of life, let us try a bit of the friendly sweetness which Horace, a reliable expert on this,[104] has praised so much" (Correspondance t. I, p. 72).

The landscape of the novel is not given in detail and exists only in the reader's imagination. He must work out in detail what exactly *à la campagne* is supposed to mean. Neither the place where the novel is said to happen nor a description of the way to it is given. This strategy has been known since the motif of the *hortus clausus* in medieval literature and is very effectively applied by Rousseau (Gerhardi 1983). Emile is an "élève imaginaire" (O.C. IV, p. 264) in a closed if extensive garden whose exact nature and boundaries remain unknown. By the example of an imaginary child the problem and the possibilities of education according to the course of nature are supposed to be paradigmatically examined. If one trusts the preface of *Emile*, this must be understood to be an instruction for the art of education.

The form is that of a literary fiction or fable[105] which Rousseau constructs (Mall 2002) without reaching back to his own educational experience or that of others, if we exclude the reference to his paternity, his short activities as a teacher of music and as a tutor, or the children of his correspondents. Rousseau never experienced a complete course of education, thus it is correct to speak of a child of *imagination*. At the same time he chooses a method of explanation which makes fiction sound realistic. Countless readers have taken the novel to recount a real-life case and from this have drawn the conclusion that it indeed explains the practical art of education.

In the preface to *Emile* Rousseau comments on this expectation of applicability. For a project such as natural education two issues had to be considered: the first is the quality of the project, which must be good in itself, and the ease of its realization; the second depends on the "given conditions in particular cases," which is not necessarily given. The circumstances of education are indefinitely different, and this is true according to both countries and social classes. That which seems to be practicable in Switzerland is not practicable in France, and that which can be realized for the bourgeoisie must be excluded for the nobility (Rousseau 1993, p. 3). In conclusion, there cannot be the same kind of education in every context, only the project.

Rousseau answers the question on quality like this: it is enough that the project should be intelligible and feasible in itself, "that what is good in it should be adapted to the nature of things, in this case, for example, that the proposed method of education should be suitable to man and adapted to the human heart" (*ibid.*). But, as a matter of fact, a practical art of education would have to offer more than trusting in the "nature of things." Also, it is not enough if the suggested kind of education fits to mankind and can be accepted by the heart. It is not sufficient if the author is convinced of the quality of his proposal: he must stand the test of practice.

Rousseau does so by describing a fiction and making it seem real. The reader is confronted with a "treatise on education" which he is supposed to take seriously. However, what is described in *Emile* is not the experienced reality of a particular case on education with real people and events but a literary demonstration of how education could best be adjusted to the *course of nature*. This is not about practical work but about the plan of a *métier* which is newly invented. Rousseau's question is about what education could achieve ideally, that is under perfect circumstances and free of all reservations. The setting of *Emile* constructs this ideal case from Rousseau's philosophical guidelines.

One part of the setting is the tutor, called in the course of the development "that educator," and introduced without a name. The fictitious child is supplied with a "good tutor" (Rousseau 1993, p. 19) or a *gouverneur*, as stated in the first book (O.C. IV, p. 263), who is supposed to form him as a man, so that he will be able to become a citizen or at least will be able to decide for or against society at the end of his education. This education is the educator's life-work. Each adult can educate only *one* person in the course of his life,[106] thus the educational relationship is restricted to two people.

In this *minimal art* of education not only are there no family nor siblings, but also there are no parents. Rousseau is not the father but the governor, and Emile is an orphan subjected to that which Rousseau in 1751 had called the robust education of the orphanages. In the letter to Madame de Francueil the reference to Plato's *Politeia* is not missing, where, as Rousseau states, an education of children in the absence of their fathers is already mentioned, only that this education is meant for the republic and not for nature, and was thus "cruel and abasing" (vile et basse). So far, the setting of *Emile* can also be understood as a projection of its author.

But this setting also shows a rational aspect. One essential reason for constructing natural education *à la campagne* is to avoid barriers of class. If the child's nature is supposed to achieve justice, education must not be tied to any social class. For Rousseau, society is divided into "rich" and "poor," that is the few who can afford luxury and the many who are excluded from it. This makes Rousseau's "social state" different from that of constitutional law, the category not used in a neutral way. Luxury spoils man's nature, so if there shall be education according to nature, it must exclude luxury of any kind. No rich man can be real, because richness spoiled the nature of man.

In one of his letter-comments[107] on *Emile* Rousseau reflects on this problem as follows:

> If I had the bad luck to be born as a prince, restricted by my class, forced to have a procession of followers, entourage, servants, that is tutors, and still had a well developed mind to be a man despite my class, in order of fulfilling the great hopes of my father, my wife, the citizens of the humanist republic, I would soon feel the difficulties to reduce this to the common denominator, most of all to educate my children for the state or to give them to the service of nature despite all those they find among their kind. (Correspondance t. XVIII, p. 115)

The best circumstances are given if an adult is able to concentrate on one child and does nothing other than to educate him according to nature and unhindered by class. As it says in the *Confessions*, the situation is free of the "rules of social decorum" (Rousseau 2000, p. 486). And, there is no "rift public" (*ibid.*) which divides into opinions that which must develop uninhibitedly and unobserved. For this Rousseau does not demand reality but the reader's imagination. He, the reader, is not supposed to see a certain reality of education but to recognize the paradigm.

Rousseau's paradigm is the first child without sin. What is described in *Emile* is the ideal alternative to the conventional kind of education, that is the child growing up naturally, which up to the twelfth year does not experience anything other than nature by its objectivity, and this without any systematic method of learning. Emile experiences and grasps nature next to him without being taught in formal lessons. He learns from the book of nature, guided by the governor, but alone for himself without needing to relate himself to others or those of his class. The child learns by all senses but without social contacts. This way, the domestication of nature (Rousseau 1992, p. 24) is supposed to be made impossible.

The setting of *Emile* is supposed to be an application of Rousseau's general theory, that is increasing the powers of nature by minimizing desires under complete control of the learning environment. Childhood is the moratorium of nature and is self-sufficient. Emile does not learn increasingly "more" but that toward which he is guided by his Spartan environment. Education *à la campagne* implies a world without social stimulation, a didactic world which is taken up in an arrangement for the child's learning. Institutions of knowledge are absent; learning happens from situations carefully prepared by the governor.

The path of education is also understood to be a *development* of nature. For Rousseau, "development" does not mean an increase or cumulation of any kind, which would contradict the fundamental skepticism toward axioms of progress; development is a sequence of ages of education reaching from birth to the twenty-fifth year. The learning environments are organized in such a way as to being appropriate to each age of education. Thus, Emile does not learn according to his individual needs but to the interests which are supposed to be typical for each age of education.

Inspired by Buffon's *Histoire naturelle*,[108] at the end of his introduction to the "Manuscrit Favre" of *Emile*[109] Rousseau identifies four ages of education.[110] This new idea is that childhood and youth are not understood according to the traditional scheme of life ages, that is they do not represent the beginning of a cycle from birth to death. Rousseau's education is orientated toward an open future without letting life end by a period of decline. The beginning of life becomes independent from the end, the course of "nature" only one of education.

Explanation for this is given by the sequence of ages of education, which is fundamental for the complete construction of *Emile* (O.C. IV, p. 60):

1. the age of education of *nature* reaches as far as to the twelfth year;
2. that of *reason* to the fifteenth;
3. that of *power* to the twentieth; and
4. that of *prudence* to the twenty-fifth.

The time of education refers to all four ages. Everything which is said about "natural education" is thus restricted to the *first* age of education, only here the rules and maxims of learning in the "natural state" are valid. The other ages require a different kind of didactics, something which has almost always been overlooked when referring to Rousseau's concept of education. His theory includes a span of four periods, different things happening in each of them. Already due to this there is not *one* principle directing Rousseau's philosophy of education.

After the completion of education life is open; at the end of the last age of education only a vague "age of happiness" is extended that should last for the rest of life (*ibid.*). Here, one could assume a connection, that is the happiness in life as the result of education, but happiness itself is not an age of *education* which might be guided by a governor. Happiness may be the result of education, but other than in many eighteenth-century sensualist tracts, education does not determine the happiness of life. In this sense, at an essential point in his work, Rousseau remains true to his theorem of freedom.

In respect of life, the ages of education are complete entities; they can be neither longer nor shorter, nor can be subject to subjective feeling. In the "Manuscrit Favre" the second age is called the "age of intelligence" (*ibid.*, p. 165). Already in this version it is the shortest age of education. Also the awakening of intelligence is not possible *before* due time. At the age of nature children are excluded from intelligence, as far as this transcends the immediate place of experience. Up to the twelfth year there are no lessons stimulating intelligence, as there is the precondition that the suitable age of education has not been reached.

The "Manuscrit Favre" is the first version of *Emile* to include the complete composition. Already here are three essential preliminary decisions for later theory. First, man's weakness results from the disproportion of his powers and his desires; only he who minimizes his desires will increase his powers (*ibid.*). Second, intelligence is not a question of knowledge; more precisely, it is not a question of the amount of knowledge, otherwise only somebody who knows everything would be really intelligent, but this is impossible (*ibid.*, pp. 166–7). And third, existing knowledge is either wrong, or waste, or vain (*ibid.*, p. 167) – that is, it is useless for education at the age of nature.

One does not learn simply to know more and more and thus to become prudent more and more, as school education assumes. Rousseau's theory is especially provocative in not assuming an increase of the amount of knowledge. The quality of learning does not improve the more, the longer it takes, simply because there is no development away from that which nature intends. Nothing is possible *before* the time set by nature. Accordingly, Rousseau finds it difficult to cope with a phenomenon which very lastingly determined the courtly society of the eighteenth century and its reflection on education, that is the existence of child prodigies who do not tally with the sequence of ages of education but obviously still follow their nature.

Nothing was more common (commune), Rousseau writes in the second book of *Emile*, than treating children as adults, that is to train them and to have their skills shown on the market. Mentioned are "troops of children" in spectacles "à la Comédie Italienne," the child pantomimes trained by the famous Nicolini,[111] drawing and calculation skills of child prodigies, a little English girl of ten doing "wonders on the harpsichord" (Rousseau 1993, p. 133) and finally, noted in an appendix of the copy from 1764, Mozart, a small boy of seven years who at his performance in Paris was able to show even more astonishing things on the piano (O.C. IV, p. 402, 1398).

Rousseau does not criticize such skills; after all they show that it is possible to do what is feasible: what can be done is done (Rousseau 1993, p. 133). He does not count the training of such skills among intellectuals but, according to the doctrine of the ages of education, among physical education. They are the result of exercises (*ibid.*), not the manifestation of genius. Physical exercises can train the body before its time, which is impossible for the mind. There is a serious warning in the construction of child prodigies in the sense of an educational expectation: "Those so gifted by nature that they rise above the level of their age" are very rare and poor at the same time because they are raised not as children but are treated as adults. They are losing their childhood (*ibid.*, p. 82). But exactly this, the genius of the *enfant prodiges*, is the counter-evidence of Rousseau's construction of a mostly ignorant childhood, characterized only by being close to nature "next to us."

As a consequence of his decision to base education only on the course of nature, finally an essential basic idea of education is negated: that education, no matter at what age, must most of all deal with positively communicating morals. For Rousseau, "natural" education means *negative* education. It does not consist of communicating positive morals to the children but in protecting them from doctrines. Paradoxically, this becomes Rousseau's essential doctrine on education. He knew what he was doing by negating positive education. For some time he considered *Emile* to be the last of his works[112] to be printed and under this pretext to be the completion of his whole philosophy (Correspondance t. XI, p. 24).

Rousseau's emphatic adoration of nature made him a cult which persists today. In the eighteenth and nineteenth centuries this cult took on strange forms. In 1908 an *Iconographie de Jean-Jacques Rousseau*[113] was published, listing more than one thousand collector's items and devotional objects, among them small statues, busts, and pictures, which all indicate not only a public but also a domestic cult (*Iconographie* 1908, tables VI, XI, XII, XIV). This cult reached a peak during the French Revolution, but lasted for the entire nineteenth century, not in officious Geneva but definitely among the reading and book culture of France.

Rousseau himself contributed to this cult. He was not only a conspicuous author but also a strange character; clothing himself provocatively and simply caused sensation. Well known is Allan Ramsey's portrait from 1766,[114] showing Rousseau wearing Armenian clothes and depicting him with a superiority which he actually never affected (Ravier 1941, t. I, fig. opposite p. 96). The French painter Maurice-Quentin de La Tour[115] saw him in a similar way, strangely non-conformist and somehow unworldly (*Iconographie* 1908, table III). Both depictions influence our image of Rousseau up to today; he is almost always seen in the former or the latter way. In contrast to this, many writers did not take into account how Rousseau's views developed and which images he had before his eyes when writing.

That which he called "nature" was based on pictures in his mind. In the *Confessions* Rousseau described the park or the landscape garden of Montmorency and directly connected it to the composition of the fifth book of *Emile* (Rousseau 2000, pp. 509–10). There, artful nature is emphasized, designed by a "skilful artist," where he had enjoyed himself as never before. With Thérèse, his cat, and his dog he would have been able to spend his whole life there without one single moment of boredom: "It was a paradise on earth; I lived there with as much innocence, and I tasted the same happiness" (*ibid.*, p. 510). In this way, the image of the place of natural education comes from the author's immediate view.[116]

Contemporary pictures of Ermenonville, the final residence of his life, show a vast, lavishly designed landscape garden designed by René-Louis de Girardin.[117] One gets an idea of good nature which can be controlled by way of cultivation (*Iconographie* 1908, tables VIII, XI, X). This idea was influenced by Rousseau: by "nature" he did not only mean a biological fact but also an extended landscape, untouched by social conflicts and social unrest. It allows a withdrawal to loneliness just as natural kinds of sociability far away from the city and its decadence (Rousseau 2000, p. 407).

Girardin (1992) himself described how natural space is shaped as a landscape garden[118] by directly using Rousseau's theory of nature. All his life Girardin was a devoted follower of Rousseau, even trying to bring up his own children according to the rules of *Emile*. Also for a garden there should be the rule that nature must direct if a reasonable order is supposed to develop. Another rule is that nature must not be over-ornate. Even a perfect garden knows reservation of luxury. If a garden is sumptuous in an exotic way, Rousseau writes to the Duchess of Portland on July 2nd, 1768, one will not recognize nature.[119]

Rousseau himself did not only perceive landscape gardens as natural paradises. On other places, St Peter's Island in lac de Bienne above all caught his eye. In the *Reveries* the island is described as the place where he had never been happier. The island was the perfect place "for solitary contemplators who like to become intoxicated with the charms of nature at leisure and collect their thoughts in a silence troubled by no noise other than the cry of eagles, the intermittent chirping of a few birds, and the rushing of torrents as they fall from the mountain" (Rousseau 2000a, p. 41). Here, in perfect remoteness, it says in the *Confessions*, he would have liked to spend the rest of his days (Rousseau 2000, p. 626).

The scene of action of *Emile* is not fixed, but Rousseau had precise ideas on what makes a natural landscape. On walks which are combined with observations of nature and "intensive botanizing" he explores St. Peter's Island (Rousseau 2000a, pp. 44–5).[120] One might also imagine the new, natural education as similar to the art of botanizing, having a lot of time, accepting no haste, and trusting in nature to develop according to its own period of growth. The art of education, as Rousseau describes it, requires long ways, patience with seemingly endless repeats, constant interest, a natural search for delicate distinction, and enjoying the fact that everything can be new if one does not already know too much (Rousseau 2000, pp. 627–8). In this sense, Rousseau's own views suggested nature to be the reason for and the way of education.

The Concept of "Negative Education"

In *Emile* Rousseau speaks of "negative education," to show not what education is supposed to achieve but what it must avoid. Negated are the two entities which are sacrosanct in the Christian tradition of education: truth and virtue. They are no longer supposed to be the objective of acting, for true education, as Rousseau says, could start out only from the child's nature. Only he who really cares about nature and imagines its development is provided with enough knowledge to be able to educate. Truth and virtue are positive entities. But they are not characteristics of nature. Thus, it says in the second book of *Emile*, "Education of the earliest years should be merely negative. It consists, not in teaching virtue or truth, but in preserving the heart from vice and the spirit of error" (Rousseau 1993, p. 68).[121]

It is not necessary to teach truth and virtue as long as the first education lasts, that is until the twelfth year (*ibid.*). This kind of education is *purely* negative, as the educationally positive – truth and virtue – can only have negative effects on the child's nature, while nature is good by itself as long as it is protected from society and and teaching at school. It is essential for "negative education" that virtue and truth are not taught and thus will take on no didactic form.

In this sense, the first education is not a "positive" one. It protects the child's nature from the unintelligible truths and incomprehending demands of virtue which children are able neither to take up nor to obey. What is essential is to guarantee that in the child's world of experience there will be no vice or errors. Neither teaching at school nor any kind of training would be able to do this because teaching aids included far too many untruths and distortions which can only be avoided if education is completely committed to nature, that is to neither truth nor virtue.

The result is expected from the perspective of the educator, not of the child: "Free from prejudices and free from habits, there would be nothing in him that counteracts the effects of your labours. In your hands he would soon become the wisest of men; by doing nothing to begin with, you would end with a prodigy of education" (*ibid.*). Rousseau wants a radical recasting of educational theory: "Reverse the usual practice and you will almost always do right" (*ibid*). "Truth" and "virtue" have been the central concepts of teaching since the Middle Ages, and these shall be taken over by *nature* – and *only* by it. Nature is not considered to be some kind of "foundation" for education but its center. From nature there comes strength, not truth or virtue, and strength involves restriction; the construction is that of a stoic child who must be protected from every temptation as unable to restrict himself, referring only to himelf and not enticed to wrong conclusions which inevitably accompany all doctrines of truth and virtue. This way, the most precious good of childhood is maintained, a life free of prejudices.

The child shall avoid the way of the savage man, that is to break the historical chain of socialization. On man's fate after the loss of the natural state Rousseau says in the Second Discourse: "In becoming sociable and a Slave he becomes weak, fearful, servile; and his soft and effeminate way of life completes the enervation of both his strength and his courage" (Rousseau 1992, p. 24). The child is threatened by this fate if education is not radically changed and based on nature alone. He must become robust and avoid any kind of effeminacy, particularly one which, like reading books, is based on doing nothing.

Consequently, during the "age of nature" education does not need to care for positive truths and virtues but must avoid them and this is pos- sible because – and insofar as – it can completely adjust to the ways of nature. *Nature* is the active entity, not lessons or formal instruction. Most of all Rousseau wants to prove the artificial nature of teaching "truth" and "virtues," which shall be replaced by the observation of nature and obeying *its* ways. "Natural" is only education *without* books; contemporary sugges- tions to provide libraries for children (e.g. Dumas 1732) would thus be the horror of childhood and not a support of education.

Whoever teaches truths or virtues teaches abstractions, while children learn concretely and immediately. The abstractions are those of philosophy, which children do not understand and which they avoid. Trying to teach truths and virtues to children is not only wrong but also senseless. The many books on education trying to do so were thus useless and unnecessary. They are worse than books on metaphysics, and one had to protect oneself from them already. It is not possible to educate by books, as they are nothing more than the "partiality of the author".[122]

In contrast to this, Rousseau formulates the rules of natural education, which are developed from the following maxim: "Fix your eyes on nature, follow the path traced by her. She keeps children at work, she hardens them by all kind of difficulties, she soon teaches them the meaning of pain and grief" (Rousseau 1993, p. 16). Other than in Fénelon's tract on the education of girls, for example, this is not meant rhetorically.[123] Nature teaches the right thing; thus it is possible to prevent children from the pain of moral education. Virtue does not need to be practiced. Nature hardens the temperament by putting children to the test, and nature teaches about the hour of effort or pain without any kind of teaching or purposeful education being necessary. "Sickness and danger play the chief part in infancy" (*ibid.*).

Whoever observes nature is able to *follow* its path. He does not need any artificial ways of teaching which are neither adjusted to the world of the child nor able to pay attention to it. And nature does not only passively show the way of education; much more, it is itself educating, by the experience of illnesses, surviving dangers, the experience of growth, or increasing powers. Illnesses should not be avoided but experienced and survived. The course of nature shows itself by the fever, every hardening makes nature stronger and every kind of softening weakens it (*ibid.*, pp. 16–17).

In this sense, education is robust, and it has a natural and not a reflexive child in mind, as was suggested by contemporary literature on education.[124] Also, Rousseau refrained from literature of fatherly advice, which was produced in the seventeenth century[125] and one century later was completed by a flood of motherly-advice books. Nothing of this is found in Rousseau's *Emile*, which by its whole construction is indeed unique. This is also true in consequence. Many passages of contemporary literature speak of "natural education," but nobody went through the situation as logically and at the same time as ignorant toward reality as Rousseau.

Natural education shall avoid the "mechanical" and thus the artificial traits of man's works. The child shall be completely subjected to the work of nature. By help of the latter that which was hidden, that is the child's potential, is transferred to reality without a third power needing to interfere. This way, every artificial interference shall be avoided, that is neither that which is divided shall be connected nor that which is connected shall be separated. Originally, the child is a unity – nature – which exists *by itself* and thus would be taken apart only by society and would have to be put together again artificially. "Man's education begins at birth; before he can speak or understand he is learning" (*ibid.*, p. 33).

At the beginning of *Emile* there is a clear statement on "natural" man being different from "civil" man: "The natural man lives for himself; he is the unit, the whole, dependent only on himself and on his like" (*ibid.*, p. 7). Natural man (l'homme naturel) refers totally to himself or to his "semblabes" (O.C. IV, S. 249), that is other natural men. In the moment of being compared to *unlike* others, that is those who are not "natural," not able or no longer able to be completely themselves, this "absolute unity" is endangered. Whoever necessarily and continually must refer to others in order to be himself is unnatural and in this sense *social* or "civil."[126]

Civil man (l'homme civil) is "but the numerator of a fraction, whose value depends on its denominator." His value is determined by the whole of the social body, not by his own unit anymore. What Christian philosophy since the Middle Ages has called "man's work" is thus the work of *society*, which sucks up the *I* (le *moi*) (O.C. IV, p. 249) and whose institutions denaturate man, that is they change an absolute existence into a relative one. As a consequence, each individual does not believe himself to be a unit on its own but understands himself to be a part of the whole to whose existence the individual did not and does not contribute: "Good social institutions are those best fitted to make a man unnatural, to exchange his independence for dependence, to merge the unit in the group, so that he no longer regards himself as one, but as a part of the whole, and is only conscious of the common life" (Rousseau 1993, pp. 7–8).

Seeing the *child* as "nature's work" is a surprising move which would never have entered the minds of the authors of literature on teaching and school reform, like Charles Rollin. Their writings never deal either with children or with their nature more closely, much more that education is determined by the authority of the sciences and by them the value of books, which is what Rousseau categorically rejects as a means of early education. For him it is essential that his fictitious pupil, Emile, learns how actively to read the book of nature, something for which sensual experience, not reading, is necessary. Whoever reads books is confronted with fancies, not with real things (*ibid.*, p. 146), but only real things will educate the senses in respect of natural knowledge, which is different from the artificial topics of lessons or reading and is thus "real" (*ibid.*, p. 160).

Learning means to "find out" real things (*ibid.*), not abstract meanings of words which no child will understand. As a general rule for teaching it is held: "Never substitute the symbol for the thing signified, unless it is impossible to show the thing itself; for the child's attention is so taken up with the symbol that he will forget what it signifies" (*ibid.*, p. 159). And more concretely as a rule of teaching: "Teach your scholar to observe the phenomena of nature; you will soon rouse his curiosity, but if you would have it grow, do not be in too great a hurry to satisfy this curiosity" (*ibid.*, p. 156).

Emile in his later childhood researches and experiences the laws of nature (*ibid.*, p. 167), and this inquiry always has to begin with the "commonest and most conspicuous phenomena" that should be taken as facts and not as causes (*ibid.*, p. 167). Education must avoid "abstract truths" (*ibid.*, p. 161) written in books. Learning should not be guided by authors who translate experiences into texts and thus take them away from the immediacy of experiencing. "Real," however, is only that which speaks immediately to the senses without needing interpretation or a philosophy – truth or virtue. Compared to this, all culture is artificial, its basis is reading, and from this children must be protected. If lost among books, they would lose their natural strength, for they would have to reduce the entirety of their senses to the particularity of reading – and what is more, to the reading of incomprehensible texts.[127] They will lose their childhood and become "little philosophers" (*ibid.*, p. 168).

This is meant in a radical sense. As mentioned above, during his first education up to his twelfth year, Emile is given only *one* book to read, Daniel Defoe's novel *Robinson Crusoe* (*ibid.*, pp. 176–7),[128] and this not due to reasons of literary teaching but because this book describes exactly the educational situation found by Emile. Rousseau speaks of the "desert island" (*ibid.*, p. 176) where the learner is forced to make his judgment by true accordance with things,[129] without being taught or educated by third parties. Robinson was forced to help himself, and that also is exactly what Emile is supposed to learn.

Fundamental to the theory of negative education is a way of learning which does not depend on others and which cannot be artificially shortened. Robinson spent twenty-eight years on his island; for Emile at the age of nature more than ten years of education under social isolation are scheduled, during which period he tries out his powers without becoming dependent. This is also and not least true for the dependency of intellect. The natural development of the child is supposed to direct learning, not spontaneous questions but the interests for his age, on which the didactic order of matters depends. Nature occurs and works as an immediate problem, which must be experienced and felt. Rousseau's understanding of nature, in other words, is the marked opposite of an order of nature which shall be taught by help of books.

Rousseau, the critic of artificial education, was both an enthusiastic and a knowledgeable botanist who understood how to follow Carl von Linné's guidelines most carefully.[130] In a short letter to Linné from September 21st, 1771 he introduces himself as his loyal student who by his advice had learned more from nature than from the books of the world: "Alone, with nature and you, on my solitary walks in the countryside I experienced blissful hours of happiness, and I took much more profit from your *Philosophie botanique*[131] than from all books on morality" (Correspondance t. XXXVIII, p. 267). Education, too, must follow the path of nature and, just as with plants, must consider the periods of growth which can be neither overlooked nor omitted.

But Rousseau's fictitious child is supposed to show more than the irreversibility of time in the growth of nature. By Emile and with his help shall be demonstrated that all evil happens because of weakness and that thus the strengthening of the child, not the teaching, must be considered the fundamental task of education: "All wickedness comes from weakness. The child is only naughty because he is weak; make him strong and he will be good; if we could do everything we should never do wrong" (Rousseau 1993, p. 39). Only he who is strong will be able to give up on being evil; he who is weak will never be good as it is weakness that makes man dependent.

This essential assumption is combined with the idea that before the "age of reason" we act while being free of morals, that is react negatively to every kind of pedagogical teaching. Children do evil or good without knowing it (*ibid.*), thus it is absurd to teach them beyond that which is according to their natural curiosity. It is essential to increase their strength, and this requires that they are prevented from being weakened by constant lessons. They shall try out their strength by themselves as far as possible and shall be prevented from educational or didactic rule (empire) (O.C. IV, p. 290). Rousseau made this theory concrete through four maxims:

1. Far from being too strong, children are not strong enough for all claims of nature. Give them full use of such strength as they have; they will not abuse it.
2. Help them and supply the experience and strength they lack whenever the need is of intelligence or the body.
3. In the help you give them confine yourself to what is really needful, without granting anything to fantasy or desires without reason; for they will not be tormented by fantasy if you do not call it into existence, seeing it is no part of nature.
4. Study carefully their speech and gestures, so that in an age when they are incapable of deceit you may discriminate between those desires which come directly from nature and those which spring only from opinions. (Rousseau 1993, p. 40; O.C. IV, p. 290)

Due to these reasons, robust education *à la campagne* suggests itself, far away from the educational demands of society, which would inevitably compare performance and thus weaken the child. The child will be strong only if he must depend on himself. On the other hand, first education in particular, that is until puberty, depends upon supervision by a constantly present, demanding, and controlling adult person, who additionally is of the same sex and must provide a paradoxical "well-regulated liberty" (Rousseau 1993, p. 66). As is Robinson for Friday, so the governor is indispensable for Emile.

Rousseau claims that only by *this* constellation – an educational relationship in a natural landscape – is it possible to educate in such a way that the "route de la nature" (O.C. IV, p. 290) is followed. During this early period Emile shall be educated only while being dependent on *things*, that is independent of social authority and the hierarchy of comparisons (Rousseau 1993, p. 58).[132] Only then, without constant contact with others, is the child *unique*, and only by this constellation will the child be able to grow according to his own strength, to be spared moral and decadence at the same time, something which requires the radical absence of any kind of organized society.

The theory of education basically refers to the original right of human nature, and in this sense we may then speak also of natural education. The first impulses of nature are always right (*ibid.*, p. 66); whoever follows them has found the way to avoid error and vice. According to Rousseau's theory of society, both – "erreur et vice" – cannot come from nature itself, for "there is no original sin in the human heart, the how and why of the entrance can be traced" (*ibid.*). This, as Rousseau says, was the unquestionable and fundamental maxim of all education (*ibid.*). In this sense, it is *natural* and "negative" only in one respect. Together with errors and vice, the evils of society can be kept away.

In respect of Rousseau's theology we may state: the Christian doctrine of original sin is confronted with natural religion and the theology of the heart, which both are the background of the setting of *Emile*. The child of nature is the pure, innocent child who is not burdened with original sin and does not belong to the Church, nor to the state, but only to *himself*. The evil must infect the child, it has not always been there; in this respect Rousseau follows his great opponent, John Locke. In the soul there are no innate ideas or "innate principles," neither good nor bad.

In more detail, Rousseau says this as follows: within the child no vice is found about which one could not tell how and by which it has come there. The only passion characteristic for man is love of himself or self-love in the wider sense. This self-love is good and useful, and as it is not naturally related to any other human it is in this respect naturally indifferent; it becomes good or evil only by its way of application and through the references it is given. Thus, until the arbiter of self-love, reason, is born, education must be anxious that the child does nothing to be seen or heard, that is nothing in respect of others but only that which nature demands from it. Then, Rousseau concludes, it will do only good deeds.

Originally, there is "amour de soi-meme" or "amour-propre" (O.C. IV, p. 322), which Rousseau terminologically distinguishes from each other as late as in the fourth book of *Emile*. There, he is interested in proving that "reason" (raison) must be considered a construction of adults which is unknown to children. The child does not have reason and thus can only be overtaxed by demands of reason. What this brings along is *nature* and *growth*; if nature is strengthened and growth is made free from all social restrictions, nothing evil will be able to affect the child, as only society is "evil."

Thus, in the *Letter to Beaumont* an essential message by Rousseau is communicated, which in *Emile* appears almost in passing. Decadence and vice exist only among adults and only in society; if children are shielded from society, they will only be able to become good. Naturally educated children keep their natural strength and stay sovereign even toward unreasonable demands of morals. "Society" means social calculation to one's own advantage, that is egotistic regulations which look like maxims of general welfare. Only he who was educated toward being strong or sovereign will be able to differentiate. He must learn to distinguish appearance from reality and thus to withstand society.

One essential reason for the moratorium of childhood results from Rousseau's criticism of John Locke. Rousseau argues that Locke does not take the child's nature into consideration and that he equates the *goal* of education – reason – with the *means* of education – reasoning with children:

> If children understood reason they would not need education, but by talking to them from their earliest age in a language they do not understand you accustom them to be satisfied with words, to question all that is said to them, to think themselves as wise as their teachers; you train them to be argumentative and rebellious; and whatever you think you gain from motives of reason, you really gain from greediness, fear, or vanity with which you are obliged to reinforce your reasoning. (Rousseau 1993, p. 63)

Children are not reasoning like adults; they act spontaneously, uncalculating. And if they must not be restricted by morals, one can only leave them to their "natural liberty" (*ibid.*, p. 62). The child is no "slave" (*ibid.*) but an active learner, although a learner that presupposes the condition of nature. "We are born capable of learning, but knowing nothing, perceiving nothing. The mind, bound up within imperfect and half grown organs, is not even aware of its own existence. The movements and cries of the new-born child are purely reflex, without knowledge or will" (*ibid*, p. 32). The acquisition of knowledge and the development of the will do not change the condition of nature.

John Locke assumed that learning was probably driven by nature, but that a child had to take care by himself for building up his mind. For this, stimulations are needed which are taken up and processed by two internal faculties which Locke (1975, pp. 104ff.) called *sensation* and *reflection*. Simple ideas turn into complex ones, which make the mind; it develops by and in the course of the child's learning and thus does not follow any superior intelligence. The mind builds up by learning, not the other way round, a thesis which, as it is well known, made Leibniz write a sharp criticism immediately after the publication of Locke's *Essay Concerning Human Understanding*.[133] It is interesting that Leibniz overlooked that which the other great critic, Rousseau, recognized at once: that *children* become the focus of epistemology and thus find their place in philosophy.

If children built up their minds by themselves, they would have to be open to arguments of reason very early and in any case much earlier than generally thought, as far as they are formulated in a way suitable to their age. "*Reasoning* with children" is what Locke (1989, p. 142) called this maxim, which Rousseau in the second book of *Emile* attacked at once. Locke's maxim was "in the height of fashion at present" but is hardly "justified by its results" (Rousseau 1993, p. 63). One cannot exchange reasons with children, let them weigh them up and then decide about them. This requires the use of reason at a period when it does not yet exist. Reason (raison) does not develop *before* due time, that is before the beginning of the appropriate age of education. "Of all man's faculties, reason, which is, so to speak, compounded of all the rest, is the last and choicest growth," and this faculty cannot be used for the child's early training (*ibid.*).

The natural sequence of ages controls the process and not, as assumed by the contemporary psychology of sensualism, the building up of habits. Locke's "mind" is built from internal habits which Rousseau understands to be restrictions of the child's spontaneity. The child always experiences anew, living in the present, without perceiving himself or his environment according to habits. Insofar as education tries to do so it just does not follow the way of nature. By this, Rousseau opposes the most successful learning theory of the eighteenth century, which fundamentally changed the view at education but which indeed has no understanding of what Rousseau meant by spontaneous learning according to nature.

Against Locke and also Condillac it is said that the only habit which Emile, the child of nature, "should be allowed to contract is that of having no habits" (*ibid.*, p. 34). No moment of the present is allowed to be sacrificed for the future (*ibid.*, p. 50). The driving forces of experience are immediate interest and the occasion or moment, which fades (*ibid.*, p. 96). Emile shall take up and be open only toward that which touches him *immediately* (O.C. IV, p. 359). The "well-regulated liberty" of education must take care for Emile's world of learning to be organized according to these demands.

Reason and morals are late achievements of man; they can be developed better, the more the early time (the experience of childhood) stays untouched by them. The child concentrates completely on himself, learns spontaneously, is only taught by nature and the consequences of his actions, that is growing according to his own strength and in harmony with experiences, left alone by the doctrines of reason or the principles of morals. Nothing distracts learning from the path of nature, as there are no other stimulations of curiosity than those which the child finds in the controlled environment.

Fundamental to the whole construction is Rousseau's theory of the child's *own* world, which by one sentence is formulated thus: "Childhood has its own ways of seeing, thinking, and feeling; nothing is more foolish that to try to substitute our ways" (Rousseau 1993, p. 54). The senses do not simply direct learning toward habits, for then it would not be possible at all to find any difference between children and adults. But the way in which children see, think, and feel is different from that of adults; in this respect childhood is a world of its own which cannot be substituted.

This means also that learning cannot simply be an increase or a constant raising of competence. One loses childhood, and Rousseau asks how it could be best used for the child in a world of his own which is closed to adults. The setting of *Emile* is also due to the fact that Rousseau assumes a foreign world of childhood which adults cannot open up by referring to their own childhood. Reason marks the boundary, nobody can go back to the age of nature, and only adults but not children are able to look at childhood in a sentimental way, only they know what is lost.

If children reached by one jump (tout d'un coup) from their mother's breast to the age of reason, there would not be two worlds and then conventional education would be enough, which appeals to the child's morality and reason (*ibid.*, pp. 67–8; O.C. IV, p. 323). Whoever wants instead to follow the "progrés naturel" (O.C. IV, p. 68) must proceed in a completely different way. Children should not do anything about their souls as far as all faculties have been developed, and reason, as stated, is the capability which is developed *last* by the soul. By this doctrine Rousseau is fundamentally different not only from Locke but from all sensualists.

Due to this doctrine, the right education during the first twelve years must give up on communicating truths and virtues. It can only be negative, as nothing else is left to it if it really wants to deal with the child and to respect his own world of perception. This world must be protected and not be additionally burdened. The child has enough to do with recognizing and trying out the ways of nature by help of the senses without being distracted. Comparisons with others would distract and weaken the child; only alone is he completely "nature": "Nature would have them children before they are men" (Rousseau 1993, p. 64).

Nature does not jump, which is why education also does not jump. Probably, Rousseau takes the ancient principle of *Natura non facit saltus* from Linné's *Philosophia Botanica* from 1751,[134] even if this sentence, which is considered to have its origins in Aristotle,[135] may also have been found in his reading of ancient texts. The idea is fundamental to the complete layout of his theory. Nature develops gradually and by uninterrupted sequences which must come one after the other and which make impossible that anything will happen *before* due time. Also, education cannot speed up the development of nature but can only follow it.

Following the definition of *éducation négative*, Rousseau addresses his professional readers: if you educators were able to do nothing and leave anything, if in other words you were able to lead your pupil up to the twelfth year in good health and strength without his being able to distinguish left from right, with your first teachings the eyes of his intellect would open to reason, that is then when this is possible and not before. This is called a miraculous effect, "un prodige d'éducation" (O.C. IV, p. 324). This effect requires nature to be able to grow according to its own pace and not to jump. Whoever cares for it does not need any artificial culture of learning but may rely on the best happening by itself if the course of time is kept. Thus, the child will not simply develop "by himself" in a psychological sense but according to his own nature.

What Rousseau does not reveal in this passage is the consequence of his construction. Natural education requires careful control. "Well-regulated liberty" is a paradox which can only be resolved by what might be called didactic channeling. The *first* mistaken idea to reach Emile is the seed of error and vice; thus there must be observing *every* first step of learning and all its consequences with meticulous precision (Rousseau 1993, pp. 62–3). Even the smallest deviation will at once result in disaster, so there must be permanent control in a very confined space. It is always the "first step that needs watching" (*ibid.*, p. 63). Thus, the fundamental maxim of childhood must be understood very ambivalently: "Leave childhood to ripen in your children" (*ibid.*, p. 68).

Emile must not make any mistakes, and he has a "prémier maître" (O.C. IV, p. 279), that is nature as its first master who must prevent coincidence. Education is not possible if the educator "acts at random" (Rousseau 1993, p. 69). He as the master of the scene can follow the path of nature and thus is not forced to leave education to chance. Rousseau is also claiming that nothing else must be done other than to leave nature alone and not to interfere with what happens. But this does not mean that everything can be possible, in other words coincidence. The idea that there is no advance without the development of nature implies its necessity. But the child does not recognize this, only the master, and it occurs within the world of learning which he provides. This world is not supposed to be any kind of didactic order, as other than teaching at school they follow nature, but they are exactly that.

Nature develops by its own pace and by organized sequences which necessarily follow one another. Time plays an outstanding role for Rousseau's theory of education, and this again by a very paradoxical escalation. One would expect some indication of naturally running time, but a famous definition in the second book of *Emile* says: "May I venture at this point to state the greatest, the most important, the most useful rule of education? It is: Do not save time, but lose it" (*ibid.*, p. 67). This thought was paradoxical, Rousseau comments, but it suggested itself if one was thinking about education, and anyway it was better, as the motto was, to think by way of paradoxes than to have prejudices (*ibid.*). But why shall there be thinking *paradoxically* about education, of all things?

The most important and "most useful" rule of education shall be to lose time. But this is anything but convincing: education, one would think, must use its time gainfully, thus one cannot simply let time, which cannot be recovered or is at hand in countless quantum, run out. With education, time must not run out but must be used and in this sense be gained or earned.[136] Otherwise, it would be impossible to organize learning. He who is only supposed to learn from things must do this in timely succession, and this makes sense only if any progress of learning is achieved. In the end one must be able to know and be able to do more than at the beginning, and this requires didactically used time.

But in Rousseau's natural space of education there is no structured running of time which would be of significance for the progress of learning. There are neither years nor months or weeks, days or hours. The absence of the calendar is a structural feature of the natural state, and also the learning space which is connected to it does not know any fixed time, without which teaching at school would be impossible. Emile, however, learns with occasions and thus by referring to each specific situation. The time of learning is always the present of experience and instruction; between two occasions of learning there is no time to be used, with the exception of Emile's governor inventing new exercises and thinking about new occasions for learning.

There is no thinking at all about time to pass. Thus, time can be neither gained nor lost and the thesis makes sense only polemically; non-natural, wrong education means a loss of time, and that is because it always tries to usefully employ the time of learning. But in the child's world, as Rousseau's thesis may be understood, there is no principle of effectiveness. Result is not an effect of effort; education will not be the better, the more means are employed. Only a few means are suitable at all, and their quality does not depend on the purpose. The natural state, in other words, is free not only of the calendar but also of economy.

The thesis that the time of first education must be lost is also to be seen against the background of Rousseau's literary construction. There is no telling a continuing story which would require gain and loss of time; much more it is about a paradigmatic plot by help of which the principle of "natural education" shall be demonstrated. This demonstration is not a narrative one; it does not need any emergencies, has no strings of action and also cannot afford the reader to be confused. In this sense, Laurence Sterne's *Tristram Shandy* is the extreme opposite of Rousseau's *Emile*. The reader is manipulated as in *Tristam Shandy*, but he is not led away from the direct path of reading by unexpected connections.

Emile and his *gouverneur* are no characters of a narration with their own biographies changing in the course of time but the two typological poles of the educational relation. The scene of *Emile*, the landscape garden, shall be understood as the natural state of education or as its paradise from which nobody is expelled but which serves only for development. A paradise, however, requires the absence of time. Thus, time cannot be lost, as it is not there at all. The passing of time in *Emile* is that of the strictly determined ages of education, a personal time and thus a continuing story of one's own biography does not exist. Due to this, Rousseau's education is not "natural" but highly artificial.

This impression is confirmed if one looks at the way in which education is controlled. As there is always danger – a very paradoxical assumption, indeed, for a paradise – the child must be protected from wrong paths as long as possible. Childhood requires a moratorium and well-protected borders, as it is a *dangerous* time of learning. The paternal way of organizing the learning space is not due to the potentials of nature but to the dangers by which the child is threatened. Rousseau says clearly: "The most dangerous period of human life lies between birth and the age of twelve. It is the time when errors and vices spring up, while as yet there is no means to destroy them; when the means of destruction are ready, the roots have gone too deep to be pulled" (*ibid.*).

Not even the seeds of errors and vice may intrude the learning space. Thus, care must be taken that all temptations are constantly absent. Free of errors, that is not simply "good" nature but *protected* and *well-controlled* nature, into which nothing can enter which might endanger the path of education.

Emile's space of experience is implicitly equated with a landscape garden which is protected on all sides. Only this way can the child be led toward virtue and truth, which must develop from itself, from its own strength. Errors and vice must be avoided as long as the dangerous time of childhood lasts.

In respect of the history of reception, this finding is irritating. The thesis of a dangerous age of nature gives up on the idea of idyllic childhood which many of Rousseau's followers had and still have in mind. But childhood is too important to be harmless. Rousseau considers it the *most* dangerous time of human life, as far as the children cannot develop according to their own nature. And even in a protected and well-controlled learning space there is the constant threat of danger, as there is no internal process of the development of nature which the children could simply follow. They must learn, and this way they could easily learn the wrong thing, which would lead them astray. The natural course of things must be controlled so exactly because children also learn what is harmful for them, which will affect them negatively.

In this theory, control is a part of nature. The only yoke allowed during first education is that of necessity and not that of any authority (*ibid.*, p. 65). Children shall be subject only to the dependence of things; all development follows the order of nature and not the order of man (*ibid.*, p. 58). Thus, childhood shall be nothing other than exercising natural liberty, which is also defined *negatively*, that is by the absence of all political sovereignty. Emile's governor, as is the theory, is tied to nature; he represents the yoke of necessity and shows the order of things without making his pupil dependent on him.

He considered it impossible, Rousseau says in the second book of *Emile*, to lead a child as far as to the twelfth year in the midst of society without giving him an idea of the relationships among men and the morality of human actions. Then, it was advisable to communicate these necessary ideas as late as possible, and, when they become unavoidable, to restrict them to their present use, so that the child would not regard himself the master of others and would not without thinking cause anybody harm (*ibid.*, p. 72). In the natural state it is possible to keep Emile ignorant and to control his learning, so that no prejudices will develop, as society is absent. And to control the child "one must often control oneself" (*ibid.*).

Many times this setting has been commented upon. One of the countless pictures shows Emile weeping at his creator's grave, adult, but capable of keeping his natural sentiment without having been spoiled by knowledge (Thiery 1992, table 33). One really sees how the heart has been protected from vice, and intellect has been protected from error. Thus, virtue and truth do not need to be *taught* but develop from the *guarantee* of the heart and of intellect. Thus, education would be a "time of liberty" (Rousseau 1993, p. 69), coming from the nature of childhood and the appropriate environment for learning. However, the precondition for this is to uncouple education from the errors of society and to completely adjust it to nature.

Because of this promise, *Emile* became a famous book and around Rousseau there developed an educational cult. In the "Edition de Boubers" of *Emile*, published in Brussels from 1774 onward, Rousseau is seen as the monument of natural education which is associated with the sun of Enlightenment and suggests a clearly female code. The fathers (tutors, in other words the wrong educators) want to distract their sons from the truth of education, to direct them toward useful or reasonable activities, while the children adore their liberator, Rousseau, who was the first to recognize that one must let them *grow* (Thiery 1992, table 1) because of their not being able to be reasonable before due time. And this is according to female care and not to male reason.

Already the first edition of *Emile* shows a female idyll of education which is even increased in the editions after 1789 (*ibid.*, tables 4, 11). Rousseau appears as the prophet of natural education, who made the child free from depending on society and led it back to the garden of nature. The altar shows the idyll of mother and child in the midst of a natural landscape; in this sense only nature is supposed to be the master of education, although really a *governor* is educating. Most often the male code of practice was overlooked for the female iconography of inwardness and probably this is also a reason for equating practice with idyll.

The cult of Rousseau is a surprising outcome which requires *Emile* to be read as a book of liberation, as indeed was always the case with his followers. As a matter of fact, the content refers rather to tough indoctrination contradicting the ideal of emancipation as it is understood today. Emile never acts by himself and learns only by didactic arrangements. He never experiences independently but is constantly controlled. Emile does not develop "himself" but his nature. He learns about the "order of things" but never utters any independent sentence. After his first education Emile is supposed to be virtuous without ever having known vice.

In the first book of *Confessions* Rousseau introduces himself as a child, before he had had his first bad experience, that is having been punished wrongly. He is clearly different from his own draft of the natural child and so the paradigm of his theory, but touches an essential topic of his entire philosophy, that of the vulnerability of the soul and thus of love of himself.

Imagine a character, timid and docile in ordinary circumstances, but ardent, proud and indomitable when roused; a child who has always been governed by the voice of reason, always treated with tenderness, equity, indulgence; who has no notion, even, of injustice, and who for the first time experiences a terrible example of it at the hands of precisely those people whom he loves and respects the most. (Rousseau 2000, pp. 18–19)

Fifty years had elapsed since this incident, but it was still hurting his soul. Heaven knew that he was innocent, but that had been of no use, the innocent was punished. "What havoc in his ideas! What confusion in his feelings! What an upheaval in his little heart, in his brain, in his whole moral and intellectual being!" (*ibid.*, p.19). The first time of experiencing violence and injustice cut deep into the soul and left the question of how it could be protected from this. "As I write this I feel the pulse beginning to race again; these moments would always be fresh in my mind, even if I lived for a hundred thousand years" (*ibid.*).

Feelings like this have their own integrity; they let self-interest step back and demand resistance against the injustice of the world. "My heart begins to burn with indignation whenever I see or hear of any unjust action, whatever its object and wherever it occurs, quite as much as if I were myself to suffer its effects" (*ibid.*). By this deeply rooted memory of the first injustice there comes to an end what Rousseau calls "the serene days of my childhood" (*ibid.*, p. 20). In no respect were they a kind of "natural education" but still produced a topic of his life, that is the question of how self-interest might appear as being strong and not as being weak.

Whoever is helplessly punished is able to imagine what injustice is. But at the same time there is the question of why one could be so vulnerable at all. He had only been able to refer to himself, Rousseau writes, and while doing so he had hardly felt physical punishment but definitely humiliation, rage, and desperation (*ibid.*, p. 19). In the *Reveries*, at the end of his life, there is still the question of how a reliable "moral instinct" develops which is not deceived and does not depend on "public interest" (Rousseau 2000a, p. 31). "It is there that I judge myself with perhaps as much severity as I will be judged by the sovereign judge after this life" (*ibid.*).

Self-Love as the Core

In a letter to Abbé de Carondelet[137] from March 4th, 1764 Rousseau notes: "The love of oneself is the most powerful, and in my opinion, the sole motive that makes human beings act. But how virtue, taken absolutely and as a metaphysical thing, is founded on that love of self, that passes my comprehension" (Rousseau 1937, p. 272). What makes love of oneself and how is it connected to a concept of virtue which is not of a metaphysical nature? This question is Rousseau's primary driving force in *Emile*; it is not saying too much to state that *love of oneself* and the problem of how one could educate toward it, if after all it is a part of nature, is the core of Rousseau's philosophy of education.

By the term of *self-love* Rousseau's concept of individuality achieves the status of a theory. "Individuality" is not the same as the respective way of life which – as shown by Rousseau's own confession about his life – is much too contradictory to take up the form of a theory. Rather, Rousseau asks what the driving force of life is and why it may take a course like the one he himself had experienced. It is not simply the single person but also his many stories which make the driving force of life. Each story might as well have had a different start, course, and ending. But then, what is it that provides the dynamics and identity of a course of life?

For Rousseau, only one fact of nature is not debatable. Each life is moved by and through *love of oneself*. It is the most elementary fact of individual existence which does not simply characterize "life" but is a positive reference of the living person to himself. This reference is original. Thus, man's nature is not a *tabula rasa* into which everything must be engraved; love of himself is nature's engraving in man. Life would not be possible if man had no love of himself, which can be distracted but not refuted. It is not a learned habit but the internal driving force of learning which lacks sensualism.

From this positive understanding of self-interest there concludes that Rousseau understood humility to be something completely different than what was meant by Christian doctrines. For him, humility is not suppression but cultivation of self-interest, moving away from the concept of vanity or of making one's own self superior at the expense of somebody else. Love of oneself takes up the form of a theorem about which Rousseau started thinking early on. The question is how love of oneself could be distinguished from being in love with oneself, that is from ancient narcissism, something which in contemporary literature and arts was almost always equated.[138]

It is reason that creates self-love, it says in the Second Discourse (Rousseau 1992, p. 37), which led Voltaire to make the marginal remark: "Quelle idée! Faut-il donc des raisonnements pour vouloir son bien-être?" (Havens 1933, p. 10).[139] But Rousseau was serious, the question of self-love was one of the topics of his life, which he could immediately connect to his own experiences. Voltaire misunderstands him; it is not about constituting self-interest by reasoning but about justifying self-love as an indispensable part of human nature. The essential argument in *Emile* is based on it, and it is planned well in advance.

In January, 1753 Rousseau published his comedy *Narcissus, or, The Lover of Himself* (Rousseau 2004, pp. 125–60), which he had written at about 20 years of age. On December 18th, 1752 the play had been staged at the king's *comédie* and Rousseau could consider it a success.[140] After all, it bears

Marivaux's trademark.[141] The story is about a young man, Valére, who falls in love with a picture showing him dressed as a woman. He looks for this woman who is himself but still cannot be himself. He is looking for himself, according to one dialog, which would mean that he would have to marry himself if he really found something (*ibid.*, p. 149). Finally, the confusions of narcissism are resolved and the true lovers find each other. Narcissism, Valére said in the end, is a "ridiculousness" that was "the shame of his youth" (*ibid.*, p. 160).

For the publication of this comedy Rousseau wrote a long preface. Here, he verbosely defends himself against all suspicions and hostilities, he presents himself as being misunderstood by his time, and closes off from "pomp scientifique." Basically, his criticism of the sciences repeats what Rousseau had already presented in the First Discourse. Following this, he accuses the arrogance of philosophers. Their self-interest (amour-propre) was increasing, the more their ignorance of the rest of the world increased. "For him, family, fatherland become words void of meaning: he is neither parent, nor citizen, nor man; he is a philosopher" (Rousseau 1992a, p. 192).

Due to the philosophical reasoning of the century we have lost innocence and morality. Even he who is of good will has no means to escape from misery, and the evils have a cause, not "so much to man as to man poorly governed" (*ibid.*, p. 194). The sciences are not able to improve him, they are part of the problem; nowhere are selfishness and vanity more common than in academies and salons. The idea of improving man's state by help of the sciences is absurd, as this way only reflection is offered. Man is "born to act and think, and not to reflect" (*ibid.*, p. 195).

> Reflection serves only to render him unhappy without rendering him better or wise: it makes him regret the good things of the past and prevents him from enjoying the present: it presents him the happy future to seduce him by the imagination of it and to torment him through desires and the unhappy future to make him feel in advance. Study corrupts his morals, impairs his health, destroys his temperament, and often spoils his reason: if it teaches him something, I would consider him very poorly compensated. (*ibid.*)

Why did Rousseau write such a dark introduction just for a comedy? And why is this introduction not an introduction at all? He himself is the answer: how, it says in the introduction, does one succeed in resisting the temptation of appreciating the love of one's own reputation more than virtue; in other words, how does one resist comparing oneself to the competitor, which forces to devaluate the others and expects them to revaluate oneself? The longing for reputation is the search for corruption, and "a vicious people never returns to virtue." Arts and sciences "destroy virtue, but leave its public simulacrum[142] which is always a fine thing. They introduce into its place politeness and the proprieties, and for the fear of appearing wicked they substitute that of being ridiculous" (*ibid.*, p. 196).

This way, the juvenile topic of narcissism has much more weight. It is no longer about reflecting the self by one's own image but about the question of how the self could stay stable if it constantly endangers itself, and this with best reason. How could one stay true to oneself if society rewards the opposite? "In a country in which it is no longer a question of honest people nor of good morals, it would be better to live with rogues than with brigands" (*ibid.*). Corruption is everywhere, disguised as virtue, and even Rousseau considered himself to be in danger "that the love of reputation makes me forget that of virtue" (*ibid.*, p. 197). So how, then, is a virtuous and truthful life possible?

On February 6th, 1759 Rousseau writes a letter to a university student from Geneva who had sent him an ode against wealth. The student was Jean-Edmonde Romilly (1739–1779), son of Jean Romilly, a Genevan watchmaker established in Paris.[143] His son's letter is about the difficulty of being truthful, and this by the example of a seemingly easy subject, that is criticism of the rich. Rousseau answered him:

> I will tell you that I do not like the end of your letter. You seem to me to judge the rich too severely. You do not consider that, since they have from the time of childhood contracted a thousand needs that we do not have, they cannot be reduced to the condition of the poor without making them more wretched than the poor. One must be just to all the world, even to those who are not so to us. Indeed, Sir, if we possessed the virtues contrary to the vices with which we reproach them, we should never even think that they were in existence, and soon they would have greater need of us than we of them. One word more, and I close. To have the right to despise the rich, one must be economical and prudent oneself, so as never to need wealth. (Rousseau 1937, p. 85)

How is virtue possible if it can be feigned and if nobody other than oneself can judge on it? And how could one be truthful in a world of prejudices? Whoever criticizes the rich, all too often wants only to be rich himself, but then criticism comes from a false need which one does not understand because one does not know about one's own needs. If one desires what one criticizes, one compares oneself without inner cohesion, that is without love of oneself which is the reason of self-respect.

Rousseau repeatedly wrote letters like this. They represent one of his essential intuitions which is gradually developed to a theorem.

Reason-giving for childhood's right of its own and its inviolability, thus for the child's special status, is essentially due to the theory of self-love, which is given a very particular meaning by Rousseau. Not coincidentally, the primary source for this theory is the fourth book of *Emile*. This book describes the development of passions and speaks of man's "second birth" (Rousseau 1993, p. 207), that is birth after childhood. For Rousseau, like many eighteenth-century writers, childhood has no sexuality (Goulemot 2002). Thus, Emile is considered to be a "child" and not a male.

> We are born, so to speak, twice over; born into existence, and born into life; born a human being, and born a man. Those who regard woman as an imperfect man are no doubt mistaken, but they have external resemblance on their side. Up to the age of puberty children of both sexes have little to distinguish them to the eye, the same face and form, the same complexion and voice, everything is the same; girls are children and boys are children; one name is enough for creatures so closely resembling one another. (*ibid.*, p. 206)

For Rousseau, there is no gradual transition from childhood to youth but a break equal to the violence of a birth. It is the birth of passions from which childhood is spared. The natural paradise is left this way, with passions waking up to disturb the good orders of childhood's learning space. Passions concern other people and thus the constitution of society. Up to now, Emile has been educated only for himself; now the problem is how he could learn to adjust to others. In this passage the two inner faculties of *amour de soi* and *amour propre* are brought up; now, however, not as a completion but as a contrast (O.C. IV, p. 493).

At the core of his theory Rousseau describes two entities which cannot be referred to each other. The first faculty is that of self-love, *amour de soi*, which concerns itself only with ourselves. It is satisfied when the true needs (nos vrai besoins) are met. The second faculty, *amour-propre*, or selfishness, is always comparing the self with others and is thus never satisfied (Rousseau 1993, p. 209). It cannot be, as this passion by preferring ourselves to others also demands of the others that they should prefer us to themselves, which is impossible. Comparison devaluates the others for the sake of one's own interests, but exactly this is also done by everybody else.

This way envy and resentment are explained, which are not naturally given but develop from social interaction. With that theory, Rousseau concludes, one recognizes how "the tender and gentle passions spring from self-love while the hateful and angry passions spring from selfishness." The key to the theory is comparison. Self-love, on one hand, leads to a self-sufficient life in accordance with man's natural needs; selfishness, on the other hand, forces man to compare himself to others and thereby develop artificial needs which have no limits. Thus, that which makes man truly good is to have only a few needs and hardly to compare himself to others. What makes him truly bad is to have many needs and to be strongly dependent on other people's opinions. "It is easy to see how we can apply this principle and guide every passion of children and man toward good or evil" (*ibid.*).

This is exactly what Rousseau does in *Emile*. The *gouverneur* directs the child in such a way that he will not compare and is also excluded from every kind of unintentional comparison, if at all possible. However, education cannot prevent adults from living together; natural education is not a means of questioning the state of society. "True, man cannot always live alone, and it will be hard therefore to remain good; and this difficulty will increase of necessity as his relations with others are extended. For this reason, above all, the dangers of social life demand that the necessary skill and care shall be devoted to guarding the human heart against the depravity which spring from fresh needs"[144] (*ibid.*).

Amour-propre is an essential topic in French literature on virtues (French moralists) after the beginning of the seventeenth century, if, however, almost always not meant as a positive, identity-supporting, but as an *indecent* faculty. Love of oneself is what contradicts the Christian commandment of humility and which must be kept at bay by help of education. The literature on education before Rousseau is full of pieces of advice and maxims on how attempts at self-love could be resisted and on what is supposed to constitute true humility. How is it that Rousseau, who has always emphasized the pathos of the heart and who in the face of the immensity of the universe has demanded man's humility, was able to move away from Christian tradition here?

One source for Rousseau is again Blaise Pascal, who in his *Pensées* described the nature of *amour-propre*. It consisted of loving and appreciating only *oneself* (Pascal s. a., pp. 375–6). By this, however, one loved also all of one's mistakes and sins, and self-love works only when confirming the *greatness* of oneself. There is no criterion for balancing the passion. Devaluating one's own self can hardly be connected to *amour-propre*, while nobody really deserves the greatness which must be built up by self-love. If there is self-love, it must be a particularly bitter kind of self-deception.

One *compares*, but one compares in the *wrong way*, that is under the precondition of a perfection which is not given. Self-love wants us to be great, but we perceive ourselves as being small; it wants us to be happy, but we perceive ourselves as being unhappy; it wants us to be the subject of other people's love and appreciation, but we see how our own mistakes make us rejected and despised (*ibid.*, p. 376). Whoever trusts in self-love must exclude a realistic perception of himself, but then self-love will deceive and hurt the feelings of whom it tries to rally.

To avoid these misjudgments Rousseau introduces a second faculty which is missing in Pascal, *amour de soi*, which represents the true needs of nature, accordance with oneself without being disturbed by comparisons to others, in this sense the stage of innocence. This faculty is fundamental, as it provides restriction. Love of oneself is satisfied when true needs are met, and this is easily the case, as they are not driven by any comparison. This way, Rousseau constructed the *homme sauvage* in 1755, as living in accordance with his needs which cannot be challenged by anybody, as apart from occasional meetings there is nobody there. The true form of living is solitude.

Pascal's pessimistic conclusion that self-awareness produced only "imperfections and vices" (*ibid.*, p. 377) is corrected by a different beginning, and this new theoretical start most of all makes education strong. Not every but a certain education can prevent vice and errors if it does not support selfishness but self-love, which will result in making comparison to others and thus to society impossible. In this sense, *loneliness* indeed guarantees the child's nature and thus the correct course of education. A key to Rousseau is his concept of *solitude*, that is living by oneself, which, as being without comparison, knows no lack. The first precondition of his theory was that only he who minimizes his wishes increases – and maintains – his powers.

Rousseau led a lonely life (Thiery 1992, table 2); contemporary engravings show him as a secluded hermit (*ibid.*, table 3) who was constantly in danger (*ibid.*, table 6) and who had to pay for his unstable life by loneliness, increasingly haunted by ideas of being prosecuted, which was not just his imagination. By his own example Rousseau demonstrated that and how "living" means in the end to have only *one* reliable inner faculty, and that is love of oneself. Only this makes one strong, as it keeps the needs at a low level, does not look for comparisons, and makes loneliness endurable.

Probably on August 4th, 1773 Rousseau writes to the Marquise de Créqui,[145] who had called him a coward and a liar. He explains that behind this accusation there are "workers of darkness," who do not appear in the open but who are still believed in by the public. This way, truth is betrayed and imputation becomes the norm of judgment. "Thus, truth accompanied by deceit, by power and its numerous satellites, disguises, creeps and works in the underground, only illusion, left alone, betrayed, but fearless and proud, challenging it loudly and wandering in the light of the sun. This seems to be natural enough for you, to judge on me without listening to me, not to have an open debate with me, in order of tearing my heart apart just for the fun of it, by the inner restlessness of insecurity" (Correspondance t. XL, p. 59).

Given such experiences, there must be a reliable, supporting entity in the face of the insecurity of life. Rousseau was not the first in French literature to consider love of oneself the deeper basis of human identity: others state that from the emotion of love of oneself there come all other emotions, for example Pierre Corneille (1606–1684).[146] And the founder of the French moralists, François de la Rochefoucauld (1613–1680), noted at the beginning of his *réflexion morales* that *amour-propre* interpreted everything for itself and must thus refer them to itself, which resulted in tyrannic consequences: "It renders all men to become idolatrous of themselves and makes them tyrants against others, if fortune gives the means for this" (La Rochefoucauld 2001, p. 307).

Amour-propre never lies at rest and never stops desiring; from everything it drains what is useful for it; nothing is as intense (impétueux) as its desires, nothing is as hidden as its intentions, and nothing is as confident as its behavior (conduite). Often it is invisible and works against us; it makes us monstrous, leads to ridiculous convictions (*ibid.*), and is still the greatest flatterer (*ibid.*, p. 309) whom we love to obey. It hides what we could discover in its country (*ibid.*), and it is much more skilled than any educated man could ever be (*ibid.*, p. 310). The strongest of our passions is an indispensable part of our lives; *amour-propre* will not even lie at rest when it has made a fool of us (*ibid.*).

Also in Pascal (s. a., p. 378) *amour-propre* was the cause of human "corruption." Whoever wants to restrain himself, to find a way back to the right path, who wants to find virtue, cannot reconcile this with self-love (*ibid.*). Rousseau wanted to show that it was not necessary to withdraw to a monastery, like Pascal, to find the path of restraint or repentance. The "route of nature" can only be found and determined *within ourselves* if in the beginning, that is with education, the right way is found. In this sense, everything depends on education; only it can make man strong, as it excludes all weaknesses and makes sure that the child's sovereignty is maintained.

Emile is led *through* nature, and he is led *as* nature, accompanied by only one person to whom he must compare himself but in whom he may trust to do and initiate the right things for him. Thus, the illustrators of *Emile* have always used landscapes and metaphors of pathways to depict natural education. In these pictures one sees educational leadership which at the same time is *avoidance*; going outside must not happen too early, accordance with one's own strength must always be found anew (Thiery 1992, tables 13, 17), and ultimately a young man must be released into society who is able to live exclusively by his own powers.

This, however, is not at all without difficulties and has its price. The freedom of first education is not, as Rousseau says, "well-regulated," that is paradox; freedom is an illusion. Emile learns only that which he is supposed to learn, a living machine without a biography, without a culture, and without a face. Building up his mind is sacrificed to the doctrine of the ages of education; until the end of his age of nature Emile does not really listen to music, must be happy with two scales (Rousseau 1993, p. 136), does not see any picture, does not watch any play, is not told to write constantly, and, as already mentioned, reads only *Robinson Crusoe*, and this not to raise his own literary standards.

The didactic direction does not allow his reading to create suspense and thus uncensored joy; Emile shall learn that, like him, Robinson bases his judgments on the true relationships of the things, independent of prejudices and as a "solitary man" (*un homme isolé*) (*ibid.*, p. 177; O. C. IV, p. 455).[147] One truly lives by oneself only if no prejudices touch the soul. Rousseau's phobia about society and his appreciation of natural education require a theory of prejudice which is characterized by the idea that public exchange and justice are incompatible. Who is judged, exposes himself to prejudices.

Prejudices determine public exchange as far as to private existence. Only one who is able to protect himself from this will maintain his own strength and thus his objective judgment. Whoever joins society will make himself dependent and will endanger his soul, as others are able to command it. On July 25th, 1768[148] Rousseau writes to Thérèse: "Freedom and peace are not found in community: if you get used to the first of them you will need the second. To be free and in peace one must be by oneself and must not allow anybody to bind one" (Correspondance t. XXXVI, p. 26).

Whoever wants to live freely and with inner quietness can rely only on himself. If transferred to education, from this there concludes the maxim of panic-stricken avoidance of prejudices. Social isolation educates because it forces the child to be restricted to himself, not touched by anything which might affect his own strength. Natural education shall be guided only by this experience. By the description of this education the two other preliminary decisions of the theory are also fulfilled: you will learn nothing from books, as they are untrue and vain, and intelligence grows independently of amount of knowledge; more precisely, it is formed by self-restriction.

Books are the chief cause of children's sorrows, and reading is the "curse of childhood." Emile, twelve years old, "will hardly know what a book is" (Rousseau 1993, p. 95). Free from obedience, children will "only learn what they perceive to be of real and present value" which reading books is not. Letting children learn what they want, directed only by their immediate interests, has no bad consequences as the amount or even the quality of knowledge does not matter. One reason for this is Rousseau's treatment of the child's talents. Even though education should follow the route of nature, there are no natural gifts. "Silly children grow into ordinary men. I know no generalisation more certain than this" (*ibid.*, p. 83). Natural education will not render the child stupid, because there is no stupidity in childhood. To be exact:

> It is the most difficult thing in the world to distinguish between genuine stupidity, and the apparent and deceitful stupidity which is the sign of a strong character. At first sight it seems strange that the two extremes should have the same outward signs; and yet it may well be so, for at an age when man has yet no true ideas, the whole difference between the genius and the rest consists in this: the latter only take in false ideas, while the former, finding nothing but false ideas, receives no ideas at all. In this he resembles the fool; the one is fit for nothing, the other finds nothing fit for him. (*ibid.*)

To distinguish between the genius and the fool is possible only by chance, "which may offer the genius some idea which he can understand, while the fool is always the same" (*ibid.*). Apart from this, genuine stupidity can be excluded from childhood. A "stupid child" is a misconception, developed by adults who don't know about children. "Those who judge children hastily are apt to be mistakes; they are often more childish than the child himself" (*ibid.*, p. 84).

If nature is given time to work (*ibid.*), formal lessons are not necessary, except those by nature itself. "Childhood is the sleep of reason" and because of this the child will not accept abstract ideas. The apparent ease of children's learning is in reality their ruin. Adults, again, fail to see that "this very facility proves that they are *not* learning. Their shining, polished brain reflects, as in a mirror, the things you show them, but nothing sinks in" (*ibid.*, pp. 84–5; italics J.O.). For this another far-reaching reason is given:

> Before the age of reason the child receives images, not ideas; and there is this difference between them: images are merely the pictures of external objects, while ideas are notions about those objects determined by their relations. An image when it is recalled may exist by itself in the mind, but every idea implies other ideas. When we image we merely perceive, when we reason we compare. Our sensations are merely passive, our notions or ideas spring from an active principles which judges. (*ibid.*, p. 85)

Children are "incapable of judging" (*ibid.*), and this also explains why it is the best education to isolate them and to learn only from things. Things can be perceived and connected with images, ideas can come later. All knowledge of children is "on the sensation-level" and "nothing has penetrated to their understanding." Their memory is little better than their other powers, "for they always have to learn over again, when they are grown up, what they learnt as children" (*ibid.*). That does not mean that children have "no sort of reason," but they reason very well only "with regard to things that affect their actual and sensible well-being" (*ibid.*). They learn in and for the present not for the future. And "complete ignorance with regard to certain matters is perhaps the best thing for children" (*ibid.*, p. 213).

The child's own world of learning is also the basis for Rousseau's rejection of paternalism. The false prudence of fathers changes children into slaves (*ibid.*, p. 179), while children are happy only if they can play with time and do not know its value (*ibid.*, p. 180). This requires the absence of educational goals and intentions. The idea of social relations is "gradually developed" in the child's mind (*ibid.*, p. 187), and it is not an object of education. Only nature, it says in the third book of *Emile*, can form indelible characters, "and nature makes neither the prince, the rich man, nor the nobleman. [149] The satrap whom you have educated for greatness, what will become of him in his degradation?" (*ibid.*, p. 188)

Sentences like this have been quoted time and again without considering the implications of the theory. Rousseau claims that this Spartan childhood knows no loss and that it was important to extend it as far as possible (*ibid.*, p. 232). Studying society may follow (*ibid.*, p. 236), just as studying literature, and every lesson which Emile might still have during his age of intelligence must be adjusted to *his* experiences and *his* mind (*ibid.*, p. 239). In the end, Emile has learned to live by himself and enjoy his own society (vivre avec lui-même) (*ibid.*, p. 254; O.C. IV, p. 543), and that is his preparation for society up to that moment. It is not enough but this is what counts.

Rousseau is proud of the result of his education. This is summed up at the end of the third book:

> Emile's knowledge is confined to nature and things ... (He) is industrious, temperate, patient, steadfast, and full of courage ... He thinks not of others, but of himself, and prefers that others should do the same. He makes no claim upon them, and acknowledges no debt to them. He is alone in the midst of society, he depends on him alone, for he is all a boy can be at his age. (Rousseau 1993, p. 204)

Emile has not been able to decide about the mode of this education, and also he has not really contributed to its implementation. But Rousseau's last sentence of the third book is meant only as a rhetorical question asking the reader: "Do you think that the earlier years of a child, who reached his fifteenth year in this condition, have been wasted?" (*ibid.*, p. 205) This question is answered by his arch-enemy Voltaire, whose marginal remark on this passage is famous: "Yes, it is a loss, because the product of education is a brute who knows (!) not one social virtue" (Havens 1933, p. 89). Rousseau had written: "In a word Emile possessed of all that portion of virtue which concerns himself. To acquire the social virtues he only needs a knowledge of the relations which make those virtues necessary; he only lacks knowledge which he is ready to receive" (Rousseau 1993, p. 204). "Il lui m(anque) tout" (He lacks everything) Voltaire commented (Havens 1933, p. 89).

The setting of "negative education" and of the "natural child" becomes understandable only if the polemics are included, that which is rejected and fought. Through a fictitious example Rousseau wants to show and to go through literarily what education *without* the dualism of self-love and selfishness would be like. Ultimately, *Emile* demonstrates the disadvantage of social contact in the face of the advantages of solitude. If it is said that education is good if it maintains the children's innocence (Rousseau 1993, p. 214), this means learning according to natural needs which shall be maintained as long and as purely as possible. The consequence of self-love as the basis of education is what Rousseau called "happy ignorance" (*ibid.*, p. 212).

Man's *weakness* is what makes him sociable, every social relation is "a sign of insufficiency." If each man had no need of others, "we should hardly think of associating with them. So our frail happiness has its roots in our weakness. A really happy man is a hermit" (*ibid.*, p. 218). Whoever has no need of others is able to maintain his *amour de soi*, and this is enough for being happy. Our frailty is the consequence of being constantly forced to compare when in society. So only a lonely being is truly happy, avoiding the *frêle bonheur* (O.C. IV, p. 503) of social relations.

But relations to others are unavoidable. Those who are relating to each other are "imperfect creatures," hence it follows "that we are drawn towards our fellow-creatures less by our feeling for their joys than for their sorrows" (Rousseau 1993, p. 218). This is the way out of the isolation of childhood, growing empathy for others and the development not of love but of pity:

> At sixteen the adolescent knows what it is to suffer, for he himself had suffered; but he scarcely realises that others suffer too; to see without feeling is not knowledge, and ... the child who does not picture the feelings of others knows no ills but his own; but when his imagination is kindled by the first beginnings of growing sensibility, he begins to perceive himself in fellow-creatures, to be touched by their cries, to suffer in their sufferings. It is at this time, that the sorrowful picture of suffering humanity should stir his heart with the first touch of pity he has ever known. (*ibid*, pp. 219–20)

Morality also makes one unhappy, insofar as it ties the love of oneself to others. Then, as one compares each other's virtuousness, morals would be a competition and would allow no real virtue. Virtue and morality are not the same. Rousseau understands virtue to be stoic, as bearing life without looking for one's own advantage. Morality must be shared and thus can always be an illusion. Morals are full of prejudices and can hardly be distinguished from self-interest. Because of this, Rousseau makes humility strong, abandoning advantage and gain. Being the goals of education, virtue and morality require comparison and thus moral competition. Never are there two people being exactly as good as each other, while morality *by* being different demands following the respectively *better* one and finally the *best* one, that is never to be satisfied. Thus, morality does not make one happy but only dependent.

Happiness requires the absence of comparison, as every comparison and, even more, moral comparison stimulates new needs which do not exist in nature. If thus education rallies around the banner of morality, it *can* only make children unhappy. And this not because it pursued the wrong goals but because happiness cannot be the topic of any kind of education, unless it may be a negative one which right from the beginning gives up on pursuing goals, except that of protecting nature from the yoke of comparison.

"Happiness" is an outstanding topic in the reflection on education in the eighteenth century, wherever education becomes independent of Christian doctrines. It is *no* topic of this literature if and how happiness may break. It is education, as is the assumption behind these theories, which makes man happy; it is out of the question that it could also make him unhappy. Rousseau is one of the few to be skeptical toward this approach and to negate it without referring to original sin. What if "happiness" is not an optimum for man, as and insofar as every society spoils every kind of happiness and makes it impossible? And what if education could only serve for *society*, that is if Rousseau's option for nature is dropped or was never given?

Questions of this kind trouble the educational discourse since Rousseau. This discourse has never been as self-confident as it pretended to be; it works by simple relations which are tied to moral oppositions. The "good" in education is supposed to be clear and reliably *good* and the "bad" is supposed to be as clearly *bad*. "Good nature" would be the *guarantor* of new education, providing security which is often lacking. But it is barely possible to deal with Rousseau's guidelines in this legitimizing way. His theories are much too paradoxical to guarantee anything in the long run and without self-objection.

The guidelines must thus be determined differently and deeper: if society is the home of sin, only a new kind of man will be able to overcome it, who must be God's image in nature. Then, God and man will be forever innocent, in the sense of the evil not having to be understood as a part of creation or as inherited characteristic of man. But this has consequences: the first wrong idea to enter Emile's mind is, as already shown, the seed of error and vice, thus everything depends on controlling his experiences in such a way that the purpose of education is purely and undisturbingly achieved. This expectation of the "pure" lies still at the heart of "modern education" (Hofmann *et al.* 2006).

The first "wrong" starts the chain of all wrongs – one sees how the scheme of original sin still works even in its negation. Nature is good only if it stays pure, which by the first wrong step will be radically endangered. But then, education would require a natural *quarantine* of the good, at least so long as childhood lasts, which must be protected in its own way. Childhood shall be able to mature within children, without being disturbed by future goals which are alien to them. Thus, it is a key problem how education should deal with the *future*, particularly if this is connected with a new and radically different association while at the same time, due to protecting childhood, everything in education must be referred wholly to the present. Rousseau finds a famous paradox for this: "What is to be thought ... of that cruel education[150] which sacrifices the present to an uncertain future, that burdens a child with all sorts of restrictions and begins by making him miserable, in order to prepare for some far-off happiness which he may never enjoy?" (*ibid.*, p. 50). It is "barbarous" if education tries to surpass the present for a future which cannot be foreseen. The future is insecure, thus it cannot be the goal or the subject of education which cannot bear insecurity. Barbarous education – and that is every kind of education *not* following Rousseau's guidelines – chains the children in every possible way and makes them unhappy in order to prepare them for future happiness they will never experience because education cannot bring it about.

The process of education, however, makes sense only if *going beyond* the present, and this requires – in Rousseau's sense – a promise which can be distinguished from real happiness or unhappiness of the future. If the *process* decides about achieving the goal, then there is no connection between the beginning and the end of education which would be *simple, linear,* and *progressive.* But what could be done then? How could we avoid the present to be sacrificed to the future if every kind of education is directed toward improving the present? Rousseau helps himself by a far-reaching theory of two worlds, which in a certain way is based on Augustine but radically rejects the latter's doctrine of original sin.

The "good" and the "bad" are considered two radically different spheres, one of which may never touch or affect the other. Other than in Augustine, both worlds are *earthly.* Rousseau does *not* distinguish the state of the world from the state of God,[151] like this life from the hereafter; much more nature and society are understood to be horizontal analogies. Nature is not above or below man, just as society is not heaven or hell. Much more, the one, good world is *nature*, while the other, bad world is *society*, without the two of them forming a hierarchy. They are parallel, and are so close that at least in respect of education there must be an artificial and constantly stabilized distance.

Whoever grows up in the good world will be able to change to the other one without loss, provided he finds a place *in it* which is appropriate to his identity. The topic of loneliness is supposed to point to the fact that every integration into society bears the risk of *not* finding the place suggested by natural education. Without identity being affected, society can then be left again. A retreat to the world of education, however, is impossible, Rousseau does *not* think childhood can be repeated or is some kind of natural regression. Childhood has a definite result, both negative and positive; thus whoever is not successful in society in the sense of natural identity can only retreat to loneliness. The experiment of good nature has no second chance.

Every education is unique and must be completed. As its results cannot be corrected – nature offers only *one* way – neither is it possible to draw new conclusions from it and change its course. Whoever does not find an appropriate place in society *must* opt for loneliness and nothing else. In the world of education everything depends on leaving nothing to chance (*ibid.*, p. 213). Whoever wants to educate, it says, must well know "the laws of chance," to be able to calculate the probabilities (*ibid.*, p. 313). But this is only a new paradox, for the probability calculus prevents from chance only in the sense of statistics, not in the sense of everyday events, of their causes and consequences.

Education, however, if understood as a fragile practice and real *frêle bonheur*, builds up and goes on as the result of events, not strung on the chain of nature. The following event *may* be undetermined, the consequence is *not definitely* the next determinedness, and the process changes due to *unexpected* experiences. Whoever rules out chance must replace it by the plan, which on the other hand will only result in being forced to make the plan open for the next coincidence. This is not compatible with the goal of education and for no general purpose, but definitely to practice. Human action is not determined by a natural plan and insofar as education is a field of action it cannot be guided by nature.

The deeper reason for the predominance of loneliness in Rousseau's concept of education is the shifting of sin to history and thus to the development of society. Rousseau, to use Ernst Cassirer's (1932) words, solves the problem of *theodicy* because a sinful society cannot be a hereditary fate. Augustinian original sin was a part of man's *nature*, who like Rousseau projects sin or evil on society; paradoxically he has the chance of being able to change this state because and as far as nature is not open to the access of politics.

In this sense, good nature is the condition for society to improve. Under the condition of man's constitutive sinfulness evil can be neither lessened nor increased but always only stated anew. If one makes nature free of sinfulness, it will not only be good but sociable at all for the first time, with the new paradox that existing society is not ready for this while at the same time needs it. And only then the problem can be stated *if* and, if yes, *how* society could be *changed*, or, more precisely, *improved* by way of education.

The front cover of an edition of *Emile* from 1792 (Thiery 1992, table 20) shows how this educational experiment was perceived, that is as a political message. In the picture one sees Rousseau's monument as that of the prophet of natural education who from the midst of nature rose to the pantheon of eternity because and as far as he stood up against the false doctrines of the Church. One sees how he buried original sin, that is the doctrines of the ecclesiastical teachers, under his body. They have been refuted by innocence and purity, the angel state of children. The children leave the underground and are liberated, they themselves sweep aside the filth of original sin and then it will be possible to make them free in the name of revolution. However, one sees two children, and one sees both sexes.

This picture introduces the *fifth* book of *Emile*, where Rousseau describes how Emile is prepared for society, in this context and decisively for the other sex, which up to that point has not held any educational significance. The critical test of the theory of self-love is unification with the other sex, which requires the sociability of a couple and thus demands mutual dependence, which, other than in the Second Discourse, demands permanence. No social tie is more dangerous than love, and education is least able to prepare for this precisely.

On August 12th, 1769 Rousseau writes to Thérèse and comments on their relationship. This unusual letter after twenty-four years at each other's side – Rousseau speaks of "notre union" – tries to explain his honesty and that he wants to live in this "perfect union" until the end of his days. In a world of hostility and envy all that was left for him was her. "It is certain that, finding only closed or false hearts anymore, the only foundation (ressource) of my life, my entire trust is in you; I cannot live without the opportunity of speaking my mind, and this I can do only with you. It is certain that if you gave up on me and I was forced to live completely on my own; but that is impossible for me and I would be a dead man" (Correspondance t. XXXVII, p. 121).

A dependency could hardly be greater, more so as Rousseau even complains on living together "en misalliance," which he felt to be a great burden. He mentions her "project" to move to another community because she could no longer stand at his side. Rousseau speaks of an "asylum" where she was taking refuge, giving the choice of leaving him to her free will but still offering a reason for her to stay.

> But what concerns your decision which you wanted to make in your state of rage, that is to leave me and to disappear without my saying anything on this and without my knowing where you would go, never in my life would I accept this because this would be shameful and dishonorable to the one of us and the other, and against all our obligations. (*ibid.*, p. 122)

Society as an Objective of Education

Rousseau criticizes and denies existing society in favor of a social association which is dependent on the success of natural education. Its real objective is society; it is not simply an end in itself, as sometimes assumed. The social contract assumes the *citoyen* and thus a sovereign subject, as being identical with itself and not having experienced any loss of natural power in the course of its upbringing. Rousseau supposes that maintaining natural power is constantly endangered and thus constructs the concept of "negative education." The reason for this is the "pure" relation between individual and society, which is stated in the fourth book of *Emile*: "The man and the citizen, whoever he may be, has no property to invest in society but himself, all his other goods belong to society in spite of himself" (Rousseau 1993, p. 189).

But how should individual and society be related? There are only some hints in *Emile*, not a theory. Basically, the relation is not two-sided but mutual: "Society must be studied in the individual and the individual in the society; those who treat politics and morals apart from one another will never understand either" (*ibid.*, p. 236). But there is a growing dependency of the individual because of his increasing needs. Primitive relations show how men are influenced by them and what passions should spring from them. "We see that it is in proportion to the development of these passions that a man's relations with others expand or contract (*ibid.*, pp. 235–7).

At the end of his education Emile must be able to do more than just enjoy his own society:

> To live in the world he must know how to get on with other people, he must know what forces move them, he must calculate the action and re-action of self-interest in civil society, he must estimate the results so accurately that he will rarely fail in his undertakings, or he will at least have tried in the best possible way. (*ibid.*, p. 254)

But "social intercourse" as opposed to "private life" (*ibid.*, p. 375) is not the same as the state of society for which Rousseau developed a theory.

Society as it exists is bad, but the *state* of society can be described in a non-empirical way. Rousseau's *Contrat Social*, written and published in parallel with *Emile*, is an ideal-type theory that dealt with the framework of the social state as such. Rousseau is looking for the conditions not of historical societies but of *good* society, and society at its normative core is *one*, not many.

The state of society entails the loss of "natural liberty" in favor of "civil liberty and the legal right of property" (Rousseau 2004a, pp. 20–1). Also, man acquires with civil society the state of "moral freedom"; citizens must be capable of using their freedom according to law and virtue. "Citizens" are defined as "participans à l'autorité souveraine" (O.C. III, p. 362) who "share in the sovereign power" (Rousseau 2004a, p. 17). Together they form an "association" or a body politic or a people (*ibid.*, p. 16). Rousseau uses two criteria for measuring a "body politic": the extent of its territory and the number of its people. By both factors the appropriate or best size of a state must be designed. This "certain balance" is not an exact mathematical proportion but an equilibrium which must be secured against, inside and outside. Two other conditions for instituting a people are plenty and peace; it is no alternative merely to do business or wage war (*ibid.*, pp. 54ff.).[152]

In the *Contrat Social* Rousseau does not say anything about what makes man a citizen. The difficulty arises from the preconditions of natural upbringing and criticism of state education. Unlike many authors after the mid-eighteenth century, Rousseau – in *Emile* – does *not* try to achieve general school education for all children of a people, who this way are prepared for their laws and duties as future citizens. This alone is not according to their nature, an argument which is mentioned nowhere, for example in his opponent Jean-Robert Tronchin's (1761) theory of state. Also Voltaire in the *Idées républicaines*, directed against Rousseau's *Contrat Social*, did not consider nature the main problem of qualifying citizens but ignorance and brutishness (Voltaire 1961, p. 513; *Idées républicaines* XXXV).[153]

Rousseau's way of thinking about this problem was completely different. Virtue is not a question of knowledge, citizens arguably need political virtues to join a society, but these virtues do not arise from teaching but from that which is demanded by the *general will* (*volonté générale*) and thus by the foundation of society. For this it is not public education that is necessary, but definitely a kind of education which makes virtues possible at all, as this keeps childhood free from dependency and thus maintains natural sovereignty. Common schooling can only be harmful because it subordinates the child and weakens his natural powers. Reading books is not preparing future citizens.

Also, school knowledge is not useful for civil virtues. The people form a political body as a moral person; this body demands citizens who must learn how to overcome their particular interests and to act according to the common interest. The citizen must submit to the general will. "Fancying that the artificial person which constitutes the state is a mere fictitious entity (since it is not a man) he might seek to enjoy the rights of a citizen without doing the duties of a subject. The growth of this kind of injustice would bring about the ruin of the body politic" (Rousseau 2004a, p. 19). Ruling a society goes back to an original covenant (une première convention) (*ibid.*, p. 13), and the general will cannot err (*ibid.*, p. 30).

The metaphor of "contract" does not refer to a legal relationship but to an act of foundation. The members of society do not sign a previously nego-tiated paper. The metaphor is a signal for the equality of contract partners, without an existing formal contract. There is only the original act, by which "people become *a* people" (*ibid.*, p. 13). With contracts, however, there is not only the problem of equality of partners; without mutual agreement it is not possible to decide about each other. At the same time there are the problems of how fixed contracts are to be kept and of what secures their keeping. The situation becomes even more difficult if contracts do not assume a social order but are the first to originate its existence.

The *Social Contract* is Rousseau's most thought-out work, based on more than twenty years of studying and reflection. On December 23rd, 1761 he writes to Antoine-Jacques Roustan (1734–1808) in Geneva[154] that the *Contrat Social*, about whose genesis he states to have kept quiet, is likely to be published only after the *Traité de l'Éducation* but that it is many years ahead of it (Correspondance t. IX, pp. 344–5).[155] Work on the problem of society precedes studying education, the theories are written almost in parallel, but Rousseau never said anything about how the two books from the year 1762 fit together. About this there is no explanation by the author but only the interpretation of a puzzle.

This interpretation may start out from the fifth book of *Emile*, that is the end of the novel and the result of the literary experiment of "natural upbringing." Many interpreters, examining Rousseau's theory of education, ignore the end, for which long passages from *Contrat Social* were taken over and didactically processed. Often it has been overlooked how Rousseau composed the end and that for this the theory of society plays an essential role. In the first four books of *Emile* society is denied to be a fact, and now it is suddenly made strong, not coincidentally beginning with the intimate social behavior of the couple. The first real "society" Emile is about to experience is that of the union between a man and a woman.

Since Pierre Burgelin's essay "L'éducation de Sophie" (1962)[156] the *begin-ning* of the fifth book has been debated. The discussion makes clear that in *Emile* two ways of upbringing are described, that of a man and that of a woman, while until the fifth book there was the pretense that "natural upbringing" serves man in general and thus the two sexes (Martin 1981; Meld Shell 2001 and others). For decades, the interpreters of *Emile* have indeed overlooked or not taken into consideration that the protagonist of the novel bears a male name. Nature's order is referred to him, which thus is not the foundation of educating "man" but the *male*. At the end of the "natural upbringing" of man a principle of inequality is introduced (Rousseau 1993, pp. 384ff.), which previously was not announced at all.

The reason for this is a very natural one. From the age of strength Emile must be led toward the age of prudence, and this is no longer possible in a state of social isolation but requires the presence of the other sex. The fifth book starts with laconic sentences "We have reached the last act of youth's drama; we are approaching its closing scene. It is not good that man should be alone. Emile is now a man. We have promised him a companion and we must give her to him. That companion is Sophie" (O.C. IV, p. 692).[157] The governor chooses Sophie for Emile (Rousseau 1993, p. 441) according to the indirect method of education, that is she is introduced in such a way that Emile is not only able to form an opinion about her but believes her to be his own choice.

Rousseau mentions that he originally intended to educate both, Emile and Sophie, together and for each other. "But on consideration I thought all these premature arrangements undesirable, for it was absurd to plan the marriage of two children before I could tell whether this union was in accordance with nature and whether they were really suited to each other. We must not confuse what is suitable in a state of savagery with what is suitable in civilised life" (*ibid.*). Therefore both were educated according to their own nature and not under a promise of marriage, which was common practice in eighteenth-century education. Not only overseas but also European parents arranged marriages between boys and girls during their childhood (Coontz 2004 and others). This Rousseau excludes:

> Instead of providing a wife for Emile in childhood, I have waited till I know what would suit him. It is not for me to decide, but for nature; my task is to discover the choice she has made. My business, mine I repeat, not his father's; for when he entrusted his son to my care, he gave up his place to me. He gave me his rights; it is I who am really Emile's father; it is I who have made a man of him. I would have refused to educate him if I were not free to marry him according to his own choice, which is mine. (Rousseau 1993, p. 442)

Emile's search for Sophie is pretended (une feinte recherche) (O.C. IV, p. 765). She was chosen for him by the governor and this because the two *educations* fit together. "Brought up, like Emile, by Nature, she is better suited to him than any other; she will be his true mate. She is his equal in birth and nature, his inferior in fortune" (*ibid.*, p. 446; O.C. IV, p. 769). Sophie is a person and she has an image, described as follows:

> Sophie[158] is well born and she has a good disposition; she is very warm-hearted and this warmth of heart sometimes makes her imagination run away with her. Her mind is keen rather than accurate, her temper is pleasant but variable, her person pleasing though nothing out of the common, her countenance bespeaks a soul and it speaks true; you may meet her with indifference, but you will not leave her without emotion. Others possess good qualities which she lacks; others possess her good qualities in a higher degree, but in no one are these qualities better blended to form a happy disposition. She knows how to make the best of her very faults, and if she were more perfect she would be less pleasing. (Rousseau 1993, pp. 426–7)

She is not beautiful, but in her presence men forget their ideas of beautiful women and feel dissatisfied. The more often one looks at her, the prettier she becomes, and she gains where so many others lose. Her taste is modest but always suitable. She dresses appropriately, but she hates luxurious dresses. She does not stand out but arouses interest. We all like her, but we do not know why. "She does not display her charms, she conceals them, but in such a way as to enhance them." When you see her you will say: "That is a good modest girl" (*ibid.*, p. 427).

All her gifts are natural ones, and she has more taste than talent. She has a pretty voice and sings with taste and truthfulness, without being overeducated. She moves delicately, knows a little about reading music, and masters simple harmonies. She likes sewing and knitting as all other women's arts, which were carefully taught to her. "There is nothing she cannot do with her needle" (*ibid.*, p. 428). She helps her mother a lot with household chores and keeps a close eye on tidiness. She was educated for the household, without having an eye for a man. She behaves neither flirtatiously nor provocatively, she is decent and has manners. "Some day she will be the mother of a family" (*ibid.*).

Nothing about her is reminiscent of refinement or luxury: "Nothing but clean water enters her room; she knows no perfumes but the scent of flowers, and her husband will never find anything sweeter than her breath. In conclusion, the attention she pays to the outside does not blind her to the fact that time and strength are meant for greater tasks; either she does not know or she despises that exaggerated cleanliness of body which degrades the soul. Sophie is more than clean, she is pure" (*ibid.*, p. 429). Her mind is "pleasing but not brilliant, and thorough but not deep; it is the sort of mind which calls for no remark, as she never seems cleverer or stupider than oneself" (*ibid.*).

Sophie is naturally merry. As a child she was even wild and "larksome,"[159] but her mother cured her of all her giddiness, "little by little, lest too sudden a change should make her self-conscious. Thus, she became modest and retiring while still a child, and now that she is a child no longer, she finds it easier to continue this conduct than it would have been to acquire it without knowing why" (*ibid.*, pp. 429–30). In the whole book there is no image of Emile which could be compared to this. She could be described as colorful, while he remains faceless. Sophie has parents, neighbors, teachers, she grows up in company and does not need long detours of natural upbringing to be marriageable. Rousseau does not employ any ages of education for her and also needs no particular scene in a landscape garden to describe her upbringing, which in every respect is different from what Rousseau has had in store for Emile and has described on nearly four hundred previous pages.

The reason for this is the difference between the sexes and thus of a "nature" which in *Emile* is mentioned only here. Rousseau clarifies at the beginning of the fifth book: in all that does not relate to sex, woman is man. "She has the same organs, the same needs, the same faculties. The machine is the same in its construction; its parts, its workings and its appearance are similar." From whatever aspect one considers them, they differ only by degree. "Yet where sex is concerned man and women are unlike; each is the complement of the other; the difficulty in comparing them lies in our inability to decide, in either case, what is a manner of sex, and what is not" (*ibid.*, p. 384).

> In the union of sexes each alike contributes to the common end, but in different ways. From this diversity springs the first difference which may be observed between man and woman in their moral relations. The man should be strong and active; the woman should be weak and passive; the one must have both the power and the will; it is enough that the other should offer little resistance. (*ibid.*, p. 385)

Emile's upbringing thus represents *man's* nature, while Sophie's is that of the *female*; the education of the male is orientated at the world, while the woman's education is at the house; thus Emile forms Sophie, who is kept widely ignorant until meeting Emile. "She has taste without deep study, talent without art, judgment without learning. Her mind knows little, but it is trained to learn" (*ibid.*, p. 446). In fact, she has not read any books except Barrême's *Livre de comptes faits*, which is supposed to introduce her to household work, and Fénelon's *Télémaque*, which happened to fall into

Critical Exposition of Rousseau's Work

her hands as a child and which touched her heart deeply (*ibid.*).[160] Under these conditions Sophie becomes her husband's scholar (*ibid.*, p. 447). He teaches her everything he knows, "without asking whether she wants to learn it or whether it is suitable for her" (*ibid.*, p. 465).

This is reminiscent of Baron Wolmar's teachership in *Nouvelle Héloise*, although Julie d'Etange had almost equal rights. She is allowed to read, although only classical writers, no novels, and makes no decisions on her reading (Rousseau 1997, p. 49). Sophie in *Emile* is shaped after the Comtesse d'Houdetot,[161] described by Rousseau in *Confessions*. Also she is not beautiful but has a "natural and pleasing intelligence, in which gaiety, impetuosity, and naivity were happily combined" (Rousseau 2000, p. 429). She sings and dances, writes pretty verses, has an honest character, and Rousseau never tires of praising "the purity and the sincerity of her excellent nature" (*ibid.*, p. 430). But the literary model is different from experience: for Emile there are no "gestures of tenderness" and no "long and frequent tête-a-têtes" (*ibid.*, p. 433) which Rousseau claims for his relationship with the Comtesse.

The fifth book does not deal in depth with the other sex; rather, Rousseau explains how the woman's education must be to make her fit for the man. For this is assumed the dialectic of the relationship between the sexes from the male point of view: Rousseau formulates a seemingly liberal but in fact authoritative kind of education for Sophie because he believes her to be the *stronger* sex. She grants the sexual license, her appeals make the man weak, thus it is most important that *he* retains the upper hand; in other words, she is educated for *him*.

> For nature has endowed woman with a power of stimulating man's passions in excess of man's power of satisfying those passions, and has thus made him dependent on her goodwill, and compelled him in his turn to endeavour to please her, so that she may be willing to yield to his superior strength. Is it weakness which yields to force, or is it voluntarily self-surrender? This uncertainty constitutes the chief charm of the man's victory, and the woman is usually cunning enough to leave him in doubt. (Rousseau 1993, p. 387)

Thus, what makes Emile strong in the first relationship he ever had apart from that with the tutor is not the result of his education but the overcoming of his natural weakness. Sophie is told to be true, honorable, and to publicly show morality, as otherwise the man's weakness, his temptation, could not be controlled and the relationship between the sexes would be turned upside down. It is not enough that a wife should be faithful; her husband, along with his friends and neighbors, *must believe* in her fidelity (*ibid.*, p. 389). The strong sex is the weak sex because the weak one is – at the crucial moment – the strong one.

> If woman is made to please and to be subjected to man, she ought to make herself pleasing in his eyes and not provoke him to anger; her strength is in her charms, by their means she should compel him to discover to use his strength. The surest way of arousing this strength is to make it necessary by resistance. Then *amour-propre* comes to the help of desire and each exults in the other's victory. This is the origin of attack and defense, of the boldness of one sex and the timidity of the other, and even of the shame and modesty with which nature has armed the weak for the conquest of the strong. (*ibid.*, p. 385; O.C. IV, pp. 693–4)

The "union" of man and woman is not a pattern outside the intimate relationship, and it is not a contract. So if society is the objective of education it cannot be realized with a couple (here Rousseau rejects the influential Aristotelian theory of social origins, which begins many philosophical works in the Enlightenment.) Neither the relationship between sexes nor families are models for society; Rousseau clearly distinguishes "society" and "relationship," leaving open of which sex the members of society are. The citoyens in *Contrat Social* are not distinguished by their sex, while this distinction results in only Emile but not Sophie being educated for the society of citizens.

This is not congruent with the construction of the social contract. Here, Rousseau (2004a, p. 25) speaks of "a moral and lawful equality" which replaced natural inequality, "so that however unequal in strength and intelligence men become equal by covenant and by right." The condition for this is the *volonté générale*; only the general will, not the will of all (*volonté de tous*), is said always to strive for the public good (*ibid.*, p. 30). The law are "acts" of the *volonté générale* (*ibid.*, p. 41) and they are not "made" by somebody.

> The equality of rights and the notion of justice which it produces derive from the predilection which each man has for himself and hence from human nature as such ... The general will, to be truly what it is, must be general in its purpose as well as in its nature; that it should spring from all for it to apply for all; and that it loses its natural rectitude when it is directed towards any particular and circumstanced object – for in judging what is foreign to us, we have no sound principle of equity to guide us. (*ibid.*, p. 33)

Gender does not matter for this. Political congruence is not one of the natural passions, which due to the difference of the sexes are called "extreme inequal" in the second preface of *Nouvelle Héloise* (Rousseau 1997, p. 17). Only in relation to Sophie is Emile educated for his sex, otherwise for society, while Sophie is educated for her sex alone and not as a citizen. On the other hand, the social contract knows of no sexual difference; all citizens are equal because all are guided by the same general will. But for education the general will does not matter.

At the end of *Emile* there is a transition from education to politics. In the *Confessions* Rousseau emphasizes that the six years of work between 1755 and 1761 in the hermitage and at Montmorency must be understood politically, so that the end of *Emile* cannot come as a surprise.

> I had seen that everything is rooted in politics, and that, whatever the circumstances, a people will never be other than the nature of its government makes it. In other words, the great question, as to which the best possible form of government, seemed to me come down in the end as this one: what is the nature of the government most likely to produce the most virtuous, the most enlightened, the wisest, and in short, taking this word in its widest sense, the best people? (Rousseau 2000, p. 395)

In the fifth book of *Emile* Rousseau alludes to the Abbé de Saint-Pierre's[162] idea to unite all states of Europe in one single association to keep peace forever in this way (Rousseau 1993, p. 516). States should be fatherlands, but there cannot be *one* "fatherland" for *everybody*, as this association would be beyond any reasonable size. The more a state extends, the more freedom decreases (*ibid.*, p. 512), and the more numerous the population is, the less morality is in accordance with the laws (*ibid.*, p. 513); to the same extent there grows the suppressing power of the government (la force réprimante du gouvernement) (*ibid.*, p. 514; O.C. III, p. 846) because and as far as the size of the state is a cause of tempting (tentations) those controlling public power to abuse their power, while at the same time it gives them the means for doing this (Rousseau 1993, pp. 512–13).

Any democratic republic must be *small* (*ibid.*, p. 515), thus if possible its size should not be bigger than that of Geneva. Montesquieu, in the *Spirit of the Laws*, had overlooked this condition of size when wanting to connect the mode of education to the kind of government.[163] For Rousseau there is the question of what must be the best form of government to let the best kind of people develop. The problem cannot be solved analytically, by a scheme of attribution, but requires, like the project of natural education, empirical factors like size, location, or climate to be taken into account. Nevertheless, all citizens must be prepared for that which awaits them in society. If that is not supposed to be state school, there must be another solution, by which Rousseau lets Emile's education end.

The first part of the finale of *Emile* is titled "Of Travel" ("Des voyages") (*ibid*., pp. 496–522; O.C. IV, pp. 826–55). After his attempts to be her teacher Emile has to part from Sophie for one more time and starts a two-year journey with his governor, which is supposed to complete his education. Progress of the Grand Tour[164] is interrupted several times; lengthy traveling without teaching is a kind of roaming (*ibid*., p. 832); traveling by itself does not educate; the purpose of the educational tour is learning (Rousseau 1993, p. 502); and as Emile already knows physical (raports physique) and moral (raport moraux) relationships with other people, he must now be taught about civil relationships – "ses raports civil avec ses concitoyens" (*ibid*.; O.C. IV, p. 833).

The governor, in other words, uses the tour through a few of the great and many of the smaller countries of Europe, not just for learning languages (Rousseau 1993, p. 522) but for teaching the social contract. This particular "science of politics" argues against Grotius and Hobbes, says the governor; the first "relies on sophism" and the other "relies on the poets," but neither of them grasps the "principles of political law" (*ibid*., p. 505) as he – Rousseau – did in the *Social Contract*. The extended lessons are a summary of the book, whose sentences are offered in detail and commented on as if Emile were not on a journey but in a lecture on constitutional law. Thus, the book on "natural education" is politically concluded. Emile – not Sophie – must be prepared for his state of being a citizen, which requires knowledge about the general nature of government.

By coming of age, every citizen must be introduced into the social relation with his fellow citizens. This is the purpose of the teaching:

> To do this he (Emile) must study first the nature of government in general, then the different forms of government, and lastly the particular government under which he was born, to know if its suits him to live under it; for by a right which nothing can abrogate, every man, when he comes of age, becomes his own master, free to renounce the contract by which he forms part of the community, by leaving the country in which the contract holds good. (*ibid*., p. 502)

Just as one may deny one's heritage one may also give up on one's fatherland (*ibid*.). "Strictly speaking, every man remains in the land of his birth at his own risk unless he voluntarily submits to its laws in order to acquire a right to their protection" (*ibid*.).

There is an overriding reason for this: constitutional law is *not* based on an educational relationship between the king and his children (*ibid*., p. 507). The king is no father and the citizens are not his offspring. The foundation of all civil society is not a genealogy but a contract, "and it is in the nature of this contract that we must seek the nature of the society formed by it" (*ibid.*, p. 508). Members do not inherit the contract but join it, and the contract must be renegotiated in every single case. The *corps politique* is a public person (*ibid.*; O.C. IV, p. 840) and citizens are members only in this sense.

While individuals have deferred to the sovereign, the latter is no more than the general will, thus every man obeying the sovereign obeys only himself (Rousseau 1993, p. 509). This means that each *chosen* place decides on social membership and political obligation, not the *historical* place, the fatherland of birth. When, at the end of his lessons, Emile reacts with sentimentality – "where ever there are men, I am among my brothers" (O.C. IV, p. 857) – the governor points out the difference between the laws of the state and those of nature. For the wise man, eternal laws of nature replace positive laws. Eternal laws of nature are inscribed into the heart by conscience and reason, and man must defer to them if he wants to be free.

There are no slaves but only evil-doers, who act against their will and self-interest (very Socratic). But true liberty is not that of the government: "Liberty is not to be found in any form of government, it is the heart of the free man, he bears it with him everywhere. The vile man bears his slavery in himself; the one would be a slave in Geneva, the other free in Paris" (Rousseau 1993, p. 524). Thus, the question of "which is my country?" (*ibid.*) is of secondary importance, as the heart rules on virtue. Whoever has no "country" has a *land* at least to live in (*ibid.*), and morality of actions and love of virtue are most precious for man, not society (*ibid.*). Morality and virtue, above all, are what one owes to the fatherland, and there is an obligation toward these only if the fatherland is in accordance with these criteria – that it is corrupted by neither size nor decadence.[165]

The second part of the finale is composed of two last speeches from the governor. The last speech is a lesson about marriage. In the first, Emile is told that he must stay away from the big cities whose vice results from the wrong size. If the good ones are supposed to give anything to others, they need the appropriate way of living, "a patriarchal, rural life, the earliest life of man, the most peaceful, the most natural, and the most attractive to the uncorrupted heart" (*ibid.*, p. 525). The Golden Age, in the conclusion to *Emile*,[166] is an illusion only for those whose heart and taste are corrupt (gâtés) (O.C. IV, p. 859). The Golden Age of the virtuous seems to be already here, "reviving around Sophie's home" (Rousseau 1993, p. 526), and it does not exclude "service of the country" if Emile is really called to fulfill his duties (*ibid.*).

True education must be able to maintain the *uncorrupted* heart, that is the innocence of the child. Also, political virtue develops from purity of the heart, which no government can really have at its disposal. This way, Rousseau tries to avoid Montesquieu's relation between education and form of government. Virtue is not the educational law of the republic but the voice of the heart in all forms of government.[167] Thus, it is not an *idée de patrie* which characterizes *Emile*. In the end, retreat from society is thought to be the first step of the new beginning:

> All the men who withdraw from high society are useful just because of their withdrawal, since the vices are the result of its numbers. They are useful when they can bring with them into the desert places life, culture, and the love of their first condition. I like to think what benefits Emile and Sophie, in their simple home, may spread about them, what a stimulus they may give to the country, how they may revive the zeal of the unlucky villagers. (*ibid.*, pp. 525–6)[168]

Emile is presumed to be ready to live in society according to reason, which is possible as he has never lived in society, so could not be corrupted by it because of his natural strength and lack of prejudices; finally, he finds a land which demands only his *own* society, of being married to Sophie. The ideal society of *Contrat Social* does not exist in any reality which could be experienced; natural education, on the other hand, is not tied to any form of government and thus leaves choice open. There is always a country for a couple who are able to support themselves, having learned to be virtuous. And the "noble pair are united till death do part" (*ibid.*, p. 527).

But this conclusion to the novel is unconvincing. In two letters Rousseau wrote a sequel to *Emile*[169] which comes back to the topic of solitude. The letters are addressed to the governor. In a bitter voice Emile complains about his fate after the governor had left him and Sophie. In the beginning the couple were happy: two children were born, a son and a daughter, and the couple lived together in the country. But then came twists of fate: her father, her mother, and then the daughter died. Sophie succumbed to grief; Emile had to do business in a big city; the couple went there for two years and the marriage broke down. Sophie did not behave as prescribed by her own education. Contrary to convention and to the picture Rousseau painted, Sophie betrayed Emile. She confessed to him that another man had "defiled" his bed, she was pregnant and he will never touch her again (O.C. IV, p. 890).

Emile must experience that no relationship will last, not even the perfect couple. "La sublime, la noble Sophie n'est qu'une infame" ("Noble Sophie: she was nothing but a woman of shame") (*ibid.*, p. 891). In despair he realized that all his relations are broken down (*ibid.*, p. 899). Only his education saved him or at least seemed to do so:

Born with a weak soul, open to all kinds of impressions, easy to confuse, afraid to make decisions – soon after the first moments of despair in which I lost myself to my nature I became master of myself again and was able to analyze my own situation as cold-bloodedly as that of others. Subjected under the law of necessity I stopped revolting for nothing and bowed my will to the unavoidable yoke. I considered the past as something strange to me, I thought I was born again and considered my present as the guide to my behavior. (*ibid.*)

But this only added to disaster and harm. The future cannot be guided from the present; all has changed and there is no way back to her, even revenge must be ruled out. Finally Sophie died in his heart (*ibid.*, p. 904). He started again with his work as a craftsman (*ibid.*, p. 906) and lived in the house of a cabinetmaker. One day Sophie secretly visited the house without meeting him. Emile was informed by the wife of the cabinetmaker that Sophie was there with their son for a last farewell and that he will never see the son again. After that Emile fled the house for an endless journey away from civil society. "I don't need anyone; without servant, without money and without mode of travel, but also without wishes and sorrows I set out, alone and on my own feet" (*ibid.*, p. 911). "And as I broke all the bonds that tied me with my fatherland I made the whole earth my fatherland, and I became more a man [homme] the more I ceased to be a citizen [citoyen]" (*ibid.*, p. 912).

In the end Emile became a slave. First, he lived the life of a vagabond, wandering as if life were a single journey (*ibid.*, p. 914). Then he was hired as a sailor, his ship was captured by pirates, the whole crew was enslaved and they were carried off to Algiers. But the new situation – "Emile esclave" (*ibid.*, p. 916) – is only a new necessity, not the loss of natural liberty because there is none. There is only one servitude, that of nature, and men only its instrument. If liberty meant doing what man wanted, no one would be free. All men are weak and dependent on the hard yoke of necessity. Whoever is able to will what necessity demands is the freest of them all because he is never forced to do what he does not want (*ibid.*, p. 916).

Emile became a "laborious slave," who won the respect of his master and the whole town of Algiers when organizing a revolt against conditions of work. The Bey[170] of Algiers heard the story and bought the man who is no longer a citizen. He wrote to his governor: "Voilà votre Emile esclave du Bey d'Alger" (*ibid.*, p. 923). Even here the rules of conduct that Emile had learned in his education can be applied. He attained success and did not need a social contract. His new master was a wise and honorable leader of the state, his empire was in good condition, commerce and agriculture flourished, the maritime power was immense and the people had enough bread (*ibid.*, p. 924). For this second happy end no new society is necessary.

The end of *Emile* and the decision for a sequel are not Rousseau's final statements on education. The different and sometimes volatile reflections on educational problems do not result in *one* definite theory, but reveal variations which are, more than occasionally, even contradictory to that developed in *Emile*. This is true both for his published works and for numerous letters where he comments on questions of education. In these contexts one does not find the consistency of a single doctrine. Rousseau deals with completely different causes and opportunities; his motifs are adjusted to the situation without searching for unity, something he claimed always to have.

In the *Confessions* Rousseau calls (2000, p. 553) *Emile* "my latest and best work," but that does not mean that here the summing up of his reflections on education is found. He complains on the fate of the book: "Never did a work receive so much private praise and so little public approbation" (*ibid.*, p. 561). Surely this is an exaggeration: immediately after publication, at least, *Emile* aroused public attention, was bitterly contradicted but was also met with enthusiastic approval, due to the *unité de doctrine* which was almost always assumed for both the book and its author. Both damnation and adoration assume that Rousseau's theory of education could be found in *Emile* and only there.

But the end of the sequel is already a sort of self-correction. Emile and Sophie are not prepared for living together, the "history of their lives," upon which the governor is reflecting while saying good-bye (Rousseau 1993, p. 532), is not guided by the results of their upbringing, the prospect of virtue and happiness (*ibid.*) is nothing but an illusion, and passions are stronger than virtue or reason. Thus, the aim of education is not attained apart from the stoic nature that succeeds even in slavery. What remains of education is a slave and an unfaithful woman – but this cannot be the last word.

4

Variants and Contradictions

On January 12th, 1762 Rousseau writes to Malherbes that he (Rousseau) had quite clearly proven the contradictions of the social systems, with all his power revealed the evils of institutions, and finally quite simply given evidence to the fact that man was good by nature and that only the institutions of society corrupt him. These great truths had come to him during a moment of inspiration under a tree[171] and they were also to be found in his three principal writings, "that first Discourse, the one on Inequality, and the treatise On Education, these three works being inseparable and together forming one whole. All the rest has been lost; and on the spot itself there was written only the personification of Fabricius" (Rousseau 1937, p. 209).[172]

If my thesis is true, this estimation by the author is an exaggeration. His work does not form a uniform and integrated whole and at least in respect of education it is not a unity. The "rest" is by no means unimportant, and one will understand Rousseau only if this rest remains unforgotten, that is if we do not follow the author's advice. Rousseau's philosophy on education consists of a few, clearly contoured, topics and variants which are often only loosely connected to the latter. The great topics like the question of self-love, natural religion, or the nature of society are not put together to form a consistent philosophy.

Emile was supposed to do this, but before and afterward there are numerous passages deviating from it and suggesting other views. Also, it is not the case that there are variants only until the completion of *Emile* and that from then on an integrated and contradiction-free doctrine is presented. Thus, it makes sense to consider Rousseau's "theory" as a sequence of stronger and weaker "strings" which were loosely connected or not connected at all. The topics are emphasized differently, and context on arguments is very important. At one point, Rousseau reflects on the education of children, at another on citizens; on the one hand, the emphasis is of an educational nature, while on the other hand, it is of a political nature, and the reflection differs whether it is concerned with theories or with practical cases.

There are discrepancies in several respects and at various passages of the work. My focus will be on letters dealing with the topic of natural education before and after *Emile*, on the educational concept of *Nouvelle Héloise*, on the significance of books for the intellectual development of the child, which was both rejected and emphasized by Rousseau, and finally on theories on political education which Rousseau never defined negatively but always positively. That same author who wants to bring up his prime example of a child far away from society and *à la campagne* speaks of humans being able to be citizens only if being taught as early as possible about the virtues and even passions of the fatherland. For this schools are necessary and not landscapes.

In his *Letter to Beaumont* Rousseau quite firmly distinguishes "positive" from "negative" education, something which he had not done in *Emile*. This distinction is supposed to cut the core of his statements on education, and one would expect the development of the theory to be concluded by this. But Rousseau is looking for a distinction which is suitable for his justification toward Beaumont, who has attacked him for his purely negative principle of first education (Rousseau 2001, p. 6). Here, the solution is to not exclude positive education but to let it come *after* negative education, provided the thesis of childhood's "nature of its own" is true. The problem is created by *not* following his own principle.

What I call positive education tends to form the mind before maturity, and to give the child knowledge of the duties of the man. What I call negative education tends to perfect the organs, the instruments of our knowledge, before giving us this knowledge, and prepares for reason though the exercise of the senses. Negative education is far from idle. It does not produce virtues, but it prevents vices. It does not teach the truth, but it protects from error. It prepares the child for everything that can lead him to the true when he is capable of understanding it, and to the good when he is capable of loving it. (*ibid.*, p. 35)

Letters on Natural Education

In 1756, according to a letter to Louise d'Epinay, Rousseau seems to have already completed the outlines of his educational theory. This is true at least for the principle of education in accordance with age which is developed in respect of a concrete question. In this letter any "ages of education" are not yet established, as later in the "Manuscrit Favre" of *Emile*, but Rousseau must deal with a real child of a certain age. A tenet of his educational theory is that, before time, children do not understand what they are supposed to be taught, whether this is tried by way of catechisms, lessons, or letters.

Louise d'Epinay had given to him two letters to her son which Rousseau was supposed to read. Obviously, she expected an educational comment from him. In his answer Rousseau writes that by themselves the letters were good and even excellent, but only of little value for her son. The letters sounded too serious; in them a "project" of education is developed which the son would understand if he was already twenty. Even then they would perhaps be somewhat dull, that is not really a joy to read. However, this did not negate the idea of communicating with one's own son by way of letters: "I believe that the idea of writing to him is very happily conceived, and that it may shape his character and mind, but two conditions are necessary, that he can understand you and reply to you" (Rousseau 1937, p. 139).

During the eighteenth century countless letters like those by Louise d'Epinay were written, and sometimes they were also published as manuals. Rousseau judges against the background of an established culture of writing letters when saying such correspondence must indeed be written for the son. The letters which he, Rousseau, had been allowed to read were dedicated to the whole world and to everybody but not for the son, that is the real addressee. The son was not able to understand such argued letters, thus they should be put aside for a more developed age. For the time being, something different should be suggested:

> Tell him stories, tell him fables, the moral of which he can draw himself, and especially those he can apply himself. Be careful of generalities: it is only following the ordinary and futile method to put maxims in the place of facts: it is from whatever he may have noticed himself, be it good or ill, that one must start. In proportion as his ideas develop and you have taught him to reflect and make comparisons you will adapt the tone of your letters to the progress and the powers of his mind. But if you tell your son that you are setting out to cultivate his character and mind, and that in amusing him you are showing him truth and his duties, he is going to be on his guard against everything you say; he will always think he hears a lesson issuing from your mouth; everything, even his toy top will become suspect. Let your action be to that end but do keep it under cover. (*ibid.*)

The style of communication as typical for adults not only is unsuitable for education but also will result in the child's resistance. Oral or written lessons will not lead to anything, just as if there are only applying principles. Education must proceed in a way which is appropriate to the age and thus must have the gradual development of ideas in mind. One starts by moral narrations and not by letters; fables do educate but not moral lessons. What is the point if the son is told about his duties toward his mother without understanding the words? Why are words like "servility," "duty," "prudence," or "reason" presented to his ear if he does not know what to do with them?

> All that has a fearful sound at his age. It is with the actions that result from these terms that he must be made familiar; let him be ignorant of their characteristics in words until such time as you may have taught him their meaning through his own conduct; and further see to it that he appreciates above all the advantage and pleasure he has received by so acting, in order to show him that an act of submission and duty is not so fearful a thing as he may imagine. (*ibid.*)

Thus what matters is the correct moment of education, not about losing time. In 1755 there is not yet a setting of natural education as later in *Emile*; also the letter avoids any kind of paradox and shows only a few generalizations. Fables are still allowed reading. The message is simple: children cannot be taught about their duties before due time; if one tries this, one will only set them against oneself. They must be able to act according to duty, but they will not obey any abstract teaching which is only a moral appeal formulated in the language of adults.

On the other hand, one will succeed in education by making even an act of servility or duty not such a terrible thing if children are able to feel the advantage and the fun which are connected to meeting one's expectation. Children must also understand what it is demanded from them, and they will not be able to do so if they lack all qualifications, that is if they do not connect any positive ideas of their own to being forced to do something. And if they are not able to act but must only listen, they will ignore or evade what is demanded from them.

There was more success in following this rule, Rousseau continues respectfully, in the second letter which he had read. In respect of his outline the second letter was more appropriate to the age and it was also suitable for addressing younger children. Her definition of politeness was correct and sensitive, but one had to consider two things if the son was supposed to understand the whole delicacy of the statement: "Does he know what respect, what goodwill are? Is he capable of distinguishing the voluntary from the involuntary expression of a delicately feeling heart?" (*ibid.*) By both questions Rousseau indicates that here also, education by letters has missed its goal, as the son is not able to do what the letter demands. Rousseau's own letter ends with a suggestion:

> Please note, Madame, that children, if too early confronted with difficult and complicated ideas, are forced to go back to the definition of each

word. Almost always this definition is more complicated and more undetermined than the thought itself; they will use it in a bad way, and they will
keep only bad ideas in their minds. Furthermore, this shows the disadvantage of them repeating great words like parrots without understanding
their meaning at all, and of them being only big children or pretentious
blockheads at the age of twenty. (*ibid.*, pp. 183–4)

Thus, the thesis from the second book of *Emile* – that learning abstract
definitions will only feed the head with wrong ideas – comes from a concrete
correspondence, between a mother and child, who has only learned how
to repeat great words without understanding their meaning, who thus is
nothing more than a talking parrot and is said to remain a child for all
times or to become a show-off without any intellectual maturity. Complicated
sequences of words are said to be unsuitable for children, whose thinking
was directed toward concrete things and which besides this could only be
vague. Whoever wants to achieve something with children must be ready to
deal with *their* way of thinking, something which Madame d'Epinay obviously
needed to be told.

Louise d'Epinay,[173] whom Rousseau knew since 1747, married the tenant
(fermier général) Denis Lalive d'Epinay (1724–1782) at the age of nineteen,
and they were divorced in 1748. Louise, who was well compensated, had
four children, including the son mentioned in the correspondence from
her marriage with d'Epinay. At the time of this correspondence Louis-
Joseph Lalive d'Epinay (1746–1813) was nine years old. By letters such as
that to his mother Rousseau's thinking on education developed, which in
this respect required real children with whom Rousseau was confronted by
request but who were never his own. His own competence regarding matters
of education is assumed; only in the *Confessions* does Rousseau admit that
the practical work in the House of Mably had convinced him of not having
enough talent to work as the "tutor" of children (Rousseau 2000, p. 260).

Louise d'Epinay's letters to her son were published in Geneva in 1759,
without Rousseau's criticism and as an independent publication which also
shows how little Rousseau really dealt with correspondence. In August, 1757
he writes her again on children. What does being angry (chagrin) about
a child of six years, whose character one cannot know, mean to one? By
answering this question, probably for the first time in his correspondence,
Rousseau brings up *nature* as the starting point of education, which is not
mentioned in her letters. Rousseau writes: "What your children do while
they are in the charge of others proves nothing, for one can never know
whose is the fault. It is when they are no longer under nurses, governesses
and tutors that we see what nature has made them, and then it is that their
real education begins" (Rousseau 1937, pp. 114–15).

The child without persons to educate him, that is without the representatives of nutrition, of supervision and teaching, is that child of nature which is assumed in *Emile*. But then precisely it is not a real child anymore but an abstract notion, which at any cost was supposed to be avoided. Rousseau looks for what nature does with children, but no education knows such a natural state which would have to isolate the child and thus would have to experiment with him in a way that real parents would never accept. "Robust" education at orphanages is not an example for this.

Also, the nature of youth is presented in different ways, according to each cause. In spring 1758 Rousseau writes to an unknown young man and gives advice for his further education which, however, is completely different from that which the later theory of the age of youth was to prescribe. He was honored, Rousseau says, by being asked how one should organize one's own life in a moral way, but as the motif of the request was really quite simple, one had not to go very far to find the principles of morals. They are close by, from his place of staying in the garden of Montmorency, for that which is sought must be found with the heart.

Virtue is not a science which demands studies. Whoever wants to be virtuous must really want it. And once there is the will, the most important thing has already been achieved. The first piece of advice he was able to offer is never to start living a life of contemplation (deriding Aristotle), which is nothing but the laziness of the soul, this being true for every age and particularly for that of youth: "Man is not made for meditation, but for action. The life of labour God imposes on us has nothing but what is sweet to the heart of the truly good man who gives himself to it with the intention of doing his duty, and the vigor of youth has not been given us to be spent in idle contemplation" (Rousseau 1937, p. 151).

If one thing was sure, then it was this: in Paris a virtuous life was not possible. Therefore, Rousseau was going to offer a second piece of advice: to go back to his family and to try his luck in his place of origin. Only there virtue finds its concrete place, that is, as in the *Confessions*, that of origin. Thus, it was time to go back:

So, Sir, work in the station where your parents and Providence has placed you. This is the first precept of that virtue which you want to pursue, and if your staying in Paris, joined to the work you are doing, seems to you too difficult a combination, do better still, Sir, and return to your Province, go live in the bosom of your family, serve and care for your virtuous parents, – there you will really be fulfilling the duties imposed on you by virtue. You should not think yourself unfortunate at having to live as your father has done, and there is no lot in the world which works, active interest, innocence, and contentment with oneself will not make endurable, if one submits to it all with the idea of doing one's duty. There, Sir, are pieces of advice worth all those you might come to get at Montmorency. (*ibid.*, pp. 151–2)

There is no mention or any indication of "second birth" – when matters become concrete, Rousseau often recommends Calvinist attitudes toward work without having *amour de soi* in mind. The whole theory of autonomous self and social association does not play any role at all; the letter already anticipates that indeed there is no place for this. Whoever does not want to expose himself to the company of the *fripons gueux* (mean rogues) has no choice but to go back to the place where one could not bear living; an alternative location is not available. In this letter Rousseau offers less than he did in 500 pages of *Emile*, not even a new "land" (*pays*) but only the father's estate and thus the cause of conflict.

In the *Letter to Beaumont* Rousseau (2001, p. 36) writes on restraining passion in youth: "I protected my pupil's heart from the passions until adolescence, and when they are ready to be born, I delay their progress further by efforts suited to curb them." Other than love of oneself, the passions lead astray, particularly when they are increasing. However, for lessons of wisdom there was only one certain moment; before that the child is not ready for them and after that wisdom does not impress the heart anymore, which has already been abandoned to the passions (*ibid.*). And it was true that nothing is allowed to be taught to them "whose truth their judgement is incapable of feeling" (*ibid.*).

On February 6th, 1759 Rousseau answers the above-mentioned letter by the Genevan student Jean-Edmonde Romilly, who had sent him an ode. Following the not very encouraging criticism of the poem Rousseau starts speaking about his vision of simple life which had to be considered the goal of education. Whatever was done in this respect, it had to result in some way of life. The latter's description, again, echoes the end of *Emile*:

Moderate work, a straight and simple way of life, peace of the soul and a healthy body, which is the result of all these, may rather make a happy existence than knowledge and glory. If, however, you are interested in cultivating your talents as a writer, at least do not take over these people's prejudices; do not value your class more than it deserves it and your own value will be the higher. (Correspondance t. XI, pp. 21–2)

Again, there is no reservation in respect of the kind of society for which this advice is meant. Instead, the fundamental judgments are fixed – whoever is rich must be unhappy, Rousseau writes, probably on March 22nd, 1756 to Louise d'Epinay, when moving to his house La Chevrette; he was able to leave half of his few belongings in Paris and was carefree. He calls himself her "jardinier,"[174] the gardener preferring nature to every kind of luxury. A life of loneliness and poverty deserved every kind of respect. In this regard nobody was able to be more sensitive than him: "Being a loner, I am more sensitive than others ... I am poor, and it seems to me that one has to pay deference to this condition" (Correspondance t. IV, pp. 199–200).[175]

On the other hand, Rousseau corresponded exhaustively with the nobility. You are unlucky to be a prince, Rousseau writes in the above-mentioned letter from November 10th, 1763 to Louis-Eugène de Württemberg, thus seldom do you have the opportunity also to be a father. There are too many other duties, which is also true for the Duchess. From this situation there concludes the first, simple rule of education: "Take care that your child is loved by someone." If the parents are unable to educate the child, that is to be dear to him, somebody else must do it. The child needs a relation, and if this cannot be the natural one it might well be a substitute (Correspondance t. XVIII, p. 115). Realistically, the role model of the Baron de Wolmar is not considered to be suitable here, neither is the general suspicion of despotic fathers being the cause of vice and children's unhappiness (Rousseau 1997, p. 117).

In reality, the children's "reference person" in case the father is unavailable is not a governor as in *Emile* but a woman, as it is about educating a daughter. This person must match the child's sex (*ibid.*). The suitable woman is described precisely and in quintessential Rousseauist style or idealism: She must be neither too young nor too beautiful,[176] a widow would be better than an unmarried woman, she cannot simply educate by her emotions, even less by some "bel esprit," and she should use her intellect to obey her orders. "It is important that she is not to be handled too easily, and it is not important for her to be accommodating. On the contrary, one shall have her as an aid, considering one's own interests. It is impossible to put a squanderer in his place, while misers are kept under control by help of their own mistakes" (Correspondance t. XVIII, p. 116).

Nothing would be worse and to fear more for education than her having "humeur." Humor is only a quality of fools. Also, she should not be too lively, as often this is symptomatic of people too easily enraged. If a perfect choice cannot be found, there must be compromises. In any case, this woman must have strength of character; a brilliant character, however, is not necessary (*ibid.*). "Besides this, do not look for a cultivated mind; the mind will develop in the course of learning, that is all. She would put on an act if she is knowing; you can handle her better if she is ignorant; if she did not know how to read, even the better; she will learn this together with her pupil. The only intellectual quality to be demanded should be a sense of justice" (*ibid.*).

In comparison, the governor in *Emile* was not described like this at all. And for Sophie an educator of her own, demanded here by class, was not necessary. The mother was enough, as for Henriette in *Nouvelle Héloise*. However, Julie d'Etange also educates her two sons, so in this case sex does not need to match for education. And the effort Rousseau suggests for the education of the daughter of the Prince of Württemberg is not according to that which Rousseau usually suggests for girls: "They obey their mothers until they can imitate them. When wives do their duty, be sure that daughters will not fail in theirs" (Rousseau 1997, p. 17).[177]

His first rule, as Rousseau writes further to the prince, was the choice of the reference person, which could not be done too carefully. Then there follow further rules of an education which by no word is connected to nature. Not in any situation may the educator love the child or may be loved by him (Correspondance t. XVIII, pp. 116–17). This is forbidden by social status. Also, the relationship between the child and his *gouvernante* must not be characterized only by carefulness, as this indicates dependence. "We want the child to be precious for his governess. This is necessary to have the governess's fate being tied to that of the child" (*ibid.*, p. 117).

The governess must offer a "real service," that is she must educate the child neither toward flaunting nor toward representation. And she shall be rewarded according to the success of her efforts and not for her good intentions, something which the righteous father and not the mother must decide upon. "The judgment of women is too little accepted, and motherly love is blind" (*ibid.*). Choosing the judges for education, as Rousseau says, is a special problem demanding careful work. The governess must trust in the reliability of the judgment. She may never forget that the success of her work is judged and that this is no punishment; she is not judged to cause her pain (*à sa peine*) (*ibid.*, p. 118). And the question is not how her work is rewarded but whether education succeeds (*ibid.*).

The governess shall not educate by intellect or interest but by her imagination. Money incentives are tempting, but their power will fade away in the far future (*ibid.*). Her imagination can be put to the test, and if the long duration of education makes her tired, her tasks can still be divided and be rewarded in the interim (*ibid.*, p. 119). The child will love the governess, provided she will handle her with seriousness and not pamper the child. For everything else this principle will be valid: "The effect of habit is natural and reliable; never has it failed due to the tutors' mistakes" (*ibid.*). There is no mention of it being essential for education *not* to take up habits.

On the other hand, here also the dangerous moment in education is mentioned, this time in respect of a girl. "At a certain age the little girl will be capricious and obstinate. Let us suspect such a moment when the girl does not want to listen; this moment will happen seldom, one feels why. In this unpleasant moment the governess lacks any means. Thus, she will be irritated and look at her pupil and say: now the moment has come, you rob me of the bread of my old age" (*ibid.*). But the child of such a father cannot be a monster, thus one warning will be enough (*ibid.*). "This is the course of nature" (*ibid.*).

The second rule refers to instructions. The governess needs a special directive (mémoire instructif), according to which she must proceed. It does not follow the "path of nature" (route de la nature) but the "route" prescribed by her master the prince, and this incessantly and without any deviation. One must not allow discussion, Rousseau says, the governess is nothing more than a means of carrying out her master's directives, which must be reasonable, simple, and comprehensible (*ibid.*, p. 120). And she must internalize these instructions, that is she must not have only the words at hand but must know what to do (*ibid.*). If circumstances change, she must be instructed afresh to avoid even the slightest mistake. This is most of all the mother's task (*ibid.*).

The third rule concerns the distribution of power. Also here, Rousseau is certain: within the framework of her responsibilities the governess has absolute power (un pouvoir absolu) over the child (*ibid.*). She acts like a second mother (*ibid.*, p. 121) in the context of that economy of the house as described in *Nouvelle Héloise*, something which Rousseau explicitly points out to the prince (*ibid.*).[178] The maxims of good housekeeping require also control of servants, who may never influence education (*ibid.*, p. 121). This must be clearly expressed by help of speeches (*ibid.*, p. 123). Only this way will one remain as master in one's own house (*ibid.*).

Many thousand means concluding from these rules, thus Rousseau finishes the longest letter on education he ever wrote. Finally, he wanted to offer only one more important piece of advice: "It is important to always check the child most accurately, and to carefully watch the progress of his body and his heart. If something around the child is done contradicting the rules, this impression will be remembered by the child. As soon as you see a new sign for deviance, look for its causes with care, and you will find them without fail" (*ibid.*). Freedom for the child is not intended, insofar as the setting of *Emile* comes to bear.

The first letter to the prince dates from September 29th, 1763 (Correspondance t. XVII, pp. 286–7). The prince asks Rousseau in more detail about his daughter's education on October 4th, 1763 (Correspondance t. XVIII, pp. 13–16), and Rousseau answers on October 17th, at first in a very formal way (*ibid.*, pp. 43–5), before then sketching his educational schedule for the prince's daughter. On December 15th in respect of his letter having been received positively, Rousseau answered by a flattering letter which does not offer any new argument, except that the father is warned not to consider his daughter to be "precocious" (précoce) (*ibid.*, p. 213), something which was against nature. He is told to observe, examine, and verify her, Rousseau here not forgetting to point out the empire of habits (*ibid.*).

A letter from January 21st, 1764 (Correspondance t. XIX, pp. 74–5) gives further observations on education and diet, but again does not mention *Emile*, the book by which Rousseau advanced to be an educational expert. Later letters to the prince do not mention the topic or if so, then only in passing. In other letters Rousseau deals with these questions without ever presenting a comparable educational schedule. Some letters are very short; others are detailed and focus on the given case. In contrast to his writings for his defense, they are not about a doctrine but questions of his readers. Rousseau's answers sometimes try to develop suitable solutions which, although showing certain basic motifs, vary according to each case.

Some letters doubted whether Rousseau's method of education was applicable. On June 2nd, 1762, immediately after *Emile* had been published, the Marquise de Créqui wrote to Rousseau: "I have read your novel on education; I call it a 'novel' because it seems to me that it is impossible to realize your method. But reading the novel gave me much to digest, to contemplate and to profit for my own views on education" (Correspondance t. XI, p. 11). The relationship between Emile and Sophie in particular is regarded as far from reality (*ibid.*, p. 12). The process of marriage will be directed against him, because she will find it necessary to join the world and not just to stay at home (*ibid.*, p. 13). After this letter Rousseau started to write the sequel.

On February 14th, 1763 Charles-Hubert Mérau wrote to Rousseau about a very special topic, dancing and the movement of the body (Correspondance t. XV, pp. 176–83). Mérau advocates lectures on dancing as being according to nature and defends his teacher, François-Robert Marcel,[179] against an attack that Rousseau wrote in *Emile* (Rousseau 1993, pp. 123–4; O.C. IV, pp. 390–1). Here the "monkey tricks of Marcel" came under fire with which children are drilled for the stage. Emile "should emulate the mountain goat, not the ballet dancer" (Rousseau 1993, p. 124). He is not the "enemy of his art," Rousseau writes in his answer to Mérau, but M. Marcel has only written phrases that have died with him. What he did for children was to teach them how to please the crowd and stimulate jealousy; what he did not do was to encourage the right to their *amour-propre* (Correspondance t. XV, pp. 248–9).

On March 16th, 1764 Madeleine-Elisabeth Roguin[180] wrote a letter in which she said that she, a pregnant wife and soon-to-be mother, had read Rousseau's book and became convinced not to give away the child but to nourish him herself. He – Rousseau – was one of the first men to show the way (la route) to make children happy. It is not that she pretended to educate an Emile or his Sophie, because only Rousseau could form them, but reading the book informed her of all the details necessary to start natural education. She asked him for more details such as whether she could use a wicker basket for the baby, what was the best hour to bath the child in cold water and at what age should one start with the method of natural education (Correspondance t. XIX, pp. 219–20).

Rousseau answered on April 6th that she surely will be a good mother with her zeal for motherhood and her caring for children that spoke out in her letter. He gave good advice on natural education. It is not very important, he said, if the child lies in a wicker basket or something else provided that he sleeps not too soft, slightly slanting and often in the open air. If he grows up in liberty he will not hesitate to acquire all the strength that is necessary to give himself the attitude that suits him. Good nutrition by her will keep him in her arms. And when to start with cold baths? After birth, Madame! (Correspondance t. XIX, p. 276)

In the letters like this[181] the systematic part of the theory of education as developed in *Emile* is applied, if at all, indirectly and fragmentarily. This is not surprising, as this theory is distinctive by playing with paradoxes and by violating common views of education, which for a direct discussion with parents or readers is not a strategy to be followed. Here Rousseau is as rigorous as he is helpful, but not paradoxical. The theory of education itself shows different versions, each of them according to the chosen emphasis. If one starts with Rousseau's most read work, *Emile* may also be considered a shift in emphasis. In fact, the original view of education was not nature but the house.

Education in the House

It is definitely no coincidence that Rousseau for the first time worked out the idea of natural education in the epistolary novel *Julie ou La Nouvelle Héloise*. The *New Héloise* was published a little under a year before *Emile*[182] and became Rousseau's greatest literary success. He himself comments on how the two works are related to each other in the *Confessions*: "Everything that is daring in *Emile* was already to be found in *Julie*" (Rousseau 2000, p. 397). This is meant in the sense of a thesis on a basic theme in his work. That which looked daring in *Contrat Social* was already found in the Second Discourse, it says, and Julie's confession of faith on her dying bed at the end of *Nouvelle Héloise* was the same as that of the Savoyard vicar in the middle of *Emile* (*ibid.*).

The analogy of "daring assumptions," however, refers only to the way in which certain doctrines of "natural education" are formulated. The setting of education in *Nouvelle Héloise* is completely different. One year before *Emile* the doctrines are also true for home and society: a natural paradise *à la campagne* is not necessary, father and mother educate, a governor or a governess is not necessary, servants are kept at bay, there are a number of siblings and sociability is not a disadvantage – only the difference of the sexes is already clearly present. "Natural education" is only meant for boys.

Despite the title, in this novel Rousseau does not go through the medieval drama of Abaelard and Héloise with new protagonists. The story is mentioned in passing (Rousseau 1997, p. 70), but only in respect of morals: unfaithful Abaelard is sentenced and Héloise is met with sympathy, without using the drama for anything more than choosing a similar introduction, that is a noble girl being taught by a master who is brought into her house. Rousseau shows how Julie d'Etange falls in love with her tutor St Preux, who is a commoner, starts a relationship with him, but then – unlike the original Héloise – does not disappear behind the walls of a monastery, and instead marries within her social class and becomes an example of a mother whose marital virtues are not affected even by the surprising return of her former lover and their newly arousing love.

Julie is happily married to the Russian emigrant and philosopher Baron de Wolmar and lives on the estate of Clarens at the foot of the Alps, following his principles. The estate represents a model society. Only in this sense is the title justified; the *New Héloise* is not a repeat of the old one but marks a new beginning. The narrative of the story and its end are very different: Julie dies after trying to rescue her younger son from drowning (*ibid.*, p. 577), so doing her duty as a mother; in the medieval drama, Héloise gives birth to a son before joining the monastery, with the knowledge that Abaelard, who is castrated by her uncle, becomes estranged from her. Motherhood in Rousseau's sense does not play any role in this story.

Baron de Wolmar shows understanding for past emotions which Julie reveals to him. He asks St Preux into his house as a guest and shows him how exemplarily his estate is run, which is both a clear hierarchy and a well-organized community (*ibid.*, pp. 365). Natural education is a part of this "domestic economy" (*ibid.*, p. 379). In the third letter of the fifth part Julie's three children are described. This letter is written by St Preux to Milord Edward, a young British philosopher who is a part of the correspondence. St Preux is welcome, and impressed by the "peaceful days between living reason and sensible virtue" which he is allowed to spend at the estate (*ibid.*, p. 432).

Rousseau's depiction of the children starts with a scene when Henriette, the daughter, teaches her younger brothers. They skip through a picture book whose topics the older brother tries to explain to the younger one. Henriette knows the book by heart. Each time the older one makes a mistake she interferes, corrects him, and tells them the correct words. These are, as it says, "little lessons which were given and received without much care, but also without the slightest inhibition" (*ibid.*, p. 457). Meanwhile, the adults continue with their conversation, after they had experienced "a morning in the English manner," "gathered in silence" (*ibid.*, p. 456).

Then a quarrel between the two brothers is described. The younger brother has hidden some boxwood jackstraws under the picture book, the older one seeing how the younger is distracted from leafing through and looking at the prints; he waits until his brother has collected his jackstraws and then hits him so that they fall out of his hands. The mother watches the incident, gives an instruction and corrects the situation without the younger one weeping or the older one triumphing. How does the mother achieve this with so little effort? "One never sees her urge them to speak or to keep quiet, nor prescribe or forbid them this or that. She never argues with them, she does not contradict them in their games; one would think that she was content to see them and love them, and when they have spent their day with her, her whole duty as mother is fulfilled" (*ibid.*, p. 459).

Other than in *Emile*, the experiment has already been made. Julie and Wolmar report on the result of educating according to nature. This does not require a natural state "next to" society but happens within society, however, in an unusual environment and realized by a couple with particular maxims. More exactly: natural education follows the principles of the landlord, "an enlightened observer, who combined a father's interest with a philosopher's detachment" (*ibid.*, p. 460). "Philosopher" is not meant negatively here. Wolmar assumes "that the first and most important education, the one precisely that everyone overlooks, is to prepare a child for receiving instruction" (*ibid.*).

Here, the motif from the letter to Louise d'Epinay is seized, which was that everything must be done avoiding "premature instruction" and letting nature take its course without using a language which children do not understand and which makes them "argumentative and rebellious" (*ibid.*, pp. 460–1). Then there appears the essential argument from *Emile*: childhood has its own ways of seeing, of thinking, and of feeling, which cannot and must not be replaced by the adult way (*ibid.*, p. 461). Also here, avoiding lessons before the due time is combined with the ban on reasoning with children.

Reason begins to shape only after several years, and when the body has assumed a certain consistency. Nature's intention is then that the body be strengthened before the mind comes into play. Children are always in motion; repose and reflection are the aversion of their age; a studious and sedentary life keeps them from growing and thriving; neither their mind nor their body can bear constraint. Forever closed up in a room with books, they lose all their vigor; they become delicate, feeble, sickly, rather stultified than reasonable; and the soul is affected for life by the atrophy of the body. (*ibid.*)

Julie Wolmar's two sons demonstrate that nature is right only if all kinds of premature instructions are avoided. The natural disposition of each individual must be the foundation of education, not the scheme of school education (*ibid.*, p. 462). To St Preux's objection on whether it was not more advisable for education to assume "a perfect model of the reasonable and honorable man," so that the character could be cultivated and nature corrected, Julie answers that "character" and "nature" cannot be separated. Also, both cannot be influenced according to a model. "The question is not to change the character and bend the natural disposition, but on the contrary to push it as far as it can go, to cultivate it and keep it from degenerating" (*ibid.*, p. 464).

However, before one can cultivate a child's character one must study it; it becomes visible, and must have ample opportunities to become so. These opportunities must be adjusted to the individual "genius" (*ibid.*); they do not require a model and have no effect before due time: "Let us await the first spark of reason; that is what brings out the character and also what gives it its genuine form; it is through reason that we cultivate it, and before reason there is no genuine education for man" (*ibid.*). Formation of the character requires personal maturity (*ibid.*, p. 465); natural growth must thus be completed before the growth of intellect can start.

From these maxims there derives Julie's "method" (*ibid.*) which she explains to St Preux in detail. Her application of this method, she says, was guided less by a philosophical principle than by the love of a mother who wants to see her children happy (*ibid.*). While in *Emile* it is the nameless governor who educates, here it is the natural mother who does not simply apply her husband's principles but modifies them by her love. Only from this do they become effective. Her method, she tells St Preux, is "a new and sure path to make a child at once free, patient, affectionate, docile, and this through a very simple means, which is to persuade him that he is *but* a child" (*ibid.*, p. 466; italics J.O.).

Emile, the orphan, must not be convinced that he is nothing other than a child, as the ages of education determine his status as a child. But he grows up in the state of nature. Under the conditions of a house and a social community other precautions are necessary. The children must not perceive themselves as the servants' masters, and the servants must not be false authorities (*ibid.*, pp. 467–8). The children must accept necessity and their dependency, just as their misery and their frailty (*ibid.*, p. 468). Every rejection they live to see is irrevocable, and the children must be used to being rejected, and to experience this as less cruel (*ibid.*).

From the outset, the child must accept what is told to him, and for all that he suffers or which distresses him, he must recognize the "empire of necessity, the effect of his own frailty, never the working of someone else's malevolence" (*ibid.*, p. 469). This is not explained; the children are made subject to a necessity the reason for which they are not told: "The only means of rendering them amenable to reason is not to reason with them, but to convince them thoroughly that reason is beyond their age" (*ibid.*, p. 470). She never argued with them, Julie says, she never explained why she refused anything, but she acted in a way which made her children rely on the existence of good reasons which they did not need to know (*ibid.*).

For a tender-loving mother this was very rigorous, St Preux contests; Pythagoras would not have been able to handle his students more strictly (*ibid.*).[183] How could there be any freedom under all these restrictions, if there had been constantly talk of freedom? (*ibid.*, p. 471) She answers that it was not only about "restricting their freedom to prevent them from infringing on ours" (*ibid.*). Much more, one had to prevent vanity from springing up, that is showing a kind of attention to the child which was inappropriate, "a whole circle of rational people listening to him, leading him on, admiring him, awaiting with fawning avidness the oracles issuing from his mouth, and breaking forth in resounding joy at every impertinence he utters" (*ibid.*). This way, one would only form "marionettes", not children (*ibid.*).

Questions are not categorically banned, but children will learn more from questions they are asked than from those they ask themselves (*ibid.*, pp. 471–2). A kind of "happy sterility" is good for them (*ibid.*, p. 472) by which they can be prepared for their education. This determines her role as a mother, Julie says, "not to educate my sons, but to prepare them to be educated" (*ibid.*, p. 473). This distinction is not made in *Emile*; there, education is an integrated business running along the lines of the ages of education, of which there is not a word in *Nouvelle Héloise*. The problem is defined by the maxim of avoiding too early education by books which are stored badly in the children's memories and affect the maturing of their power of judgment (*ibid.*, pp. 474–5). "This method, it is true, does not create young prodigies, and does not allow governesses and preceptors to show off; but it creates judicious, robust men, healthy in body and understanding, who, without having attracted admiration during their youth, attract esteem when they are grown" (*ibid.*, p. 476). One learns how to read by being read to, learning by heart is unnecessary, a catechism is not needed, and only the children's natural dispositions come to bear (*ibid.*, p. 477) – this way "happy and free children" will develop (*ibid.*, p. 478). It is assumed, however, that to make this kind of education successful certain conditions must be met.

> It required the understanding of an enlightened father to sort out amidst established prejudices the genuine art of governing children from their birth; it required all his patience to lend himself to its execution, without ever giving the lie to his lessons by his conduct; it required children well born in whom nature had done enough so that we could love its handiwork alone; it required having around us only intelligent and well-intentioned domestics, who never tire of entering into their master's views; a single brutal or flattering servant would have been enough to spoil everything. (*ibid.*, p. 479)

The most important precondition, however, is the mother's power, which overcomes all obstacles and which is an example for everybody. Rousseau finds a dramatic formula for this: "Ah do but be women and mothers, and earth's sweetest empire will also be the most respected!" (*ibid.*) Thus, it is the more remarkable that although *Emile* is supposed to address mothers, its scenario does not need a mother at all. Why according to nature a governor must educate a boy, whereas a mother is as successful with two boys, remains incomprehensible.

Only in one respect Rousseau treats the case of natural education in the same way. Henriette, the sister, is the two brothers' "first governess," but she herself is exclusively educated by the mother. The boys are prepared for their later studies by the father and the teachers; the girl receives a kind of education whose principles are completely different. The reason for this is also found in the fifth book of *Emile*: with education for girls, it is said, it was "difficult to add to nature's gifts." It was important "that she will be as worthy as her mother, if anyone on earth can be" (*ibid.*). However, this is further explained only by the description of Sophie's education.

At the end of *Nouvelle Héloise* is Julie's confession of faith, which is in no way the same as that of the Savoyard vicar, as it is not burdened with philosophical problems but justifies her own mode of belief, even against the suspicion that she "did not entirely agree with Church doctrine" (*ibid.*, p. 580). Wolmar reports on her final hours and also thinks about how children react to the death of somebody they love: "Although children are taught the name of death, they have no notion of it; they fear it neither for themselves nor for others; they are afraid of suffering and not of dying" (*ibid.*, p. 583). In one last letter on the education of her sons after her death, Julie writes: "Do not make scholars of them, make them into charitable and just men" (*ibid.*, p. 610).

Voltaire (1961, pp. 396–409) wrote a statement on *Nouvelle Héloise* which
to a certain degree is also true for *Emile*. The book, he wrote, was not a novel
but a kind of moral teaching. A novel, however frivolous this kind of literature may be, entailed preparing events and forming them to a chain, then
connecting them with an intrigue and finally solving the puzzle. Rousseau
had no intention to form a novel; he succeeded in putting approximately
one thousand moral discourses into his book without offering anything
more for the narration than a minimum of action with no suspense. This is
not *Télémaque*, not the *Princess of Cleves*, not *Zaide*,[184] it is "JEAN-JACQUES
tout pur" (*ibid.*, p. 404).

But probably the mixture of morals and sentiment was the precondition
for the success of *Nouvelle Héloise*. Indeed, Rousseau does not write a frivolous
novel, but he touches the ideas of moral perfection with his mostly female
readers. When he lets Julie say "A reasonably vigilant mother holds her
children's passions in her hands" (Rousseau 1997, p. 476) he touches on
contemporary ideals, not empirical facts. It is a similar scenario when he
describes how she listens carefully to her children despite her moral rigorism
and notes everything they say. And the final metaphor has, so to speak,
become proverbial for the communication of the ideal mother. She is said
to be only "the Gardener's servant; I weed the garden, I remove the bad
seed, it is for him to cultivate the good" (*ibid.*, p. 478).

Finally, who is not tempted to believe in the result of education if it seems
to be exemplary and is according to one's own wishes?

Consider my children and especially the elder, do you know any on
earth who are happier, gayer, less troublesome? You see them leap, laugh,
run about all day without ever bothering anyone. What pleasures, what
independence are accessible to their age that they do not enjoy or that
they abuse? They restrain themselves as little in front of me as in my
absence. On the contrary, under their mother's eye they always have a bit
more confidence, and although I am the instigator of all the strictness
they experience, they always find me the least strict: for I could not bear
not to be what they love most in the world. (*ibid.*, p. 473)

In the *Confessions* Rousseau offers a correction to his educational theory
which has hardly been considered although it clearly aims at *Emile*:

A common mistake among educators, and one that I have not avoided in
my *Emile*, is to try to make young people attentive to what you want to say
to them by promising at its conclusion some object that is of particular
interest to them. Struck by the object that is just displayed before him,
the young man becomes wholly intent upon it and has soon, with one

bound, leapt over your preliminary talk in his eagerness to arrive at the place towards which you are leading him too slowly for his liking. If you want to hold his attention, you must not let him see from the start where it is all tending. (Rousseau 2000, p. 189).

Not that the domestic education in *Nouvelle Héloise*, which, however, is only indicated by very few scenes, does proceed according to this maxim of the promised object or the promised reward but definitely the whole practical part of *Emile*. Every time the governor acts, that is he asks questions, names tasks, or reveals a problem which is supposed to stimulate learning, some object or success is promised or at least indicated. Only because Emile does not behave as Rousseau thinks real "young men" do, his attention is never faster than the promise and in the end is always reaching the original goal.

Another, even more different, variant is the idea of explaining one's own life by one's own childhood. Rousseau presents the most concise version of this idea by the third walk of the *Reveries of a Solitary Walker*. The perspective is not, as with natural education, looking ahead but back. Childhood is not supposed to be newly organized; it happened and now must be connected to life. It is also used as an explanation, which means that it must be shortened to a certain basic feature. It is not about remembering and its more or less influencing power but about one's own fate.

The third walk is the only one in the *Reveries* to start with a quotation, by Solon. In the English translation this quotation is "I continue to learn while growing old" (Rousseau 2000a, p. 17).[185] Rousseau argues against this principle, which does not lead to any way of completing one's learning and thus of using one's knowledge. As always, the evidence for the invalidity of this principle by Solon is from Solon himself. Learning, Rousseau says, had not changed him. Thrown from childhood to the troubles of the world, he had to learn early that he was not born for living in this world. All the time he had been looking for an anchorage where he might find rest and had not to look for happiness in the midst of crowd (*ibid.*, p. 18).

This feeling nourished by education from the time of my childhood and reinforced during my whole life of this long web of miseries and misfortunes which has filled it, has at all times made me seek to know the nature and the destination of my being in a more interested and careful manner than I found any other man seek to do. (*ibid.*)

For him, learning had always been the root of knowing, not teaching. Whoever wanted to teach or even enlighten others would need to know enough, something which he had never been able to claim for himself (*ibid.*). His curiosity had developed during his childhood and had to do with the "study of good books" (*ibid.*, p. 19). He had not found happiness by this, and at the age of forty he had decided to give up on the world and to choose the "less uncertain route" of loneliness (*ibid.*, p. 20). Since then he had been living in accordance with his principles (*ibid.*, p. 23), which would not change anymore, that is would not be influenced by further experience. He stopped learning.

In this sense, life is not an open process, as one might have thought at the end of *Emile*. One day the "vigor of age" and the "complete maturity of mind" demand truths to be found and no longer to be a problem. This is also meant as self-restriction. "I therefore limited myself to what was within my reach, without getting myself involved in what went beyond" (*ibid.*, p. 25). Childhood and youth are constructive and also determining experiences which lead to a result, to a form of life which cannot be given up. From then on it is important to maintain one's course (*ibid.*, p. 26). "Confined thus within the narrow sphere of my former knowledge, I do not share with Solon the happiness of being able to learn each day while growing old and I even ought to keep myself from the dangerous pride of wanting to learn what I am henceforth unable to know well" (*ibid.*, p. 27). Only one task stays. To the end of one's life the virtues must be kept. Knowledge becomes uninteresting, and one will regret the moments when trying to achieve it. Only virtues support life, and this particularly when facing death. It is not possible to part from life as a better man, only to be more virtuous than at the start (*ibid.*).

Such passages have nothing to do anymore with the project of "natural education." Rousseau remembers intensively how he had been impressed as a child by reading Plutarch (*ibid.*, p. 28), at the same time describing his "natural temperament" which was developed during childhood but never changed (*ibid.*, p. 35). Again, he refers to his children and reports on a dinner when he denied paternity but everybody knew that he was lying (*ibid.*, p. 36). Finally, he considers to supplement the *Confessions*, which had been entirely written from his not always reliable memory (*ibid.*, p. 37). The practical topic of his old age is botany, not education.

The topic between 1755 and 1765, "natural" or "negative" education, has two principal versions: one is enacted in the house, the other *à la campagne*. For each version there is the essential question of how reason could be developed if that is not possible before due time, as childhood's "own ways" prevent it. It is now interesting what Rousseau thinks about education when *not* referring to this doctrine. In both versions childhood's "own ways" are combined with criticism of reading too early and the maxim of keeping books away from children. If his daughter was really "precocious" (précoce), Rousseau writes to the Prince of Württemberg on December 15th, 1763, this was indeed worrying, but the problem could be solved by doing everything to protect the child from methods which demanded learning "avant le temps" (Correspondance t. XVIII, p. 213).

Education with Books

In various passages Rousseau commented on questions of man's education independently of his main doctrine. The complete First Discourse is dedicated to proving that modern education, as represented by science and philosophy, affected morals and was by no means able to contribute to educate the nature of man. Thus, ignorance is better than constant refinement of knowledge which would only result in even more corruption (Rousseau 1992a, p. 21).

> What shall we think of those Compilers of works who have indiscreetly broken down the door of the Sciences and let into their Sanctuary a popular unworthy of approaching it; whereas it would be preferable for all who could not go far in the world of letters to be rebuffed from the outset and directed into Arts useful for society. He who will be a bad versifier or a subaltern Geometer all his life would perhaps become a great great cloth maker. (*ibid.*)

This topic is also a motif of many of his letters: what is the value of education? And for whom shall it be? For the theory of education the answer is clear: "learned man will rarely think of great things, Princes will more rarely do fine ones, and People will continue to be vile, corrupt and unhappy" (*ibid.*, p. 22). But this rigorous ban on science, arts, and learning by books cannot always be maintained.

This way, questions are approached which concern both the cultivation of the mind and the morality of authors and a raging flood of books. These questions are discussed by a man who was able to laboriously work out his own cultivation, independently of educational institutions. For this, books always played a crucial role. Childhood being protected from books is a construction which has Rousseau's biography against it and which can hardly be understood if one has in mind how successful the autodidactic walk through the world of books was for Rousseau himself. But this topic reveals further different facets, one of which is the education of people by way of books, something which Rousseau judges on comparatively consistently.

In his answering letter from September 10th, 1755 to Voltaire Rousseau asks his arch-enemy if he was seriously of the opinion that the great minds (les grands génies) of literature and philosophy should be educators if they then had also to teach the big crowd. But if everybody interferes with education, what do we get? Whoever limps cannot move his body sufficiently,

Montaigne says, and he whose mind was didactically practiced, so his mind limps: "But in this century of knowledge we see only people walking with a limp trying to teach others how to walk properly" (Correspondance t. III, p. 165). This goes against the idea of having to educate the people and of thus providing knowledge to march in step. But this, Rousseau says, was missing the point.

The people take up the writings by the wise in order to be able to judge, not to be taught (*ibid.*). He himself, Rousseau says, would not have needed education at all if he had stayed in his original trade. "What concerns me, had I followed my destination, I would neither have written nor read, and doubtlessly I would have become happier" (*ibid.*). But primarily this is meant rhetorically. "The philosophy of the heart will cost the mind dear if it has to be crammed with such trash," Rousseau (1937, p. 133) writes to Jacob Vernes on April 2nd, 1755 and one had to ask what the public benefit of all those boring readings is which one must go through because one must pay good money for the spirit of education (*ibid.*). But Rousseau bows exactly to this, he who in his letters never reveals any passion for reading.

In his second letter to Malherbes from January 12th, 1762, where he continues to account for himself, Rousseau describes himself as an ambivalent mind, awkward and slow on the one hand, quick-tempered and vivacious on the other hand:

> An indolent spirit that fights shy of every care, a temperament that is ardent, bilious, easily affected, and excessively sensitive to all that affects it, these two things do not seem capable of uniting in the same character; and yet they are the basis of mine. Although I could not resolve such as an opposition by any principles, it exists for all that: I am conscious of it, and nothing is more certain; and I can at least give by the facts a kind of history which may serve to make it conceivable. (*ibid.*, p 207)

Already here, this is put into the context of his childhood, and more exactly of his reading behavior as a child. His childhood, Rousseau says, was abnormal, as unlike other children it was spent with books. For him there was no ban on books, without this resulting in the damage suspected by the theory of natural education. At least, Rousseau himself explains by the course of his reading:

> I was more active in my childhood, but never in the same way as another child; that tiring of everything threw me early into reading. When I was six, Plutarch fell into my hands; at eight, I knew him by heart, I had read all the stories, and they made me shed buckets of tears before the age when the heart really has an interest in such things. It was thus there was

formed in me that love of the heroic and romantic which has only grown stronger up to the present and which will end with a dislike of everything save what resembles my own foolish dreams. (*ibid.*)

His own education was in fact a result of the books he had read. The stages of education are carefully depicted in the *Confessions*. Even the place of reading is given. Already as a child he had experienced sleeping problems at night, Rousseau writes (2000, p. 567). "Since then I had got into the habit of reading every night in bed, until I felt my eyelids drooping." That which Julie, the ideal mother, bans strictly under the maxim of "not studying in books" (Rousseau 1997, p. 475), something which also the governor in *Emile* obeys, for the author of these two books, who after all believed only in the evidence of his own self, it is a precondition of his success. Without any formal training in schools Rousseau had to read books to satisfy his ambitions.

At the beginning of the *Confessions* he describes – moving far away from his own theory – how by way of books he learned how to read, being dependent on his own reading and not on being read out to. Until 1719, that is until his seventh year, he read romances his mother had left to him.[186] Later, the library of his grandfather, Samuel Bernard (1631–1701), was open to him, and "fortunately it contained some good books" (Rousseau 2000, p. 8). He carefully lists the titles which were important for him[187] and also recounts that he used to read them out to his father, the watchmaker, in the latter's workshop and to discuss them with him. No one prevented him from reading; his father was not a governor with an educational principle in mind but only an artisan who was proud of his son and his unusual interests.

The list of books includes at the beginning ancient classical writings, like Ovid's *Metamorphosis* and Plutarch's *On Famous Men*, which indeed became a point of reference for Rousseau's thoughts to which he always referred. Also mentioned are Jacques-Bénigne Bossuet's *Discours sur l'histoire universelle* (1681), Jean le Sueur's two-volumed *Histoire de l'Église et de l'Empire* (1686), Jean de la Bruyère's *Les charactères* (1688), a French edition of Giovanni Battista Nani's *Historia della repubblica veneta* (1660), Bernard de Fontenelle's *Nouveau dialogues des morts* (1683), and also Fontenelle's *Entretiens sur la luralité des mondes* (1686), as well as different editions of Molière. Rousseau read all these books as a child and they obviously cultivated his mind.

In retrospect, Rousseau understands this experience of early reading to have been a decisive influence for his self-education. He developed a kind of taste for these works which was rare and maybe even unique for a boy of his age (*ibid.*). But his estimation of the effect of education by books, which is supposed to be strictly out of the question during the age of nature, goes even further. It concerns his political mind. Rousseau writes: "These interesting books, and the conversations they occasioned between my father and me, shaped that free, republican spirit, that proud and indominable character, that impatience with servitude and constraint, which it has been my torment to possess all my life in circumstances not at all favorable to its development" (*ibid.*, p. 9).

Independently of judging on his education for later circumstances, for which it was favorable: here reading, particularly Plutarch, stimulates imagination; here also, it allowed to put oneself in the place of the ancient heroes and to let oneself be encouraged by their example, just as before it was not affecting and not against nature to develop a "passion for romances," that is a kind of reading of which Julie definitely did not want to know anything (*ibid.*, p. 8). But why should it be true only for Rousseau's own education that it is an indispensible experience of childhood that reading transforms to imaginations and the characters of the stories come to life in one's mind? "I became the person whose life I was reading" (*ibid.*, p. 9).

The mentioning of book titles plays an important role for the *Confessions*; obviously, they are supposed to refer to stages in a course of education which has to do with the occasion and the choice of reading. In Louise de Warens's library Rousseau discovered not only his dislike of "medical books" (*ibid.*, p. 107), something which did not exclude them from being consulted later, but also books which permanently influenced him, like the writings by Samuel Pufendorf (1632–1694), one of the founders of natural law; books by the philosopher Pierre Bayle (1647–1766); or those by the Seigneur de Saint-Évremont, who is of interest for the development of Rousseau's esthetics (*ibid.*, p. 108).[188] There was also reading together, for example La Bruyère, whom "Maman" appreciated more than La Rochefoucauld, not forgetting the moral "digressions" developing from this reading (*ibid.*, p. 109).

Rousseau also describes Louise de Warens's course of education, which has also to do with books. However, her education is said to have been "erratic" and "ill-directed," as she had learned less from her father and her tutors than from her lovers. "But so many different kinds of instruction merely impeded one another; and since she herself introduced no order into her various studies, they did nothing to further her natural intelligence" (*ibid.*, p. 49). It seems as if she knew some principles of modern philosophy and physics, but she shared her father's tending toward alchemy and was surrounded by charlatans who ruined her financially. The bright light of her reason became obscured, but "her excellent heart withstood every test and remained always the same" (*ibid.*).

Rousseau gave advice on what good education is all about. In a letter to Genevan compatriot Jacob Vernes, his attitude is that of a teacher who passes on his educational experiences. Great and important works teach intellect, Rousseau says, not forgetting to point out the difference between the educational levels in Geneva and in Paris:

> Serious and profound writings may do us honour, but all the glitter of that trifling philosophy which is the fashion of the day is ill-suited to us. The great themes such as virtue and liberty enlarge and strengthen the mind; the little things, like poetry and the fine arts, impart to it more delicacy and subtlety. For the former a telescope is needed, for the latter, a microscope; and men accustomed to taking the measure of the heavens would not know how to dissect flies – behold the reason why Geneva is the land of wisdom and reason, and Paris the seat of taste. Let us leave the refinements of taste, then, to those myopic literary lights who spend their lives looking at mites at the end of their noses: let us learn to be prouder of our lack of such taste than they are of possessing it; and while they are composing journals and trifling pamphlets for the ladies' salons, let us try to write books that will be useful and worthy of immortality. (Rousseau 1937, p. 133)

The great books are mentioned in the *Confessions*. Bernard Lamy's (1640–1714) *Entretiens sur les sciences* (1683) opens up Rousseau's access to modern sciences (Rousseau 2000, p. 226); Jean-Phillipe Rameau's (1683–1764) *Traité d'harmonie réduite à ses principes naturels* (1722) offers insights into the theory of the fine arts to him (*ibid.*, p. 180); of contemporary philosophy besides Locke, Descartes, Leibniz, and Malebranche, also Port-Royal's *Logics*[189] are quoted, that is the foundation of his discussions on Jansenism (*ibid.*, p. 231). The most difficult of all studies was that of the Latin language (*ibid.*, p. 233), probably because there were no school lessons and he had to teach himself Latin. It was arduous for Rousseau to learn to translate texts without ever being able to write or even speak, something which was of no advantage when dealing with the arrogant "men of letters" in the *salons* of Paris (*ibid.*).

But classical education is used. For example, on April 12th, 1765 he gives a lesson on a sequence in Cicero[190] to the much younger Pierre-Alexandre DuPeyrou and follows this by reflecting on the French art of writing letters or books:

> If an expression is that what we understand to be "French" or of "good taste," that is of no interest: one speaks or writes only for the sake of communication; provided one is understandable one will achieve one's goal; if one is clear, even the better. Thus, speak clear for everybody who understands French; that is common, and be sure, if beyond this you produced five hundred barbarisms, you would not have written less well. I go further and claim that sometimes grammar mistakes are needed to

be clearer; this is the real art of writing, and not the pedantry of purism. (Correspondance t. XXV, p. 84)

Thus, the significance of certain books for cultivating one's mind is highly appreciated, while on the other hand books may be morally condemned. The former is the case for the benefits of books for that which Rousseau (2000, p. 229) calls his "plan of study," that is the course of his intellectual cultivation. The benefits of studies developed only gradually and by help of a special method of learning (*ibid.*, pp. 228–9). This is the case for what is later called cultural criticism. Most books are not only dangerous for children but also do not contribute anything to virtue. Sciences and arts in their popular form have negative effects on morals (Rousseau 1992a, p. 40) and they do not contribute to cultivating the mind. Both disciplines remain unconnected.

It is often overlooked that even *Emile* contains a plan of studying books, albeit not for the child but for the young man. Reading is necessary for cultivating a young man's taste, although the place of cultivation has to be considered carefully. Paris is not Geneva (Rousseau 1993, p. 367). The course of reading recapitulates his own: "Speaking generally Emile will have more taste for the books of the ancients than for our own, just because they were the first, and therefore the ancients are nearer to nature and their genius is more distinct" (*ibid.*, p. 369). What contemporary authors like La Motte[191] or Abbé Terrasson[192] have to say is of no real advance to human reason "for what we gain in one direction we lose in another" (*ibid.*).

Teaching the good books of the ancients also has an instrumental aspect: "All minds start from the same point, and as the time spent in learning what others have thought is so much time lost in learning to think for ourselves, we have more acquired knowledge and less vigour of mind. Our minds like our arms are accustomed to use tools for everything, and to do nothing for themselves" (*ibid.*). So what should be learned must be chosen carefully, and to learn the ancients is of more use than the moderns.[193] But classical literature is the only way to promote education. Theater is another object, not to study morals but to study taste (*ibid.*). The same holds for the study of poetry (*ibid.*, p. 370). The study of languages, old and new, will be pure and "unlimited amusement," and the main object for all of these studies will not be fame but the "love of beauty" (*ibid.*).

Also this course of literary education should strengthen Emile's confidence and capacity to judge. Here Rousseau refers to his main principle of education – that of independence by the way of "pure" experiences:

After I have led Emile to the sources of pure literature, I will also show him the channels into the reservoirs of modern compilators; journals, translations, dictionaries, he shall cast a glance at them all, and then leave them forever. To amuse him he shall hear the chatter of the acadamies; I will draw his attention to the fact that every member of them is worth more by himself than he is as a member of the society; he will then draw his own conclusions as to the utility of these fine institutions. (*ibid.*, p. 369)

So as a young man Emile underwent a course of classical education not very different from that of his peers. Now the time was right for reading books and to cultivate the mind, although not a mind that chatters in academies. Rousseau did not say a word on how natural strength as the result of childhood and the cultivation of taste of a young man can be harmonized; it is just the age that makes literary education necessary. But there are no doubts that for forming the mind books are necessary.

In the *Letters Written from the Mountain* Rousseau wrote a verdict against books, not against his own but those "that are not written for the people such as mine has always been" (Rousseau 2001, p. 211).

Many books are written; few are written with a sincere desire to further the good. Out of a hundred Works that appear, at least sixty have motives of interest or ambition as their object. Thirty others, directed by the spirit of party, by hatred, proceed, under the cover of anonymity, to bring into public the poison of calumny and satire. Ten, perhaps, and that is much, are written with good intentions: one says in them the truth that one knows, one seeks in them the good that one loves. Yes; but where is the man in whom one pardons the truth? Thus one must hide oneself in order to say it. In order to be useful with impunity, one let one's Books loose among the public, and one ducks. (*ibid.*, p. 219)

Whoever is afraid of being punished should not write any books; conformity will never have truth on its side. This is also a criticism of authors, among whom he himself counts. In the *Reveries* a passage is found which is telling in this respect: "I never had much of a bent for amour-propre, but this factitious passion had become magnified in me when I was in the social world, especially when I was an author" (Rousseau 2000a, p. 73).

Thus, criticism of authors is also partly criticism of himself. On January 12th, 1762 he had told Malherbes that as a matter of fact he, Rousseau, was an author against his own will (auteur malgré moi) (Correspondance t. X, p. 26). Here, he even doubts his talent of writing and already here he mentions that *amour-propre* may be led astray and enticed by success. Neither does he omit to point out the cause: "After I had discovered the people's false opinions to be the source of their misery and their malice, or at least believed to have discovered this, I felt that these were just those opinions which made me be unhappy, and that my misery and my vice were rather due to my situation than to myself" (*ibid.*, p. 27).

In *Letter to Beaumont* Rousseau describes two kinds of wrong education, which have both to do with the cult of books which played such a major role in his own course of education. Here, Rousseau summarizes what he rejects: public education by the state on the one hand, dogmatic education by the Churches on the other hand. "Public education" is the program of Enlightenment, and doctrinaire learning that of catechist lessons. Both concepts are sharply criticized: "Men should not be half taught. If they must remain in error, why not leave them in ignorance?" And what are schools and universities good for "if they teach nothing about what is important for men to know?" (Rousseau 2001, p. 53)

It seems to be the goal of the established institutions of education "to mislead the People, modify its reason at the outset, and prevent it from proceeding to the truth" (*ibid.*). Teaching the people serves to confuse them; the people are being enlightened to destroy them (*ibid.*). "I have always seen that public education had two essential defects that were impossible to remote. One is bad faith of those who give it and the other is the blindness of those who receive it" (*ibid.*). By help of "professors of the lie," who only pursue their own interests, it will not be possible to accomplish the only task which might justify public education, that is to get rid of prejudices. This is a central topic for Rousseau, explained thus:

> If men without passions taught men without prejudices, our knowledge would remain more limited but more certain, and reason would always reign. Now whatever one does, the interest of public men will always be the same, but the prejudices of the people, being without any fixed basis, are more variable. They can be modified, changed, increased, or diminished. It is only on this side, therefore, that education can gain some hold, and it is there that the friend of truth should aim. He can hope to make the people more reasonable but not those who lead it more honest. (*ibid.*)

The teaching of doctrines without true belief is also dangerous. "A person who professes a senseless doctrine cannot tolerate its being seen for what it is. Reason then becomes the greatest crime" (*ibid.*, p. 55). In this case reason would be the same as doctrine, while on the other hand the deist attempt at "teaching them to reason about Religion" (*ibid.*) does not lead any further because, as is the core of the doctrine, religion can only be grasped by the heart and thus by personal belief. "A person who loves peace should not have recourse to Books. It is the way to finish nothing" (*ibid.*).

Books result in endless dispute. The language of these discussions is vague and inaccurate, at the same time tied to passions, particularly with religious matters, so that in the end there will not be clarification but the discussion on doctrines will go on in a completely different way, that is by way of violence instead of words. "There will be debates that generate, in accordance with custom, into wars and cruelties" (*ibid.*, p. 56). Not all deeds demand explanations; it is not costly to follow dogmas and it costs dearly to practice morality, something which is even more true if behind religious practice there is no belief at all and thus no compassion anymore (*ibid.*, pp. 56–7).

Given the contradictions of experience, doctrinaire education requires endless refinement of dogmas and thus distancing from morals (*ibid.*, p. 57). The sense of duties is lost. Whoever follows the catechism does not ask about God but about the right understanding of dogmas: "A Christian is no longer asked if he fears God, but rather if he is orthodox" (*ibid.*, p. 58). But this comes to nothing except dealing with questions every day to which there are no other answers than referring to dogmas, which themselves dissolve into endless branches of scholasticism.

> We spend our lives arguing, quibbling, tormenting, persecuting, fighting each other for the things that are least understood and least necessary to understand. Decisions are piled on decisions in vain; in vain are their contradictions plastered over with unintelligible jargon. Each day we find new questions to resolve, each day new subjects for quarrels, because each doctrine has infinite branches, and each person, obstinate about his little idea, believes essential what is not at all so and neglects the truly essential. And if we propose to them objections they cannot resolve – which, given the structure of their doctrines, becomes easier from day to day – they sulk like children. (*ibid.*, pp. 65–6)

This can also be understood as a political comment, again referring to Rousseau's criticism of public opinion. Whoever depends on it, and in society this is everybody, is prevented from forming his own opinion. Rousseau summarizes this criticism in a letter from January 15th, 1769 as follows:

> I know that common reason is very narrow-minded; that at once one comes up to its close limitations, each man to his own, as he may have them; that opinions make statements on opinions only, not on reason; and that everybody who is defeated by somebody else's argumentation, which is rare anyway, is defeated by prejudice, by power, by preference, by laziness but seldomly, maybe never, due to his own judgment. (Correspondance t. XXXVII, p. 13)[194]

On the other hand, influencing public opinion is an important aspect of Rousseau's theory of political education, which is probably the one to show the greatest distance from *Emile*. If Rousseau saw a unity of education and politics, it is here, and in many respects this unity contradicts the concepts of his theory of natural education. Here childhood is not a moratorium; political education does not take the children's "own ways" into account, it is not "negative" but *positive*, that is it communicates truths and virtues, and the way in which it is formulated is not paradoxical.

Political Education

In his second introduction to *Nouvelle Héloise* Rousseau explains the poor state of common education by parents' "avarice and vanity," which set a bad example at home. Then he asks: "Would you cure this evil? Go back to the source. If there is some reform to attempt in public morals, it must begin with domestic morals, and that depends absolutely on fathers and mothers" (Rousseau 1997, p. 18). This model becomes clear in the epistolary novel, which besides the love story shows most of all how domestic morals could be reformed and what, in respect of education, an example of parents is like who are *not* dominated by avarice and vanity. Some years before, however, Rousseau had already presented a model on reforming public morals which is hardly compatible with that described in *Nouvelle Héloise*.

Rousseau's *Discourse on Political Economy*, which in 1755 was published in the fifth volume of the *Encyclopédie*, gives – in addition to the *Contrat Social* seven years later – an elaborated theory of political education. In the *Contrat Social* it is indicated by only a few passages that molding the people requires education: "Nations, like men, are teachable only in their youth; with age they become incorrigible" (Rousseau 2004a, p. 49). For both cases, a period of maturing must be assumed, which must be used "before they are made subject to law" (*ibid.*, p. 50). How this is supposed to be done is not explained in more detail in this passage. There is only the general statement that success was rare because of "the impossibility of finding the simplicity of nature together with the needs that society creates" (*ibid.*, p. 58).

At the end of *Contrat Social*, among the remarks on civil religion, Rousseau, as mentioned, speaks of dogmas, which are supposed to express a profession of faith "purely civil," that is they must be understood to be a catechism without religion[195] (*ibid.*, p. 166). They are expressions of social conscience – "sentiments de sociabilité" to be precise (O.C. III, p. 468) – "without which is it impossible to be either a good citizen or a loyal subject" (Rousseau 2004a, p. 166). Thus, the principle of *équité* alone – equality of all citizens – is not enough. As in Montesquieu,[196] an additional condition, that is emotional agreement among citizens, must secure social cohesion, without any other educational concept than the assumed catechism.

In more detail and more unequivocally Rousseau comments on education toward sociability in other political writings, without the theory of natural education as well. Obviously, the political problem demands different conclusions than the educational one. While already discussing the idea of natural or age-appropriate education in his letters, in Rousseau's political economy text any reference to this is missing. The topic there is the relation of law, government, and "general will," the essential argument still being strongly influenced by Montesquieu's thesis that the government molds the people and, depending on its influence, may mold them toward the good or the bad: "It is certain that people are in the long run what the government makes them" (Rousseau 1992, p. 148). In this context the maxim is formulated "Form men ... if you want to command men. If you want the laws to be obeyed, make them beloved, so that for men to do what they should, they need only think they ought to do it" (*ibid.*).

The basic rule for political economy is not the market but the rule of virtue. "Make virtue reign" (*ibid.*, p. 149) is the maxim of political education. Being good citizens, the people must love their duties, and this not due to permanent demand but by public agreement: "Good public morals replace the genius of leaders. And the more virtue reigns, the less necessary are talents" (*ibid.*, p. 150).

The citizens must incorporate the political virtues. Carelessness in the law is not the same as moderation; whoever wants to be just must be strict and severe, and whoever tolerates wickedness "that one has the right and the power to repress is wicked oneself" (*ibid.*). To make virtue reign education is necessary:

> It is not enough to say to citizens, be good. It is necessary to teach them to be so, and example itself, which is the first lesson in this regard, is not the only means that must be used. Love of fatherland is the most effective, for ... every man is virtuous when his private will conforms on all matters with the general will, and we willingly want what is wanted by the people we love. (*ibid.*, pp. 150–1)

Love of the fatherland is declared "the most heroic of the passions," which is said to combine the power of self-interest (*amour-propre*) with all the beauty of virtue (*ibid.*, p. 151). Positive teaching by help of good examples from history supports the love of the fatherland which this way becomes the "common mother of the citizens" (*ibid.*, p. 153). Self-confident, free citizens must be formed for this task, and "forming citizens is not accomplished in a day, and to have them as men they must be taught as children" (*ibid.*, p. 154). This is said to be particularly true for emotions: "A man who had no passions would certainly be a very bad citizen" (*ibid.*, p. 155).

Passions are educated by directing the people to compare themselves and to prefer differently, that is to love one object more than another. One can only love a certain thing, but one is able to learn to prefer this certain thing to others if it has turned out to be beautiful and not deformed. Passions for the fatherland this way are passions against other lands. Rousseau's theory does not offer a choice on this; passions are not supposed to be formed to let the people decide on their own. Much more, they are supposed to become one with the political body to whom they belong.

> If, for example, they are trained early enough never to consider their persons except as related to the body of the State, and not to perceive their own existence, so to speak, except as part of the State's, they will eventually come to identify themselves in some way with this larger whole; to feel themselves to be members of the fatherland; to love it with the delicate feeling that any isolated man feels only for himself; to elevate their soul perpetually toward this great object; and thereby to transform into a sublime virtue this dangerous disposition from which all our vices arise. (*ibid.*)

The dangerous disposition is *amour-propre*, which is reshaped or "sublimed" as love of the fatherland. Thus, the solution here is completely different from the later one in *Emile*. It is not about preventing early social ties but about their definite support, and there is no mention here of the dangers of comparison. In the year of the letter to Louise d'Epinay on wrong education *before* due time, political education cannot be started too early, without asking if the children understand what is done with them: "It is from the first moment of life that one must learn to deserve to live; and since one shares the rights of citizens at birth, the instant of our birth should be the beginning of the performance of our duties. If there are laws for maturity, there should be some for childhood that teach obedience to others" (*ibid.*).

That which will later become the necessity of nature, is the law of the state here. "Obedience to others" is completely excluded in *Emile*, whereas state education is mentioned in *Political Economy*, to which Rousseau had already alluded in his notes on the Second Discourse, where the "paternal rights" (*ibid.*, p. 77) were doubted. If fathers and mothers spoil education, they will have lost their rights. Their relationship to their children is one of the "ill-formed unions" of our civilization (*ibid.*), by way of which the citizens cannot be molded. Consequently, at the end of the Second Discourse the citizens are said to be *deformed* if compared to savage man (*ibid.*, p. 66).

The opposite shall be achieved by political education toward the fatherland. Bearing in mind the criticism, this is not done by the fathers. Children would only be exposed to the fathers' prejudices, and state and government would have to bear the damage done by the fathers. Thus, the business of education must be transformed from the fathers to public authorities (*ibid.*, pp. 155–6). Rousseau mentions *state education* in this sense in 1755; this does not necessarily mean school education, but education by the government and for the state, upon which – as in Plato's *Politeia* – nothing less than the existence of the state is said to depend (*ibid.*, p. 156).

> If children are raised in common in the midst of equality, if they are imbued with the laws of the state and the maxims of the general will, if they are taught to respect them above all things, if they are surrounded by examples and objects that constantly remind them of the tender mother that nourishes them, her love for them, the inestimable benefits they receive from her, and what they owe in return, there can be no doubt that they will learn from this to love one another as brothers, never to want anything except what the society wants, to substitute the actions of men and citizens for the sterile, empty babbles of sophists, and one day to become the defenders and fathers of the fatherland whose children they will have been for so long. (*ibid.*)

This is also true in the negative respect: everywhere where the lessons of love of the fatherland are *not* supported by the state's authority and behavior is *not* influenced by heroic examples, teaching is fruitless, "and virtue itself loses its credit in the mouth of the one who does not practice it" (*ibid.*). Here, the negative is not paradoxical, so the positive may then simply appear to be the opposite of the negative.

> But when illustrious warriors, bent by the weight of their laurels, preach courage; when upright magistrates, grown gray in dignity and at the tribunals, teach justice; all of them will train their virtuous successors, and will transmit from age to age to the generations that follow the experience and talents of leaders, the courage and virtues of citizens, and the emulation common to all of living and dying for the fatherland. (*ibid.*)

Yet another version of *bonne éducation* (O.C. III, p. 968) is offered by Rousseau in *Considerations on the Government of Poland*, contracted work from 1770–1.[197] Here, it is not, as in Rousseau's ancient frame of reference, about positive examples from history, through which civil virtues are supposed to be demonstrated as credibly as possible, but about a concept of national education through schooling. Almost ten years after *Emile*, the purpose is determined similarly to that in *Political Economy* and also repeats the argument of lifelong obligation starting with birth:

It is education that must give the national form to souls, and direct their opinions and their tastes so that they will be patriots by inclination, by passion, and by necessity. Upon opening its eyes a child ought to see the fatherland and until death ought to see nothing but it. Every true republican imbibes the love of the fatherland, that is to say, of the laws and of freedom along with his mother's milk. (Rousseau 2005, p. 179)[198]

For an expert's report Rousseau had to be more detailed and could not present only a rhetorical statement. How could there be influence on opinion and taste in such a way as to have patriots develop who feel inner passion for the republic?

The idea of influencing public opinion by government action is already found in the *Letter to d'Alembert* on the theater in Geneva from 1758. To the question of how the government might influence the people's morality Rousseau answers: by "public opinion" (Rousseau 2004, p. 300). As an explanation, he says:

If our habits in retirement are born of our own sentiments, in Society they are born of others' opinions. When we do not live in ourselves but in others, it is their judgments which guide everything. Nothing appears good or desirable to individuals which the public has not judged to be such, and the only happiness which most men know is to be esteemed happy. (*ibid.*)

This is very close to what David Hume had described as the mechanism of public praise and blame. The "instruments" of influencing public opinion are said to be "neither laws nor punishments nor any sort of coercive means" (*ibid.*), which again comes close to Hume. Force has no power over minds (*ibid.*), whoever wants to extinguish public prejudices needs great authority in respect of the questions under discussion (*ibid.*, p. 301), and nothing is more independent of power than public judgment (*ibid.*). "Neither reason, nor virtue nor laws will vanquish public opinion, so long as the art of changing it has not been found" (*ibid.*, p. 302).

As this art was missing, it says further, it was difficult to rule public opinion, but it was easy to influence it, however less by way of reason or power than by way of factors like "chance, countless accidental causes, countless unforeseen circumstances" (*ibid.*, p. 305). From the government's point of view this results in consequences, as this process cannot be controlled. The effects are unforeseeable. "All that human wisdom can do is to forestall changes, to arrest from afar all that brings them on. But once they are tolerated and authorized, we are rarely master of their effects and cannot be held answerable for them" (*ibid.*).[199]

In the *Plan for a Constitution for Corsica* from 1764,[200] Rousseau deals with vanity as a result of public opinion. But vanity is only one aspect of *amour-propre*; another is pride. Vanity is due to prejudices; pride has to do with appreciating goods. Both aspects can be influenced, without Rousseau thinking about "effects which are difficult to be influenced on." In this political context he says clearly: "The arbiters of a people's opinion are the arbiters of its actions" (Rousseau 2005, p. 154). And from this he concludes: "One can thus make a people prideful or vain according to the selection of the objects upon which one directs its judgements" (*ibid.*).

In *Considerations on the Government of Poland* this solution is differentiated and further developed in terms of national education. What is assumed is a free man who needs school, not nature, to learn how to love his fatherland: "He leaves school already completely formed for license, that is to say for servitude" (*ibid.*, pp. 179–80). Learning by things and independently of authorities was fundamental in *Emile*; here it no longer plays any role. Also, childhood – as in *Nouvelle Héloïse* – is no longer a kind of preparation but consists of lessons. And now the ages of education are projections of targets:

> At twenty years of age a Pole ought not to be a different sort of man; he ought to be a Pole. I wish that in learning to read, he might read things about his country, at ten years of age he might be acquainted with all his products, at twelve all the provinces, all the roads, all the cities, at fifteen he might know all of its history, at sixteen all the laws, that there not be in all Poland a fine action or an illustrious man about which his memory and heart are not full, and about which he cannot give an account at a moment's notice. (*ibid.*, p. 180)

Thus, teaching follows a strictly national curriculum, the teachers are citizens, that is laymen, and not representatives of an educational class,[201] of which Rousseau assumes that they would not feel sufficiently obliged to the future nation. National education is the same for all children and free. Unlike other writings, here Rousseau does not differentiate according to either origin or sex. The poorer children will be funded, which will be considered an honor. These children will be called "children of the state" and will receive special signs of honor to distinguish them from others (*ibid.*, pp. 180–1).

In respect of lessons and the moral objective, one field of education is of outstanding significance which, as Rousseau says, is always neglected: that of "physical exercises" (*ibid.*, p. 181). By them there will develop "robust and healthy temperaments," and then the core of his educational theory also seems to obtain justice.

I shall never repeat enough that good education ought to be negative. Prevent the vices from being born, you will have done enough for virtue. The means for this is of the greatest simplicity in good public education. It is always to keep the children on alert, not by boring studies of which they understand nothing and for which they acquire a hatred by the sole fact that they are forced to stay put; but by means of exercises that please them by satisfying their body's need to act while it is growing, and the pleasure of which for them will not be limited to that. (*ibid.*)

Explicitly, "physical exercises" are not meant to allow children "to play separately at their whim." Much more, they play commonly and "in such a manner that there is always a common goal to which all aspire and which excites competition and emulation" (*ibid.*). This, however, assumes that which in *Emile* was said to be "against nature," that is comparing to each other and to sting the *amour-propre* of being better than others. Here, there is no mention of strictly excluding comparison; instead, there shall be *one* political goal of education for *all*, without the conflict of self-love with society playing any role.

All the children's games require an audience. Games are thought to make the children used to striving for public (and, ironically, adult) praise early and "under the eyes of their fellow citizens." The prizes for the victors are not awarded by teachers or headmasters "but by acclamation and by the judgements of the spectators." The audience's decisions will be the more just, the more the games become a spectacle, as then all "decent people and all good patriots" will take part (*ibid.*). Everything will be supervised by an educational board. A "College of Magistrates of first rank" (*ibid.*, p. 182) will administrate and supervise national education, on whose success the hopes of the republic, the glory and the fate of the nation, are said to depend.

Dramatically, this is expressed as follows:

Direct the practices, the customs, the morals of the Poles in this spirit of education, you will be developing in them that leaven that is not yet made flat by corrupt maxims, by worn-out institutions, by an egoistical philosophy that preaches what is deadly. The nation will date its second birth from the terrible crisis out of which it is coming and, seeing what its still undisciplined members have done, it will expect much and obtain more from a well-pondered establishment; it will cherish, it will respect laws that flatter its noble pride, that render it, that maintain it happy and free; tearing from its bosom the passions that evade them, it will nourish there the ones that make them loved; finally renewing itself, so to speak, by itself, in this new age it will reacquire all the vigor of an nascent nation. But without these precautions expect nothing from your laws. (*ibid.*)

The ancient examples of this concept have already been named in *Political Economy*. There, it says: "I know of only three peoples who in former times practiced public education: namely the Cretans, the Lacedemonians, and the ancient Persians. Among all three it was the greatest success, and produced marvels among the latter two" (Rousseau 1992a, p. 156).

Why these "miraculous things" have not been repeated by the history of education is explained by considering the development of big nations, for which this method was no longer practicable. Furthermore, there is reference to a historical counter-example; the Romans achieved the same purpose by domestic education by the fathers (*ibid.*, pp. 156–7). The task itself, however, that is educating the children toward the virtues of their fatherland, remains (*ibid.*, p. 157). And of all of Rousseau's educational concepts, this one has probably had the most lasting effect when we consider the practice of political education during the two centuries since Rousseau's death in 1778. Natural education must be distinguished from that.

Notes

1. After a splendid career, the Protestant jurist Chrétien-Guillaume de Lamoigon de Malherbes (1721–1794) became First President of the Cour des aides, that is the French Court of Appelation. Lamoigon de Malherbes was guillotined in 1794 because he had defended the French king. His voluminous correspondence with Rousseau was published as an edition of its own (Rousseau 1991).
2. This is formulated in the third of the five articles on rational faith which Cherbury formulated in 1645 in *De religionis Gentilium errorumque apud eos causes*.
3. *Christianity not Mysterious* (London 1696).
4. Starting from William Whiston's (1667–1752) book *The True Text* (1722) where the lack of coherence between the New and Old Testaments is proven. Also Rousseau (2001, p. 155) speaks of "free interpretation of Scripture."
5. For example, in *Le rêve de d'Alembert* (1769).
6. *An Essay Concerning Human Understanding* (1689).
7. *Pensées sur la religion et autres sujets* (published posthumously in 1670). English translation under the title of *Pascal's Pensées* by W. F. Trotter (1910).
8. In the contemporary theological and political debates the Jansenists were also called *Parti molinisti*. This refers to the Spanish Jesuit Luis de Molina (1535–1600), who had tried to make the Catholic doctrine of mercy compatible to man's free will. "Molinism" was banned in 1607 by Pope Paul V.

9. And rightly so, as Lefebvre (1966–1968) explained.
10. Letter to A. Audoyer from May 28th, 1763.
11. Letter to J. Burnand from March 21st, 1763.
12. The literary figure of the Catholic vicar from Savoy was inspired by real people. In the *Confessions* Rousseau explains that the Savoyard vicar was inspired by two French Abbés: Jean-Claude Gaime (1692–1761) and Jean-Baptiste Gâtier (1703–1760). After his conversion to the Catholic faith Abbé Gaime visited Rousseau at Turn, and Rousseau met the Abbé Gâtier during his stay at the seminar. Both died during Rousseau's work on *Emile*.
13. *A Discourse Concerning the Unchangeable Obligations of Natural Religion, and the Truth and Certainty of Christian Revelation* (1705). Later, these Boyle Lectures are used for Clarke's essential text *A Discourse Concerning the Being and Attributes of God, the Obligations of Natural Religion, and the Truth of Certainty of Christian Revelation.*
14. In Samuel Clarke this is identical with the accusation of "materialism."
15. Important documents of the ban were published for the first time by Gustave Lanson in 1905 in the opening volume of *Annales de la Société Jean-Jacques Rousseau.*
16. Paul-Claude Moultou was a priest in Geneva. In the city he was one of the defenders of Rousseau and *Emile* after the 1762 ban. Together with Pierre-Alexandre DuPeyrou (1729–1794) and René-Louis de Girardin (1735–1808), Moultou was also responsible for the posthumous edition of Rousseau's first *Oeuvres complètes* (1780–9).
17. The flight is decribed in detail in the *Confessions* (Rousseau 2000, pp. 567ff.).
18. After the stop at Yverdon, Rousseau went to the Prussian town of Neuchâtel. The Prussian king's Scottish governor there, Lord George Keith (*c*. 1693–1778), 10th and last Earl Marischal, granted him asylum. In July, 1762 Rousseau moved into a house in the remote mountain village of Môtiers above Neuchâtel. From 1707 to 1805 Neuenburg was Prussian.
19. The *Premier Syndic* is the spokesman for the magistrate of the Republic of Geneva. Jacob Favre was born *c*. 1685; his date of death is unknown (Société genevoise de Généalogie: http://www.gen-gen.ch).
20. After Rousseau's decision to give back his citizenship an opposition formed. On June 18th, 1763 a group of Geneva citizens handed in a first "representation" which demanded that the *Petit Conseil* reconsider its proceeding in Rousseau's case. They formed a party of "Representatives" which wanted to support Rousseau with his "letters from the mountain." The constitutional and thus political problem was due to the system of *four councils* in Geneva (General Council, Council of the Two Hundred, Council of the Sixty, and Small Council), which had

practically not changed since the Reformation, that is the edicts from 1534, and which did not represent the real power situation anymore. The rule of the small group of patricians had led to civil-war-like situations as early as 1737. Young Rousseau watched them when staying at Annecy.

21. Jean-Robert Tronchin (1710–1792) headed the investigation by the *Petit Conseil*, which on June 17th, 1762 had resulted in the damnation of the two books. The sentence called Rousseau's writings "comme téméraires, scandaleux, impies, tendant à détruire la religion chrétienne et de tous les gouvernements" (O.C. III, S. CLXII). From 1760 to 1767 Tronchin was Procureur Général of the Republic of Geneva.

22. *De la religion civile* is the title of the eighth (second last) chapter of the fourth book of the *Contrat Social* (O.C. III, pp. 460–9). The *Profession de foi du vicaire savoyard* is found in *Emile* in the middle of the fourth book (O.C. IV, pp. 565–635).

23. "Regarding a specific fact, a miracle is an immediate act of divine power, a tangible change in the order of nature, a real and visible exception to its Laws" (Rousseau 2001, p. 173).

24. "Superstition is the most awful scourge of the human race. It brutalizes the simple, it persecutes the wise, it puts Nations in chains, it does a hundred horrible things everywhere. What good does it do? None. If it does some, it is for Tyrants. It is their most terrible weapon, and that in itself is the greatest harm it has ever done" (Rousseau 2001, p. 140).

25. "Miracles … are the proof of simple people, for whom the Laws of nature form a very tight circle around them. But the sphere expands as men learn more and sense how much more there is for them to learn" (Rousseau 2001, p. 178).

26. "A sign in itself proves nothing, then" (Rousseau 2001, p. 180).

27. On December 23rd, 1761 Rousseau writes to Moultou: "You will easily understand that the confession of the *Savoyard vicar* is mine" (Correspondance t. IX, p. 342).

28. Letter from December 7th, 1763 to Conzié.

29. In the first book of the *Confessions* Rousseau says: "I had feelings before I had thoughts: that is the common lot of humanity" (Rousseau 2000, p. 8).

30. In this letter Alexander Pope talks to his friend, the Scottish physician and writer John Arbuthnot (1667–1735), about contemporaries in order to demonstrate the principles of his satires.

31. Meant here is Arthur Moore (1666?–1730), a man of great experience who represented the town of Grimsby in the British Parliament. His son was the writer and bon viveur James Moore Smythe (1702–1734), whom Pope suspected to be a plagiarist.

32. See Van Berkel and Vanderjagt (2006).
33. For example, Konrad von Megenburg: *Das Buch der Natur* (*c.* 1350).
34. Jacob Vernes was a Calvinist reverend in Geneva.
35. The best-known work of the famous English writer and poet Samuel Johnson is *A Dictionary of the English Language* (1747–55). Johnson, who is often simply referred to as "Dr Johnson," met his later biographer Boswell for the first time in London on Monday, May 16th, 1763 (*Boswell's London Journal* 1950, pp. 259ff.).
36. George Dempster (1732–1808) was a member of the British Parliament after 1762 and later became one of the chairmen of the East India Company. Boswell calls him a "republican" (Boswell's *London Journal* 1950, p. 316). Indeed, Dempster opposed British colonial policy in North America and supported the colonies' independence.
37. As early as 1757 Diderot had developed a similar argument in *Le fils naturel ou les Epreuves de la vertu*, and by just two lines: "The good man lives in society, only a wicked man lives alone."
38. William Petty (1623–1687): *A Treatise of Taxes and Contributions* (1662).
39. "And, Sir, if six hundred a year procure a man more consequence and of course more happiness than six, the same proportion will hold good as to six thousand, and so on as far as opulence can be carried" (*Boswell's London Journal* 1950, pp. 314–15).
40. Rousseau's remarks against wealth and luxury are countless. See, for example, the collection of early fragments *On Wealth* (Rousseau 2005, pp. 6–18).
41. *Essai de théodicée sur la bonté de Dieu, la liberté de l'homme et l'origine du mal* (1710).
42. *Essay on Man* (1732–4).
43. The idea of the partially bad and the "universal Good" originates from Alexander Pope (*Essay on Man*, Epistle I, 290). Voltaire (1756, p. 6) attacks him personally.
44. Rousseau wrote a long letter to Voltaire on the latter's poem; Voltaire confirmed receipt of this letter on September 1st, 1756. Against its author's intentions, Rousseau's letter was published in Nos. 53 and 44 (1760) of Samuel Formey's magazine, the *Secretary of the Berlin Academy*. Rousseau reports on this incident in detail in the *Confessions* (ninth book O.C. I, pp. 429ff.).
45. "Tout est bien."
46. "To think rightly in this respect, it seems that things ought to be considered relatively in the physical order, and absolutely in the moral order: with the result that the greatest idea that I can give myself of Providence is that each material being be disposed the best way possible in relation to the whole, and each intelligent and sensitive being the best

way possible in relation to himself; which signifies in other terms that for whomever feels his existence it is worth more to exist than not to exist. But it is necessary to apply this rule to the total duration of each sensitive being, and not to several particular instances of its duration, such as human life" (Rousseau 1992, pp. 116–17).

47. "Nature showed me a scene of harmony and proportion; the human race shows me nothing but confusion and disorder. The elements agree together; men are in a state of chaos" (Rousseau 1993, p. 288).

48. "Man's first language . . . is the cry of nature" (Rousseau 1992, p. 31).

49. *Almanzor and Almahide, or The Conquest of Granada* (drama in two parts, first performance 1670–1). Here, the following lines are found: "I am free as Nature first made man,/Ere the base laws of servitude began,/When wild in woods the noble sauvage ran."

50. The story of a gentle, naïve Huron from Canada is told, who is civilized in France and this way becomes unhappy.

51. *Manners of the American Natives Compared with the Manners of Earliest Times* (London 1724) (Latifau 1974–7).

52. *Dialogues ou Entretiens d'un savage et du Baron de la Hontan* (Paris 1704).

53. On the use of the *âge d'or* in Rousseau see the study by Terrasse (1970).

54. For example, James Thomson: *The Castle of Indolence* (London 1748).

55. In English literature most of all following John Pomfret's poem *The Choice* (1700). Also Albrecht von Haller's poem *Die Alpen* (1729) is famous, and in respect of Rousseau Hans Peter Hirzel's *The Rural Socrates* (German 1761, English translation 1770).

56. On these passages Voltaire commented drily: "Le sauvage n'est méchant que comme un loup qui a faim" (Havens 1933, p. 10).

57. Rousseau had particular trust in DuPeyrou, as in 1765 the latter had published matter on Rousseau having been persecuted and mistreated at Môtiers.

58. Leonhard Usteri was a teacher and professor of theology at the Zürich grammar school.

59. Christophe de Beaumont du Repaire, an outspoken enemy of the Jansenists, was Archbishop of Paris after 1746.

60. The Mandement exists in an English translation in Rousseau 2001, pp. 3–16.

61. Marc-Michel Rey (1720–1780) came from Geneva and later lived in Amsterdam, the center of European book-printing. Rey was Rousseau's principal publisher, in whom the latter could trust in a time when there was no copyright. The correspondence between Rousseau and Rey was published for the first time in 1858 by Johannes Bosscha (see Turnovsky 2003).

62. Christian communities may count among this, also Muslim and Jewish, but no pagan ones (Correspondance t. XVI, p. 261).

63. However, Augustine was often misunderstood by the clergy. For example, he denied a time structure for the Book of Genesis and assumed simultaneous creation instead of one in the course of seven days (*The Literal Interpretation of Genesis*). This has consequences on the assumption of the date of expulsion from Paradise and on the development of the sinful body, which played a major role in Catholic dogma.

64. Romans 5:12–17.

65. Sir Richard Steele was co-founder of two famous British magazines: *The Tatler* (1709–1711) and *The Spectator* (1711–1712).

66. *The Spectator*, No. 11, March 13 (1711).

67. Like Alain-René Lesage's (1668–1747) play *L'Ilse des Amazons* (Paris 1721) or Varennes de Mondasse's novel *La découverte de l'empire de Cantahar* (Paris 1730). There are hundreds of such sources, some of which even give concrete suggestions on constitution. One example is Jean-Baptiste de Boyer, Marquis d'Argens (1703–1771): *Le législateur moderne ou les mémoires du chevallier de Meillcourt* (Amsterdam 1739).

68. *Essays, Moral and Political* (vols. I–II Edinburgh 1741–2) (at first anonymously, seventeen editions until 1777).

69. *Enquiry Concerning the Principles of Morals*, written in 1751 and part of *Essays and Treatises on Several Subjects* (six editions until 1777).

70. "La Patrie" (O.C. III, p. 364).

71. O.C. III, pp. 460–9.

72. The first Nicean Council was in AD 325 and formulated the first Christian confession of faith.

73. Aurelius Augustinus (AD 354–430), born in North Africa, worked for some years as a teacher of rhetoric at the court in Milan. Here, he experienced his conversion to ascetic life, and here he was baptized on Easter night in the year AD 387. In AD 396 Augustine became Bishop of Hippo Regius in what is today Algeria; here the *Confessiones* were written.

74. "My confessions are not written for publication during my lifetime or during that of the other people concerned" (Rousseau 2000, p. 391).

75. "For who among men knows the thoughts of a man except the spirit of the man which is in him? Even so the thoughts of God no one knows except the Spirit of God" (1 Corinthians 2:11).

76. "Physician of my most intimate self" (Saint Augustine 1998, p. 180).

77. This idea originates from a correspondence between Rousseau and his publisher, Marc-Michel Rey.

78. The first integral edition of the *Confessions* by Pierre-Alexandre DuPeyrou was produced together with an edition of Rousseau's letters in 1790 in Neuchâtel.

79. Letter to Malherbes from January 4th, 1762.
80. "I was born with a natural love of solitude which has only grown stronger as I came to know men better" (Letter to Malherbes from January 4th, 1762) (Rousseau 1937, p. 204).
81. Louise d'Epinay explained this in her *Histoire de Madame de Montbrillant*, which was published as late as 1818. Diderot was also truly shocked, as can be read in the second edition (1782) of his *Essai sur les règnes de Claude et de Néron*.
82. "To know a character properly, one must distinguish what is natural to it from what is acquired" (Rousseau 2000, p. 644). Rousseau should be able to do this for himself.
83. Suzanne Bolliou de Saint Julien (d. 1754) was the first wife of Charles Louis Dupin de Francueil (1716–1780). He was the stepson of Louise-Marie-Madeleine Dupin (1706–1799). For her Rousseau served as a secretary from 1745 to 1751. Rousseau was introduced to Madame Dupin probabaly in March, 1743 by Louis Bertrand Castel (1688–1757). Castel, a Jesuit, was a famous author who also wrote textbooks, including one *géométrie naturelle* (1737).
84. Madeleine Angélique de Neufville (1707–1787) was married to Charles François Frédéric II de Montmorency-Luxembourg (1702–1764). Both the Duke and the Duchess of Luxembourg served as Rousseau's patrons.
85. "A father's duty" (Rousseau 1993, pp. 18–19).
86. Letter to Jean Dusaulx (1728–1799) from February 16th, 1771.
87. "Yes, the cruel moment when this letter was written was the one to make me believe for the first and only time to be able to break through the dark veil of the incredible plot I was involved in. Despite my efforts of understanding these secrets I have not had the slightest idea up to this moment, and its traces disappear in my mind in the midst of the indefinite absurdities I am surrounded with" (Correspondance t. XXXVIII, p. 137).
88. In the *Letters Written from the Mountain*, due to Tronchin's criticism the good mother becomes the intellectual mother: "That mother, as young and amiable as she is, has philosophy and knows the human heart; in looks she is an ornament of her sex, and in genuis an exception. It is for minds of her caliber that I took up the pen" (Rousseau 2001, p. 212). Probably this refers to Louise-Alexandrine-Julie de Chenonceaux (Rousseau 2000, p. 350).
89. "L'art de former des hommes" (O.C. IV, p. 241).
90. *Mémoire présentée à Monsieur de Mably sur l'éducation de M. son fils*, written in 1740 (O.C. IV, pp. 1–32). After April, 1740 Rousseau worked for one year as a *précepteur* in the de Mably household. His contract was not renewed (Cranston 1991, pp. 150–1.).

91. "Children are reluctant to respect a tutor, as bad loyalty and disgusting servility look despicable to them" (Correspondance t. I, p. 117).
92. Real work started in October, 1758 (Jimack 1960, p. 37). In a letter to Lenieps from January 18th, 1762, that is before the publication of the book, Rousseau had pointed out that this was eight years' work (Correspondance t. X, p. 39). Ravier's thesis, orientated along the *Confessions*, that the basis of *Emile* reached back to the time after having worked as a tutor, overlooks the development of almost twenty years (Jimack 1960, p. 36).
93. *De la manière d'enseigner et d'étudier les belles lettres, par rapport à l'esprit et au coeur* (1726–1731). Charles Rollin (1661–1741) was a professor of rhetoric at the Collège de Plessis and after 1688 at the Collège de France in Paris. From 1699 to 1715 he was the Head of the Collège Beauvais. Rollin had to give up this position in 1722, as he had defended the doctrines of the Jansenists. In 1739 Rollin opposed the bull *Unigenitus dei filius*, which was edited by Pope Clement XI, and obtained on September 8th, 1713 by Pasquier Quesnel (1634–1719), who was head of the Jansenist movement.
94. This thesis originates from Variot (1926); see also Rudolf (1969) and various others.
95. The fact that Rousseau also understood medicine "à la mode" (O.C. IV, p. 269) does not contradict this.
96. Also, the first texts on medicine for children after the fifteenth century always include educational statements and thus served as educational manuals, often distinguished and closed off from the rigid moral tracts of Christian education.
97. Robert James's *Medical Dictionary* was published in three volumes in its original English edition between 1743 and 1745. The French translation, published in six volumes between 1746 and 1748, was produced by Denis Diderot. The front page of the print-run names co-translaters, that is Marc-Antoine Edous and Francois-Vincent Toussaint, who did not contribute, however.
98. For example, the fifth volume of the *Encyclopédie* contains three relevant notes, that is by Louis Jaucourt "emmailotter," by Amulphe Daumont "enfance" (médecine), and by Antoine-Gaspard Boucher d'Argis (enfant) (Jurisprudence).
99. For example, Dubois 1726, S. 18–54.
100. Morelly's two influential writings were published in 1743 and 1745. First, the tract on education of the mind was published, then that on education of the heart.
101. The wet-nurse of the first years is mentioned only in passing.
102. "Emile" according to *The Life of Aemilius Paulus* in Plutarch's *Vitae parallelae* (Shanks 1927). There is sufficient evidence of Rousseau's

reading of Plutarch. He himself calls Plutarch "mon maître et con-sulateur" (letter to Madame d'Epinay from May, 1754). The giving of the name of "Emile," however, is debated; Rousseau himself never commented on this.

103. "Men are devoured by our towns. In a few generations the race dies out or becomes degenerate; it needs renewal, and it is always renewed from the country. Send your children to renew themselves, so to speak, send them to regain in the open fields the strength lost in the foul air of our crowded cities" (Rousseau 1993, p. 30).

104. The concept of rustic, simple life is described by Horace in his *Sermons* (Book II:2).

105. This is appropriate to a general definition by Rousseau (2000a, p. 32): "Fictions which have a moral purpose are called allegories or fables; and as their pupose is or ought to be only to wrap useful truths in easily perceived and pleasing forms, in such cases we hardly care about hiding the *de facto* lie, which is only the cloak of truth; and he who merely sets forth a fable as a fable in no way lies."

106. "People seek a tutor who has already educated one pupil. This is too much; one man can only educate one pupil" (Rousseau 1993, p. 21). The reason is thus: "With more experience you may know better what to do, but you are less capable of doing it" (*ibid.*).

107. Letter to Prince Louis-Eugène de Württemberg (1731–1795) from November 10th, 1763. The prince, son of Duke Karl-Alexander von Württemberg, was a cavalry officer and in French service since 1749. The cause for his correspondence with Rousseau was his marriage with the Saxony lady of the court, Sophie Albertine von Bleichlingen in 1762.

108. Georges Louis Leclerc Comte de Buffon (1707–1788) was the director of the Jardin du roi in Paris after 1739. The first volumes of *Histoire naturelle* were published in 1749. One part of this voluminous, finally 36-volumed, natural history was the *Histoire de l'Homme* from which Rousseau takes his distinguishing of ages.

109. The Geneva Indologist and patron Léopold Favre (1848–1922) reported on finding, authenticating, and publication of the manuscript in the eighth volume of *Annales de la Société Jean-Jacques Rousseau* (Favre 1912).

110. "Les âges de l'éducation" according to Jimack (1960), ch. 7.

111. Grimaldo Nicolini was an Italian dancing master, in whose pan-tomimes children also appeared.

112. Letter to Jean Néaulme from June 5th, 1762.

113. This is René-Louis de Girardin's collection, Rousseau's later patron.

114. After years of apprenticeship in Italy, the Scottish painter Allan Ramsey (1713–1784) had founded a studio in London in 1738. Soon he was considered one of Britain's best portrait painters of the age. He painted Rousseau during the latter's stay in Britain.

115. Maurice-Quentin de la Tour (1704–1788) was a famous portrait painter in Paris, who had his first exhibition in 1737 and became a member of the Academy of Fine Arts in 1746. In 1750 he was appointed Royal Court Painter. Well known is his portrait *M. Rousseau, citoyen de Geneve*, which was presented in Paris in 1753. La Tour was a convinced follower of Rousseau's theories, whose writings he knew well.

116. Another "earthly paradise" was Bossey, the place of Rousseau's own childhood (Rousseau 2000, p. 20).

117. Since 1754 Girardin was in military service. Between 1761 and 1766 he visited landscape gardens in Britain; from 1765 on he started developing the garden of Ermenonville. See *Le parc Jean-Jacques Rousseau*: http://perso.club-internet.fr/cesarigd/parcsafabriques/erm/dErm1.htm

118. *De la composition des paysages, ou des moyens d'embellir la nature autour des habitations, en y joignant l'agréable à l'utile* (1777).

119. What is meant is the garden of the veterinary school of Lyon.

120. Here, he also considers himself "a second Robinson Crusoe" (Rousseau 2000, p. 630).

121. The French original is stronger: "La première éducation doit ... être *purement* négative. Elle consiste, *non point* à enseigner la vertu ni la vérité, mais à garantir le coeur du vice et l'esprit de l'erreur" (O.C. IV, S. 323; italics J. O.).

122. Letter to Dom Léger-Marie Deschamps from September 12th, 1761.

123. "Il faut se contenter de suivre et d'aider la nature" (Fénelon 1983, p. 99). Before this, it says clearly: "Avant que les enfants sachent entièrement parler, on peut les préparer à l'instruction" (*ibid.*, p. 96).

124. One example is *Conversations d'Emilie*, which Louise d'Epinay had published in 1774 as an anti-book to Rousseau's *Emile*. Here, there is education by conversation and thus by common reflection, not – like in Rousseau – by sensually understanding things (Epinay 1774/1996; see also Caron 2003). Until the end of the eighteenth century *Les charmes de l'enfance* (Jauffret 1794) became a popular topic of manual literature in France.

125. Like *Testament ou conseils fidéles d'un bon père à ses enfants* (1648) by Philippe Fortin de la Hoguette (1582–1668). There are hundreds of such titles.

126. The French word *civil* refers to "socially disciplined," to somebody influenced by morality or good behavior, that is he must consider

the interests of third parties without having the possibility of being completely himself or being allowed to be himself.

127. Even La Fontaine's *Fables*, a popular entertainment for children in the eighteenth century, are excluded (O.C. IV, pp. 352ff., shown by the analysis of "le Corbeau et le Renard"). Books are the tools of greatest misery during childhood: "Reading is the curse of childhood, yet it is almost the only occupation you can find for children" (Rousseau 1993, p. 95). *Immediate interest* – "present interest" (*ibid.*, p. 96) – is lacking. Learning, however, will only be successful if it employs this driving force (le grand mobile). Thus, the method of education must be *passive* (methode inactive) and wait for each thing to arouse immediate interest (*ibid.*, p. 97). For training the senses – "to learn to feel" (*ibid.*, p. 115) – "to teach . . . to read" (*ibid.*, p. 135) is unnecessary.

128. Daniel Defoe (really Foe) (1660–1731) published *Robinson Crusoe* in 1719. The book was extremely successful; until 1799 alone 134 English editions have been proven.

129. "The true relations of things" (Rousseau 1993, p. 177).

130. *Lettres sur la Botanique* (1771–1774) (O.C. IV, S. 1149–97).

131. Carl von Linné's (1717–1778) book *Philosophie botanique* was first published in 1751.

132. "Keep the child dependent on things only. By this course of education you will have followed the order of nature" (Rousseau 1993, p. 58).

133. *Neue Abhandlungen über den menschlichen Verstand* (1706).

134. Carolus Linnaeus: *Philosophia Botanica*, ch. 27.

135. Aristotle: Historia Animalium, 8.1.588b; De Partibus Animalium 4.5.618a.

136. *Gagner* means "to gain" and "to earn."

137. Alexandre-Louis-Benoît de Carondelet was born September 15th, 1744 in Noyelle (Flanders). The Abbé later served as Father Alexandro Luis Benito Carondelet in the Diocese of Louisiana and the two Floridas. (University of Notre Dame Archives: http://archives.nd.edu/mano/17960115.htm)

138. Since Michelangelo Merisi's (Le Caravage) (1573–1610) painting *Narcisse* from 1595 at the latest, love of oneself is *self-mirroring*.

139. "What an idea! Do we need reasoning to want our well-being?"

140. Between 1732 and 1754 Rousseau wrote seven plays, comedies and tragedies, of which only *Narcisse* was staged.

141. Following Rousseau's request, the famous theater writer Pierre de Marivaux (1688–1763) read the play and worked on it.

142. In a footnote Rousseau explained this expression: "This simulacrum is a certain softness of morals that sometimes replaces their purity, a certain appearance of order that prevents horrible confusion, a

certain admiration of beautiful things that keep the good ones from falling completely into obscurity. It is vice that takes the mask of virtue, not as hypocrisy in order to deceive and betray, but under this lovable and sacred effigy to escape from the horror that it has of itself when it sees itself uncovered" (Rousseau 1992a, pp. 196ff.).

143. Both, father and son Romilly, were contributors to Diderot's *Encyclopédie*. Jean-Edmonde Romilly was nominated pastor at the French Church, Threadneedle Street, in London in 1766 before he went back to Geneva.

144. "Ses nouveaux besoins" (O.C. IV, p. 493).

145. Renée-Caroline Marquise de Créqui (1714–1803) was a wealthy widow who ran a *salon* in Paris. Rousseau met her probably in 1744. He was a frequent guest in her *salon* and they had a relationship.

146. Pierre Corneille: *Tite et Bérénice* (1670), v. 279f.

147. Only "éducation solitaire" gives childhood time to mature (O.C. IV, p. 341).

148. Letter from Grenoble, addressed to "Mademoiselle Renou."

149. "La Nature ne fait ni princes, ni riches, ni grands Seigneurs" (O.C. IV, p. 469).

150. *Éducation barbare* (O.C. IV, p. 301).

151. *Vom Gottesstaat*, 18. Buch.

152. "Any people which has to choose between commerce and war is essentially weak; it depends on its neighbours; it depends on contingencies; it will never have more than a short, uncertain existence, either it conquers and ends its predicament, or it is conquered and exists no more. It can safeguard itself in freedom only by means of littleness or bigness" (Rousseau 2004a, p. 55).

153. Voltaire's *Idées républicaines par un membre d'un corps* (published in 1762) is a direct criticism of Rousseau's *Contrat Social* (Voltaire 1761, pp. 503–24).

154. In 1761 Roustan served at the Collège de Genève and three years later was nominated as pastor at the Swiss Church in London. 1791 he went back to Geneva and received civil rights.

155. As a matter of fact, the *Contrat Social* was published by Rey in Amsterdam in April, 1762, and *Emile* was published in June by Néaulme in the Netherlands and by Duchesne in France.

156. Older contributions like Oltramare (1879, pp. 121ff.) have been overlooked.

157. "Une compagne" (O.C. IV, p. 692). Barbara Foxley translated as "help-meet," which is misleading (Rousseau 1993, p. 384). In other English translations the term "companion" is used.

158. Barbara Foxley translated as "Sophy." I use the French name.

159. Folâtre (O.C. IV, p. 750).
160. The mathematician François Barrême (1640–1703) founded and headed an "École de Commerce" in Paris. His textbook *Les comptes faits du grand commerce* was first published in 1670 and had so many editions that it became proverbial as "le Barrême." The construction of *Télémaque* being a coincidental reading refers to an indication in the second foreword of *Nouvelle Héloise*: "An honest maiden does not read love stories" (Rousseau 1997, p. 17).
161. What is called "les affaires de l'Ermitage" began in January 1757.
162. *Projet de paix perpétuelle*, tomes I–III (1713–17). Charles-Inenée Castel, Abbé de Saint-Pierre (1658–1743) was a military priest (aumônier) of the Duchesse d'Orléans and accompanied the Cardinal de Polignac during the Utrecht Peace Congress in 1712, which ended the War of the Spanish Succession. After this the Abbé became an eloquent political writer whom Rousseau met in Madame Dupin's *salon*. In 1754 Rousseau took over the task of editing and newly publishing political texts by the Abbé (Courtois 1923, pp. 81, 85; O.C. I, pp. 407ff.). Rousseau's *Ecrits sur l'Abbé de Saint-Pierre* are a main source for the *Contrat Social* (Rousseau 2005, pp. 23–120; O.C. III, pp. 561–682).
163. "The laws of education will be different in each kind of government. In monarchies, their object will be *honor*; in republics, *virtue*; in despotisms, *fear*" (Montesquieu 1989, p. 31).
164. Richard Lassell's book *An Italian Voyage* (1679) introduced the term of "Grand Tour." Between the sixteenth and the twenty-second year such a voyage was supposed to be the peak of male education, mostly to learn about the "art of living."
165. "To love your native land" (Rousseau 1993, p. 525) is only true under this precondition.
166. There still follows the wedding day (Rousseau 1993, p. 526), the lesson on marriage, Sophie's "first reticence" (*ibid.*, p. 531), and Emile's final prospect of paternity (*ibid.*, pp. 532–3).
167. Rousseau distinguished between forms of government according to size and not to morals: "Generally a democratic government is adapted to small states, an aristocratic government to those of moderate size, and a monarchy to large states" (Rousseau 1993, p. 515).
168. "In fancy I see the population increasing, the land coming under cultivation, the earth clothed with fresh beauty. Many workers and plenteous crops transform the labours of the fields into holidays; I see the young couple in the midst of the rustic sports which they have revived, and I hear shouts of joy and the blessings of those about them" (Rousseau 1993, pp. 525–6).

169. *Emile et Sophie, ou Les Solitaires* (O.C. IV, S. 879–924). The two letters were written in 1762. Rousseau started the sequel immediately after the publication of *Emile* without definitely completing it. In 1768 by a letter he asked DuPeyrou to give the manuscript of the two letters back to him, which the latter had been given for commentary reading. In 1780 DuPeyrou together with Paul Moultou published the text for the first time in the *Collection complète des oeuvres de J. J. Rousseau* (Eigeldinger 1992). The English translation *Emile and Sophie or the Solitaries* was first published in 1783.

170. "Bey" is the Turkish word for master.

171. *L'illumination de Vincennes* (Cottret and Cottret 2005, pp. 118–31). In October 1749, on his way from Vincennes, Rousseau read an announcement of the *Mercure de France*, entailing the question of the moral prize of the Academy of Dijon for next year. Under an oak tree he composed a short text, the *prosopopeia of Fabricius* (Rousseau 2000, p. 342).

172. Caius Fabricius Luscinus (d. 250 BC) was a Roman general and statesman whose life was written by Plutarch. The *prosopopeia of Fabricius* is incorporated in the first part of Rousseau's First Discourse (Rousseau 1992a, p. 11). It sketches the questions of the theory.

173. Really, Louise Florence Pétronville Tardieu d'Esclavelles.

174. Letter to Louise d'Epinay from September 17th, 1756.

175. Letter to Louise d'Epinay from March 26th, 1757.

176. "Do not choose a young one and also not a beautiful one, that would be even worse: young is what you would have to fear, beautiful would attract everyone" (Correspondance XVIII, p. 116).

177. Like an excuse, it says further: "But let us be fair to wives; the cause of their disorder lies less in themselves than in our evil institutions" (Rousseau 1997, p. 17).

178. This refers to the tenth letter in the fourth part (Rousseau 1997, pp. 363–86).

179. Marcel was born in the last decade of the seventeenth century and died in 1759 after a long career as dancer and educator of dances. He was elected a member of the Royal Academy of Dance in 1719 (see Astier 1984).

180. Madeleine-Elisabeth Roguin, née Bouquin (1723–1806), was married on February 19th, 1762 to Augustin-Gabriel Roguin, an officer and nephew of Daniel Roguin, who was a close friend of Rousseau.

181. There are numerous letters dealing with education, for example Rousseau's dispute with Henriette (Correspondance letter nos. 3192, 3493, 3621, 3986, 4209, 4908, 6801). Most of the letters were written

by young parents or couples who wanted to know how to prepare for education. One curious example is John Albert Bentick (1737–1775), an English officer, who wrote to Rousseau on December 28th, 1764 and complained about his wife. She does not like his service and although she is pregnant she does not want to be a mother, being "une jeunne femmes savante" (Correspondance t. XXII, p. 312). Rousseau answered laconically that she would never love him for his merits and that a sensible heart is easy to hurt (Correspondance t. XXIII, p. 202).

182. *Julie ou La Nouvelle Héloise. Lettres de deux amants, habitant d'une petite ville dans les Alpes* was published under the date of 1761 by Marc Michel Rey in Amsterdam. The first English translation by William Kenrick appeared also in 1761. The title was: *Eloisa: Or, a Series of Original Letters Collected and Published by J. J. Rousseau.*

183. Pythagoras prescribed five years of silence to his students (Plutarch: On Curiosity, ch. IX).

184. François de Salignac de La Mothe-Fénelon's (1651–1715) *Les Aventures de Télémaque* was published in 1699; Marie-Madeleine Pioche de Lavergne, Comtesse de Lafayette's (1634–1693) *La Princesse de Clève* was published in 1678. Her novel *Zayde. Histoire espagnol* was published in 1670.

185. Plutarch: *Lives of the Noble Greeks and Romans*. Solon, ch. 2. Plutarch reports on Solon to have been a lover of knowledge for when he was old, he would say that he each day grew older, and learnt something new. At the end of Plutarch's report the quotation is repeated and connected to the joys of old age and leisure (*ibid.*, ch. 31).

186. Suzanne Bernard (1673–1712), who had married Rousseau's father in 1704, died when giving birth to her second son.

187. Also from – or maybe just because of – today's point of view this list is astonishing; provided its statements are true they shed a strange light on Rousseau's criticism of *enfants prodiges*.

188. Besides historical studies and religious tracts, Charles de Marguetel de Saint Denis, Seigneur de Saint-Évremont (1610–1703) wrote also satires like *La comédie des académistes* (1644). His tract *Sur le plaisirs*, published in 1705 in the context of an edition of his works, is a theory on taste.

189. *La logique ou l'art de penser* (Paris 1662). The authors of this "anonymous" writing were Antoine Artauld (1612–1694) and Pierre Nicole (1625–1695).

190. *Amicus Plato, amicus Aristoteles, sed magis amica veritas*. This originates from Aristotle, Nicomachean Ethics I/4, 1096a16.

191. French writer and dramatist Antoine Houdart de La Motte (1672–1731), who did not know Greek, became famous for his free translation of the Iliad, which was published in 1699.
192. Abbé Jean Terrasson (1670–1750) was Professor for Latin and Greek at the Collège Royal and one the most famous European experts on ancient literature.
193. This alludes to Bernard de Fontenelle's essay on the relationship between the moderns and the ancients (1688) in which the opposite view can be found. Progress in science and arts will devalue ancient literature because knowledge increased.
194. Letter to Laurent Aymon de Franquières (1744–1790). He met Rousseau in 1768; the main topic of the long letter (Correspondance t. XXXVII, pp. 13–24) is religion, Rousseau tries to convince the skeptical Laurent de Franquières (Blanc 2006, pp. 31ff.).
195. The dogmas of civil religion are simple, few of number, and immediately understandable without extended comments and interpretations (commentaires) (O.C. III, p. 468). This didactic rule refers to various positive dogmas and one negative dogma: "The existence of an omnipotent, intelligent, benevolent divinity that foresees and provides; the life to come; the happiness of the just; the punishment of sinners; the sanctity of the social contract and the law – these are the positive dogmas. As for the negative dogmas, I would limit them to a single one: no intolerance. Intolerance is something which belongs to the religions we have rejected" (Rousseau 2004a, p. 166). It is thus a civil confession of faith.
196. "Virtue, in a republic, is a very simple thing: it is love of the republic; it is a feeling and not a result of knowledge; the lowest man in the state, like the first, can have this feeling" (Montesquieu 1898, p. 42).
197. In the fall of 1770 the Polish nobleman Michael Wielhorski (1716–1794) asked Rousseau and the Abbé Mably to write an expert's report on the future constitution and the government system of Poland. In April, 1771 Rousseau sent his report to the client. The report was considered a diplomatic secret paper which soon became well known, due to illegal copies. Rousseau forbade it to be printed, which ensured its distribution still further.
198. The Pléiade edition says: "C'est l'éducation qui doit donner aux ames la force nationale" (O.C. III, p. 966). *Forme* instead of *force* is found in all earlier editions (Rousseau 2005, p. 254, fn. 29).
199. This argument is also found in *Contrat Social*: "Once customs are established and prejudices rooted, reform is a dangerous and fruitless enterprise" (Rousseau 2004a, p. 49).

200. In *Contrat Social* Corsica was the only country in Europe able to receive laws (Rousseau 2004a, p. 58). The Corsican officer Matthieu Buttafoco (1731–1806), who at this time was a capitaine in the régiment Royal Corse, had asked Rousseau at the end of August, 1764 to write a draft of a constitution.
201. "Above all beware of making the station of pedagogue into a profession" (Rousseau 2005, p. 180).

Part 3

The Reception and Influence of Rousseau's Work

5

The Reception of Rousseau's "Natural Education"

Rousseau had flattered the paradox too much; this is what Geneva lawyer and natural scientist Charles Bonnet (1720–1793) wrote to Berne physician Albrecht von Haller (1708–1777) on August 19th, 1755.[1] Both were naturalists and declared opponents of Rousseau. As he was contradicting himself so much, Bonnet wrote, he was the more touched (Correspondance t. III, p. 148).[2] This man cannot be taken seriously, as he cannot be caught out, and is elusive because he repeatedly uses his paradoxes as an excuse. Rousseau himself, who was a thorough reader of Haller's natural scientific writings,[3] reacted sharply to his compatriot Bonnet. Although being a materialist, he says in the *Confessions*, Bonnet supported "the most intolerant orthodoxy in anything that concerns me" (Rousseau 2000, p. 618).

In respect of religious questions, the Calvinist Bonnet cannot by any means be considered a materialist.[4] In 1762 he supported those in Geneva who wanted Rousseau's two books to be burned because they were violating Christian religion and offending the government of the Republic of Geneva. Rousseau suspected Bonnet of involvement when in 1763 his once close friend and correspondent Jacob Vernes published letters which were supposed to prove that he – Rousseau – was not a Christian (Vernes 1764). In October, 1755 Bonnet himself had published a far-reaching criticism of Rousseau's Second Discourse in the *Mercure de France*, which referred to the inconsistency in Rousseau's thoughts. This article largely determined the views of Rousseau's opponents (Bonnet 1755).[5]

Even after the publication of *Nouvelle Héloise*, being judged a paradoxical radical defined the perception of Rousseau by that part of the public which did not think well of him and reacted with hostility. However, by the success of *Nouvelle Héloise* he became a famous author on whom opinions were divided. Many of his readers did not share Voltaire's view; Rousseau's epistolary novel was a success despite or even because of its countless moral lessons. Paradoxes in the text, like natural education without nature, were overlooked in favor of the course of the love story and of the "voices of the heart." He had found a language for love and virtue and this fascinated his countless readers.

One part of the public admired Rousseau for what he wrote and deduced maxims on their own lives from it; others fought his doctrines or thought him to be a charlatan. Among eighteenth-century European intellectuals nobody was indifferent toward him. Almost every writer of importance discussed him, and besides this he found a big reading public, something which the philosophers whom he despised so much could only dream of. Rousseau cleaved the public in two: there were only admirers or enemies; he left nobody indifferent and he believed that he was important. In 1764 he wrote to Christophe de Beaumont: "My writings will remain despite you, to your shame" (Rousseau 2001, p. 65).

Samuel Johnson was of the same opinion as Bonnet and added a political reason. According to Boswell's *Journal*, Johnson said on July 20th, 1763: "Rousseau and all these people who deal in paradoxes are led away by childish desire of novelty" (*Boswell's London Journal* 1950, p. 315). The people he was talking to, Boswell and Dempster, were given a lesson by Johnson on the solid principles "the necessity and the advantages of subordination" were based on if compared to the Rousseauist madness of radical innovation (*ibid.*, pp. 315–16). At this time nobody referred to Rousseau's own subordination thesis in *Political Economy*, as the debate focused on *Nouvelle Héloise* and *Emile*, that is on natural life and education. "Naturalness" became a watchword of public debate often understood to be the same as "freedom."

However, it would be an exaggeration to consider *Emile* the educational guidebook of the eighteenth century. Impassioned, Rousseau's followers often referred only to the basic setting of "natural education," *à la campagne* understood to be an idyll or a landscape far from reality. More than a few readers tried to organize their own children's education according to it, despite – or maybe just because of – the critics' warnings. The rhetoric of the book was convincing, and hardly anyone asked about Rousseau's own paternity. Also, the paradoxes in *Emile* did not play a role for those of his followers who wanted the book to be understood as a fundamental alternative to the previous practice of education.

Rousseau's educational opponents formed immediately after the publication of *Emile* and muted its reception. So far, Rousseau had been absolutely right in his estimation that he met private attention but little public praise; indeed, mostly bad reviews were published at first. In the course of this, during the first years several standard arguments developed which continue to have an effect today. Despite Rousseau's way of perceiving reviews, these were by no means only malicious misunderstandings or misinterpretations of his theory, but papers whose objections were to be taken seriously and which could see through the construction of *Emile*.

In 1763 Samuel Formey (1711–1797), Secretary of the Berlin Academy[6] and a European intellectual of the highest reputation, published one of the numerous antipathetic writings on Rousseau's book on education. Formey's *Anti-Emile* considered the essential question of education to be not one of asking how the child's nature gets justice but in asking how man could be made *a citizen*,[7] something which did not require "nature" but training and knowledge. This position by Voltaire is formulated by one sentence: "Le vrai patriote est un homme éclairé" ("A true patriot is a man of enlightenment") (Formey 1763, p. 23). Rousseau's emphasis on nature is said to be artificial and to result in the powers of learning remaining unused. Rousseau is said to be an experienced provocateur, nothing more, at least in the field of education.

Already one year earlier, the Benedictine monk Joseph Cajot (1726–1779) had suspected Rousseau of plagiarism,[8] something which was explained in more detail in 1766 by way of a lengthy treatise. Here, Rousseau appears as an epigone who had done nothing other than exploit the educational ideas of antiquity and to mix them with more recent, most of all medical, literature (Cajot 1766, pp. 66ff.).[9] In 1769 Cajot's *Eloge de l'âne* was published, a satire on contemporary society, its customs and education, where men act as donkeys. The author of this satire introduced himself as "un docteur de Montmartre" and added a new locus to Rousseau's criticism of Paris (Cajot 1769).

In 1763 Gaspard de Beaurieu (1728–1795)[10] published his own utopia of the *élève de la nature* and with this tried to surpass *Emile*. Rousseau's damnation of luxury is found here, just as is the praise of the farmers' hard labor or simple life in the country. This was meant to be a social utopia which was understood not as a novel but realistically. Society was supposed to be rebuilt far away from the decadence of big cities. This required also a change of education. In contrast to Rousseau, the child of nature grows up with two different and separated couples and must have his first experiences without being guided by a governor, dependent only on himself and as being locked up in a cage. The child of nature must generate all the knowledge of the world by himself, even re-inventing fire (Beaurieu 1771, t. I, pp. 80ff.).

As late as the end of the eighteenth century Beaurieu's utopia was much read. In 1768 one of numerous editions was even attributed to Rousseau.[11] But besides exciting certain readers, the proverbial "child of nature" aroused mainly criticism. Rousseau was considered the founder of the *élève de la nature*, whose theories were reduced and fixed to this topic. Reaction repeatedly criticized both the theory and program of natural education as impracticable, and Rousseau's paradoxes and the many contradictions in his work.

For example, the German author Christoph Martin Wieland (1733–1813)[12] took up the arguments of criticism and also made Rousseau a debated figure in German-speaking countries.

After this, to German educationalists Rousseau looked as suspicious as to those in France or Britain. His influence on contemporary education, consisting mostly of theologians and schoolmasters, was never very great and vanished increasingly until the end of the century. If German school reformers, for example Johann Bernard Basedow (1724–1790), referred to the harmony of "Nature! School! Life!" (Basedow 1775, p. 15),[13] this was only a slogan. The revision of the educational system (*ibid.*, p. 19) was supposed to be a matter of well-made school books, of effective teaching methods,[14] and of an overhaul of the curriculum (*ibid.*, pp. 20ff). Essential for success were school organization and school life, the role of the teachers (*ibid.*, pp. 40ff), the political will, and support by the public. The child's "nature" was subject to educational work, not an entity deserving any respect *by itself*.

Similar statements are found in texts on the British and French debate (Gerdil 1764; Anon. *Remarks* 1774 and various others). Also here, if at all, "natural education" gained an acceptance as a rhetorical element, not as a goal of the practical work of teaching. This is due to a systematic reason: in all the "philanthropic" and "patriotic" drafts of the eighteenth century, education was always understood to be *positive*, never negative. Rousseau's paradoxical idea that education had to be negative at first in order to have a positive effect is hardly understood anywhere or put into practice authentically. Where the addressee of educational reform was not school, "fathers and friends of children" were addressed (von Salis-Marschlins 1775), increasingly also mothers, but never the children themselves.

Rousseau's motifs were taken up and communicated in agreement where there was complaint on school education, most of all by literature, novels, plays, and essays, which required particular readers, even there without real support of a kind of "negative education." In manuals for parents, which are a different genre, early approaches of *éducation naturelle* were extended. Rousseau's statements were placed next to those on diatetics, hygiene, or healthy diet, without understanding the setting of *Emile* to be only a literary fiction. Rousseau's *méthode* looked interesting and was discussed in respect of parents, as Rousseau had shown in *Nouvelle Héloise*.

However, contemporary perception of Rousseau among teachers was very different. In reflections by eighteenth-century school reformers, new and different schools as well as better ways of teaching were the alternatives to practice, never education according to nature. Very early the relevant passages from the second and third books of *Emile* resulted in criticism of Rousseau by educationalists and schoolmasters rather than approval (see Py 1997). The schoolmasters would be disempowered at once if one followed nature and not the guidelines of educational institutions. This does not exclude that schoolmasters referred to Rousseau rhetorically and used his catchy formulas of "natural education," which then, however, would have to happen at school and through book-related lessons.

One example is the Abbé Phillippe Serane, who founded a school at La Flèche near Angers, the *Institution de la Jeunesse*, which was declaredly supposed to be organized according to the principles of Rousseau's "natural education." In 1774 Serane published an appropriate theory which on close inspection turns out to be a description of his school and which twenty years later, again bearing "Rousseau's principles" in their title, was offered to the National Convent in Paris as a kind of *éducation républicaine*, without particularly taking Rousseau's own theories into consideration (Serane 1774).[15] Also, Serane's school books, such as *Géographie élementaire*,[16] do not contain any of Rousseau's principles. And finally Serane's utopia *l'heureux naufrage* – published in the year of the French Revolution – had apart from its anti-feudal teachings little to do with the *Contrat Social* (Serane 1789).

Thus, a fundamental conflict also became obvious, which remains today. In defense of the child and his natural development, declared Rousseauists criticize educational institutions, as they either hinder the child's nature or, if they are supposed to be legitimate, would have to be radically adjusted to this nature. In most cases, however, it is not stated how this should be done. There are reasons for this. Against what Rousseau would have wanted, the child's nature is never pure or accessible "by itself"; thus anyone who in education claims the "route de la nature" for himself is confronted with a completely different problem than someone who botanizes plants. This criticism started at the end of the eighteenth century and is connected to the French Revolution.

At the end of his long life, Rousseau's old enemy, Samuel Formey, wrote his *Souvenirs d'un citoyen*. They also were published in the year of revolution, more than ten years after Rousseau's death. Formey did not write any confessions, but simply organized his papers and tried to put them into context. On doing so, he also reflected on his literary and philosophical views, that is those authors he had repeatedly discussed, whether approvingly or critically. In this context Rousseau finds a special place: "If one thing is certain, it is that the man who most ardently held up his paradoxes became himself a paradox" (Formey 1789, t. II, pp. 114–15).

That is one mode of perception, making out Rousseau to be a radical yet regrettable paradox; the other way is that of the French Revolution, which celebrated Rousseau as its political and educational *maître penseur*. One of Rousseau's enthusiastic readers was Maximilien de Robespierre (1758–1794),[17] who on February 5th, 1794 presented the "principles of political morals" to the National Convent, according to which the republic was supposed to be ruled.[18] Robespierre calls their essential principle "public virtue," which refers to *Contrat Social* and the *religion civile*. This virtue, Robespierre said, was nothing other than love of the fatherland and its laws, by which the *volonté générale* expressed itself.

Thus, Rousseau had founded not only the objective of the revolution but also the essential means to maintain it, that is molding the people toward public virtue in line with his theory of political education. This prominent status was enough for Robespierre to have Rousseau's mortal remains taken to the Paris *Panthéon*.[19] The ceremony took place on October 11th, 1794, two days after patriotic celebrations in Rousseau's honor. The fact that all through his life he had wanted to be a *Citoyen de Genève* played no role in this posthumous honor. Rousseau was perceived as the founder of egalitarian society and of educating the people toward love of the fatherland, that is exactly along his analyses in *Political Economy*, and the idea of "natural education" was equated with this.

In contrast, conservative criticism of the revolution considered Rousseau the real originator of terror (e. g. Duvoisin 1798). Rousseau was regarded as the prototype of the politicizing, radical intellectual, something he had never been in this sense. But somebody must have spread these revolutionary ideas. The real intellectuals of the revolution, for example the physician and writer Jean-Paul Marat (1743–1793), were much closer to this image but received nowhere near as much attention as Rousseau. In an intellectual sense, Marat particularly had, much more than Rousseau, prepared the revolution, but this did not play any role, as Rousseau was the much more famous character and was much more suitable for being stylized.

The intellectual basis of conservative criticism was Edmund Burke's (1729–1797) *Reflections on the Revolution in France*, which was published in London on November 1st, 1790. At the end of that month 12,000 copies had been sold, and at the same time a hurriedly produced French translation was published, which was also a sales success.[20] In February, 1791 an unauthorized German translation was published, and in 1793 the definitive German translation produced by the diplomat and political author Friedrich Gentz (1764–1832). Illegal printings by Italian and American publishers complete the picture. What made this book such a success?

It was, after all, discussing Rousseau. In one of his first publications in 1756[21] Burke had contradicted Rousseau's thesis in the Second Discourse that man's natural state was characterized by equality and that only artificial society had provided for differences and hierarchies. Nowhere, Burke says, was the natural state found in its pure form, neither in natural freedom nor in natural religion. We only judge from the position of abstract principles which we consider "natural," whereas all experiences consist of mixtures, particularly those which are politically distorted,[22] without being able to find "pure" nature behind them. Behind our experiences there are always only other experiences, no constants like "nature" or "progress."

In 1790 this topic is again taken up by the *Reflections*. Burke (1999, pp. 8ff.) assumes that the abstract "spirit of liberty," taken in action, had put the people into a daze, the politicizing intellectuals supporting ambiguous and wavering doctrines which did not stand the test of closer observation (*ibid.*, p. 14). Given the insecurity of promises and the consequences of revolt all that was left was a return to reliable traditions, to that which is connected to experiences of success or failure and which is immune to ideologies like those of Rousseau. His theories do not take the given constitution into account and abstractly enthuse about freedom which can neither be strived for nor be achieved. In contrast to this, the Englishman emphasized: "madmen are not our lawgivers" (*ibid.*, p. 86).

Burke put forth the classical argument of a conservative: "A spirit of innovation is generally the result of a selfish temper and confined views. People will not look forward to posterity, who never look backward to their ancestors" (*ibid.*, p. 33). Guilty for the excess of revolution are the "paradoxes of eloquent writers, brought forth purely as a sport of fancy, to try their talents, to rouse attention, and excite surprise" (*ibid.*, p. 171). Rousseau is considered to be an "accurate, though eccentric observer" of his time (*ibid.*) who – were he alive – "would be shocked at the practical phrenzy of his scholars, who in their paradoxes are servile imitators" (*ibid.*, p. 172).

But this is only a kind of obeisance. In a letter to a member of the French National Assembly[23] that was published in Paris on April 27th, 1791, and which later became an appendix to the *Reflections*, Burke was unequivocal. All the leaders of the French Revolution "resemble him" – Rousseau:

His blood they transfuse into their blood and into their manners. Him they study, him they meditate; him they turn over in all the time they can spare from the laborious mischief of the day, or the debauches of the night. Rousseau is their canon of holy writ; in life he is the canon of *Polycletus*, and he is their standard figure of perfection. (*ibid.*, p. 269)

For Burke, Rousseau is nothing but "the great professor and founder of *the philosophy of vanity*" (*ibid.*, p. 270). All he wrote, especially his *Confessions*, express only vanity, and "under this philosophic instructor in the *ethics of vanity*, they have attempted in France a regeneration of the moral constitution of man" (*ibid.*, p. 271). Thus, Rousseau is the "father" of the revolution whose new system of institutions is "false and theatric" (*ibid.*, p. 272), like Rousseau himself, one has to add. The writings of Rousseau lead directly to "shameful evil" (*ibid.*, p. 274), also because he had no taste but only enthusiasm. "His doctrines, on the whole, are so inapplicable to real life and manners, that we never dream of drawing from them any rule for laws or conduct, or for fortifying or illustrating any thing by a reference to his opinions" (*ibid.*, p. 275).

As already shown, Rousseau presented a similar criticism of *philosophes*, where he rejected abstract principles and put concrete experience into focus. The fact that now he was himself made out to be an irresponsible *philosophe* is one of the many ironies in the long history of the reception of his theories. However, he would not have shared Burke's empirical argument. For Rousseau, experience does not refer simply to other experience but can be transcended. His refutation of "modern materialism," Rousseau writes in *Letter to Beaumont*, served for only one purpose: "to establish the existence of God and natural Religion with all the force of which the Author is capable" (2001, p. 75).

On the other hand, for his theory of political power Robespierre could very well refer to Rousseau and to an abstract principle founded by him. Sovereignty, it says at the beginning of the second book of *Contrat Social*, is "exercise of the general will" (Rousseau 2004a, p. 26). Essential for the sovereign is not the pragmatic quality of laws, nor the procedures of making or changing them, but that all laws and decisions are in accordance with the *volonté générale*. The general will is "always right" and always aims at the public good (*ibid.*, p. 31).[24] What is decisive is that the law unites the universality of will with that of the field of legislation (*ibid.*, p. 42) and not that they keep the balance between freedom and restriction.

But Rousseau does not say anything about who or what articulates the general will if this is not able to articulate itself. Robespierre refers to the basic principle of *Contrat Social* and at the same time claims to express this principle himself and to make it the basis of his decisions. The problem is that everybody may claim the *volonté générale*, as far as it is not understood to be an empirical entity but a principle. This way, it serves to legitimate power and not justice, for which it was originally intended. It is surely no coincidence that republican virtue, not the child's nature, became the educational model of the French Revolution. Burke (1999, p. 149) clearly recognized that this civic education requires the general will or an "interest" above empirical society.

In a way, Rousseau's criticism of intellectuals, or "philosophical fanatics" as Burke called them (*ibid.*), turned against himself. And the above-quoted idea from the *Letters Written from the Mountain*, that one could recognize the few good books, where they existed at all, by their having been written under the serious intention of supporting the good, leads nowhere. Every author may claim that, when writing his book, it had been his goal to support the good, and even the best principles from books do not reveal anything about how they will be used. Rousseau (2001, p. 224) knew this and continued in his writing, trusting that his principles would be suitable to be correctly applied, particularly in those cases he had least foreseen. On the application of his ideas by *others*, again Rousseau says nothing.

Since the French Revolution Rousseau has been considered mostly a left-wing author and during the nineteenth and twentieth centuries has been, most of all, politically perceived, by his criticism of nature's alienation from society. Although Rousseau uses the term *aliénation* in a different sense, for many authors he is the founder of the "theory of alienation," which is behind Marxist criticism of *Political Economy*. This kind of availment refers almost exclusively to the Second Discourse and to *Contrat Social*, both of which were given canonical status by left-wing Hegelianism. This holds selectively, for the theory of natural freedom, for criticism of numeric democracy (Rousseau 2004, p. 78),[25] or for the "surplus" of private production that furnishes public subsistence (*ibid.*, p. 91). The danger of the *volonté générale* did not play a role in this context.

Rousseau's theory of education can hardly be found in these political references. Left-wing criticism of society until the end of the nineteenth century increasingly occupies the topic of "education" with theories of children growing up freely, something which would have looked very strange in Rousseau's eyes. At the beginning of the twentieth century "natural education" became a point of reference for slogans of progressive politics of education which were often diametrically opposed to what Rousseau has written in *Emile*. Simultaneously, discredit on Rousseau as a person started all over again, associating, and thus assessing, his character with his *maladie* and the fate of his children.[26]

Also, by more recent analyses, often starting with Leo Strauss's (1953) interpretation of the second *Discours*[27] (like Horowitz 1987), Rousseau is found to have been an author who was the first to make an issue out of man's denaturation. Then, *Emile* appears as a kind of project on how new man could be educated for new society and could even be newly created. Doing this, the end of *Emile* is as little taken into consideration as the paradoxes of the text and also the fact that it was a fiction, not a project. It is also conspicuous that the results of "experiments" made in Rousseau's name are almost always overlooked, that is what the actual outcomes of "natural education" really were (Douthwaite 2002, ch. 4).

An early example dates back to the year 1769 and happens in the English Midlands around the Lunar Society. That was the name of a group of engineers, philosophers, authors, and inventors, who were interested in the application of experimental sciences. One of their members was the writer Thomas Day (1748–1789), who had studied law at Oxford without ever practicing as a lawyer. Day was a close friend of the Irish big landowner and later constructor Richard Lovell Edgeworth (1744–1817). Both were convinced followers of Rousseau and in their days of studying read *Emile* to find instructions for the practice of new education.

Edgeworth tried to bring up his eldest son according to Rousseau's principles because his *Emile* "had made a strong impression upon my young mind" (Edgeworth 1821, Vol. 1, p. 177). What he read he took literally and understood the book to be an explicit manual for the "education of nature" (*ibid.*, p. 178). This education lasted for several years, "notwithstanding the opposition with which I was embarrassed by my friends and relations, and the ridicule by which I became immediately assailed on all quarters" (*ibid.*). No matter what, Edgeworth isolated his son and wanted to educate him according to "necessity" and to let him learn only by things, without exposing him to a man's rule.

The boy was dressed without stockings, his arms bare, in a jacket and trousers that were very unusual in that day. He became very hardy, fearless of danger, and capable of bearing privation of every sort. He had more knowledge of things and less knowledge of books than most children of his age. He was good in mechanics and was more inventive than any other child. In the end he was "bold, free, fearless, generous; he had a ready and keen use of all his senses, and of his judgment. But he was not disposed to *obey*" (*ibid.*, pp. 178–9).

> His exertions generally arose from his own will; and, though he was what is commonly called good-tempered and good-natured, though he generally pleased by his looks, demeanour, and conversation, he had too little deference for others, and he shewed an invincible dislike to control. With me, he was always what I wished; with others, he was never any thing but what he wished to be himself. (*ibid.*, p. 179)

At the age of eight the experiment on natural education was stopped (*ibid.*). What was convincing in theory failed in practice, at least concerning social skills. Edgeworth did not raise his other children with the same principles. These principles proved to be "mistaken" (*ibid.*, p. 273). The boy became "self-willed" due to the "error of a theory" and other parents have to be "warned" not to believe "the eloquence of Rousseau" (*ibid.*, p. 274).

When visiting Paris, Edgeworth and his eight-year-old son together with Thomas Day met Rousseau in person. The meeting in the year of 1771 is seldom referred to in literature on Rousseau (see Lyons 2003). The boy was introduced to Rousseau, who immediately "took a good deal of notice" of him. Edgeworth asked Rousseau to tell him anything "that struck him in the child's manner of conversation." Rousseau agreed and took the boy with him "in his usual morning's walk." When he came back after two hours he judged favorably on the boy's abilities, which had been "well cultivated." But, Rousseau went on, "I remark in your son a propensity to party justice, which will be a great blemish in his character" (Edgeworth 1821, Vol. 1, p. 258).

Edgeworth wondered how Rousseau could form so decided an opinion in such a short time. Rousseau told him that whenever his son saw a handsome horse or a handsome carriage in the street, he always exclaimed: "That is an English horse, or an English carriage!" "Even down to a pair of shoe-buckles, every thing that appeared to be good of its kind was always pronounced by him to be English."

> "This sort of party justice," said Rousseau, "if suffered to become a ruling motive of the mind, will lead to a thousand evils: for not only will his own country, his own village, or club, or even a knot of his private acquaintance, be the object of his exclusive admiration; but he will be governed by his companions, whatever they may be, and they will become the arbiters of his destiny." (*ibid.*, p. 259)

For Edgeworth this prophecy seemed to be "sage" (*ibid.*), but he never returned to Rousseau's principles. His eldest son's education was put in the hands of a tutor, but that tutor failed (*ibid.*, p. 275). After that the course of education was completely changed: he was sent to a school, not an ordinary school but to a French Jesuit seminary (*ibid.*, p. 276). Edgeworth was impressed because of the "neatness, order," the extent and "grandeur" of the building, the regulations, and "the deportment and high characters of its masters" (*ibid.*, pp. 276–7). But the son was not prepared "for the change between the Rousseau system, which had been pursued at home, and the course of education to which he was to be subject at a public seminary" (*ibid.*, p. 353). So this education failed too. "He went to sea, readily acquired the knowledge requisite for his situation, and his hardiness and fearlessness of danger appeared to fit him for a sailor's life" (*ibid.*).

Day's story is more complex and shows two sides: Thomas Day as a father and as an author. It is pertinent to both stories that Day was more committed to Rousseau than Edgeworth.[28] The first story covers an approach on natural education which took place in Rousseau's name and during his lifetime, although he never heard of it.[29] English poet Anna Seward (1747–1809) narrated this "experiment" à la Jean-Jacques which had kept the whole community of Lichfield on their toes (Seward 1804, pp. 35ff.). This story of a "Spartan education" (*ibid.*, p. 42) has occasionally been mentioned by British autobiographical literature but did not play any role with the later reception of "natural education," although – or because – it was a practical experiment on the validity of its principles.

Thomas Day was not an outstanding figure but he was independent. His father had left a fortune to him which paid £1,200 sterling a year, the material basis for the experiment. Together with his elder friend Thomas Bicknell,[30] he visited the Foundling Hospital, an orphanage in Shrewsbury. Day adopted a twelve-year-old girl whom he called Sabrina Sidney, "Sabrina" after the river along which Shrewsbury lies, and "Sidney" after Algernon Sidney, the legendary Whig Member of Parliament from the time of the British Commonwealth.[31] From Coram's Fields in London, Day adopted a twelve-year-old girl whom he called "Lucretia," an allusion to the legendary founder of the Roman Empire.

Adoptions of this kind were by no means unusual; what was unusual was the intention behind them. Day wanted to bring up both girls according to Rousseau's methods, in order to find out if one of them would be suitable to become his wife; the other one was supposed to be provided for. However, children were only allowed to be adopted if the interested people were married. This was in contradiction to the declared purpose of the adoption. Quickly, Day decided to give the name of his friend Edgeworth, without telling him about this. Then he moved to Avignon with both girls. The reason was Rousseauist: as none of them spoke French, they were thought to be safe from the corruption of society. However, society is present even without a language. Day was to find out that nobody in Avignon was interested in his experiment in the name of the famous Rousseau and that he was continually making a fool of himself.

In France, Day experienced that which his hero, Rousseau, had lived to see in Britain. Furthermore, natural education proved to be extremely difficult. The two girls "teased and perplexed him; they quarrelled, and fought incessantly" (*ibid.*, p. 37). Also, they were bored by the lessons Day gave them, they clashed unceasingly, and finally they got smallpox and forced Day to spend whole nights at their beds instead of finding out who between them was the more natural one. Further disasters were on the horizon: during a trip a boat capsized, the quarreling did not stop, and Day even had to challenge a French officer to a duel because the latter had been all too frank toward the girls.

Thus, the experiment of educating two British girls in France in the way that Emile had been instructed was a failure. Exhausted, Day returned to Britain. At least his intention seemed to be fulfilled. He parted with Lucretia, whom he considered to be either incurably stupid or impossibly stubborn, that is not suitable to be his future wife. Sabrina became "the favourite" (*ibid.*, p. 38); she stayed with him, seemed to be promising, and with her he moved to Lichfield and to the Lunar Society in spring 1770 (*ibid.*, p. 39). Now on British soil, he tried to educate her in Rousseau's spirit.

She was thirteen years old, a growing beauty, who spoke in a soft voice and wore her hair untied. Day wanted her to harden herself and to develop Spartan virtues. One of the exercises consisted of learning how to endure hot wax on her arm. Sabrina, however, forgot about the role of a Spartan woman which was intended for her and cried out loudly instead of silently standing the pain, as according to Day would have been suitable for a wife. Also, in other ways natural education remained unsuccessful. In spring 1771 he sent her to a boarding school in Sutton Coldfield, where she was educated without Rousseau (Uglow 2003).

The second part of the story is concerned with Thomas Day the author. He published a famous children's book in three parts in 1783–9, titled *The History of Sandford and Merton*. Day's purpose in the book was to connect Rousseau's principles of natural education with social criticism. *Sandford and Merton* was much read in the nineteenth century,[32] but it had little to do with practical education. The readers were advised that wealth contributed nothing to education and that luxury was the enemy of human nature. The story tells of Tommy Merton, the spoiled and naughty son of a rich plantation owner in Jamaica, who is sent to England to be educated well. Here he meets Harry Sandford, son of a poor farmer, who with his natural and simple virtues needs no artificial schooling to become morally good. A natural life in the country is all that is needed to be able to live in harmony with oneself, provided that one is taught the few really important things in life, as the boys were – by their tutor, Reverend Barlow.

Later figures in children's literature like Tom Sawyer or Oliver Twist were conceived by their authors in opposition to the artificial morals of the followers of Rousseau, who precisely did *not* understand what children experience and feel. Thomas Day simply doubled the basic premise in Rousseau's *Emile*, by having two boys instead of one go through a "natural education," and Day did not change anything of the artificiality of Rousseau's model. If this model is called "child-centered," it should also certainly be seen as ambivalent, for although it attempted to focus on the activities of the child, at the same time it is focused on the steering of precisely these activities by well-meaning tutors or governesses.

Cases of this kind are also found in pre-Revolution France. One of Rousseau's most enthusiastic admirers was Jeanne-Marie Philopon (1754–1793), who was called Manon Roland. In 1787 she published *Réflexion sur Plutarque*, where she tried to meld Plutarch and Rousseau into one single literary character. As "young Sophie," her daughter Euroda, born in 1781, was brought up together with other girls in the Philopon house according to the example of *Nouvelle Héloise* (Cornut-Gentille 2004). The model was not Henriette, Sophie's daughter, but Sophie herself, who at the beginning of the epistolary novel is described by St Preux as an "innocent soul" (Rousseau 1997, p. 45) who follows her heart and mistrusts abstract philosophies taken from books (*ibid.*, p. 47).

Since Louise d'Epernay's *Lettres sur l'education*, educational literature has been a genre of its own in France. A well-known example is the epistolary novel *Adèle et Théodore*, which was published in three volumes in Paris between 1782 and 1789. The author was the Comtesse de Genlis,[33] who wrote numerous books and essays on education and repeatedly referred to Rousseau. One reason for this was her opposition to Voltaire. In the first book of *Adèle et Théodore* she returned to Rousseau's principle of appropriate age for the education of both children. From this principle comes a strict control of reading and knowledge. Children should learn only useful knowledge which does not exceed their mental forces. This method will surely succeed just as Rousseau had predicted. Instruction with school lessons does not belong to childhood as children will only be unhappy with this (Genlis 1782, pp. 66ff.).

Rousseau's immediate followers consist of the generation of his readers until about the end of the eighteenth century. Up to then, practical or literary experiments on "natural education" can be proven, which require thorough and detailed reading of *Emile*. These attempts by readers must be distinguished from later references to Rousseau as an educationalist. When Maria Edgeworth (1767–1849), who personally knew the Comtesse de Genlis, translated *Adèle et Théodore* into the English language by order of her father, she had a reading audience in mind, mothers and fathers, but not a profession of education, orientated toward certain philosophies.

In the course of the nineteenth century Rousseau found his way into the textbooks of education and became a "classic" of pedagogy. These books were mostly used for teacher training and soon were part of the standard repertoire of the curriculum. Thus, the interpretation by Rousseau lovers changed to being a course which was supposed to prepare for a profession (ironically, an increasingly institutionalized one) which in this context had to take the interests of novices into consideration. Thus, Rousseau was canonized, his status in the field of education rose, but at the same time he was reduced to a few, often stereotypical, statements which show neither the whole range of the problems nor the paradoxes of his work.

Curtailed and sanitized of all contradictions Rousseau became the authority of "natural education," the former expertise of his readers no longer necessary. With historical distance increasing, distortion was compounded and Rousseau could look to be the founder of a kind of education which he had never formulated. A French example of this strategy is Théodore Fritz's *Esquisse d'une histoire de l'education* from 1843, perhaps the first textbook to consider Rousseau as the historical founder of "natural education" without devaluating him. In Robert Hebert Quick's (1831–1891) *Essays on Educational Reformers* from 1868 Rousseau already belongs to the classical stock of "great educationalists" and is considered the co-founder of modern education and a genius (Quick 2003, p. 248).

Rousseau is yesterday's "master" of tomorrow's education, as stated in a publication by André Hilaire (1873). Extended studies and critical discussions on Rousseau's philosophy of education are not found throughout the entire nineteenth century; his enemies' polemics during his lifetime were continued without asking what exactly Rousseau has to do with the concept of "natural education." In the nineteenth century, not coincidentally starting out from Socialist and Anarchist groups, this concept became a slogan which resulted in numerous practical experiments, many of which felt obliged to Rousseau (Oelkers 2006a). The most famous author is Leo Tolstoy (1828–1910), who on his estate Jasnaja Poljana founded his own school, which was supposed to be organized in the spirit of Rousseau.

At the end of the nineteenth century, Rousseau is definitively tied down to *éducation naturelle*, something to which in France most of all Gabriel Compayré (1901)[34] contributed. William Boyd (1911) adapted this thesis and made it fruitful for *progressive education*, with Rousseau still today considered its founder. The "activity principle" of Rousseau's education can be proven for German studies as early as the end of the nineteenth century (Nörkow 1898) and from then on becomes the trade label for "new education," which is supposed to completely serve "the child," being psychology-based, however, and very distant from the problems which Rousseau himself pursued. The purpose of *Emile* was not simply the *active child* of international progressive education.

One of the books which mostly paved the way for "new education" in the Anglo-Saxon world was Evelyn and John Dewey's *Schools of To-Morrow*, published in 1915. Chapter 2 begins with the following statement: "Rousseau's teaching that education is a process of natural growth has influenced most theorizing upon education since his time" (Dewey and Dewey 1985, p. 222). But what has been called "theorizing upon education" since Rousseau, that is educational theory since 1762, was in fact *not* focused on the question of "natural growth." If there had been concepts of "natural growth" they were quite different from that of Rousseau. And those who favored "natural growth," like Friedrich Fröbel, had not been "Rousseauists."

But what is more important, the concept of "natural growth," as the Deweys understood it in 1915, is *not* at the heart of Rousseau's theory. His theory is read with the eyes of protagonists of child-centered education:

The child is best prepared for life as an adult by experiencing in childhood what has meaning to him as a child; and, further, the child has a right to enjoy his childhood. Because he is a growing animal who must develop so as to live successfully in the grown-up world, nothing should be done to interfere with growth, and everything should be done to further the full and free development of his body and his mind. (*ibid.*)

Even if it is meant only as a principle, a "full and free development" of the child cannot be found in Rousseau's writings, let alone such a development of both, the body and the mind. The principle that all learning must be "meaningful" to the child is Rousseau's, but not in the sense of the child having a right to "enjoy" his childhood. Again, it follows that Rousseau's child is not that of psychological theories. "Spartan" experiments could no longer be done.

One year later John Dewey in *Democracy and Education* criticizes some concepts of education which he considered to be wrong. For the second of these concepts Dewey uses the term *Education as Unfolding*. This doctrine is associated with the names of three authors, that is Fröbel, Hegel, and Rousseau, representing three concepts which despite being different in many respects share a common essence: "Development is conceived not as continuous growing, but as the unfolding of latent powers toward a definite goal. The goal is conceived of as completion, perfection. Life at any stage short of attainment to this goal is merely an unfolding toward it" (Dewey 1985, p. 61). "Goals" may as well be ideals. They are absolute in the sense of the complete development being supposed to develop toward them and only them. As in Fröbel's *formation of man* or Hegel's *philosophy of history*, ideals are latently present in development, in the form of "potentials" or "undeveloped gifts" which gradually lead toward their completion. "What is termed development is the gradual making explicit and outward of what is thus wrapped up" (*ibid.*, p. 62). Thus, that which is supposed to be development is nothing other than "the unfolding of a ready-made latent principle" (*ibid.*, p. 63).

Indeed, some educational theories of the nineteenth century are structured this way. Goals are final states which may be achieved or missed without any possibility of changing them by way of actual process. These goals are secured by metaphysical theories or by the "nature" of "history," of "spirit," or of "society." Empirical theories on education are hardly found on the European continent at the turn of the twentieth century, or they are counted as psychology. But psychological theories also tend to understand "development" in a teleological way, something which cannot ultimately be shown by Piaget and the Geneva *éducation nouvelle*.

Consequently, Dewey also criticizes Rousseau, to whom Piaget always referred. Rousseau, Dewey says, plans the child's "natural development" as a development of potential with whom no third party is allowed to interfere, as far as society is unnatural (*ibid.*, p. 65). But nature is not the "standard" of education, as many reformers of education assumed at the end of the nineteenth century. Indeed, referring to natural education may be used for criticizing educational practice, but nature does not simply do its work "within" the child. It is not an agent, whereas Rousseauists understand nature to set its law and its goal in advance for human development, education then only having to follow it. "The constructive use of intelligence in foresight, and contriving, is then discounted; we are just to get out of the way and allow nature to do the work" (*ibid.*, p. 119).

Rousseau, Dewey summed up, was right in that the structure and activities of the organs furnish the *conditions* of all teaching to use the organs. But he was "profoundly wrong" in intimating that they supply not only the conditions but also the *ends* of their developments (*ibid.*, pp. 120–1). This is "pure mythology." Natural or native powers "furnish the initiating and limiting forces in all education; they do not furnish its ends or aims" (*ibid.*, p. 121). Rousseau's concept of nature is that of creation, not that of biology. "There is no learning except from a beginning in unlearned powers, but learning is not a matter of the spontaneous overflow of the unlearned powers. Roussseau's contrary opinion is doubtless due to the fact that he identified God with Nature; to him the original powers are wholly good, coming directly from a wise and good creator" (*ibid.*).

Child-centered education had two main sources: the Kindergarten movement from the mid-nineteenth century on the one hand, and the new child psychology at the end of the nineteenth century on the other hand. The sources often mingled: Fröbelian motives were at the heart of psychological child studies, and empiricial results often seemed to verify the principles of child-centered education, which was mostly a reaction against schooling at the end of the nineteenth century. Modern *schooling* in this view contradicted modern *education*, because it was held that schooling did not respect the natural growth of the child. It *interfered* with growth and *did nothing* to support the "full and free development" of the child.

This contradicts the stoic picture of education Rousseau himself gave. It is *not* what "modern education" is made of. Rousseau became its hero mostly due to cult and legend, not because he was read but because he found admiration. Even an extensive *reading* of Rousseau, like André Ravier did in 1941 in his magistral doctoral thesis, meant studying him as a source of "new education." Ravier, who in the first half of the twentieth century wrote by far best work on Rousseau's theory of education, concentrated on two themes: first, the mal-reception of *Emile* in eighteenth-century-literature[35] and second, its rediscovery within the context of new education. In this context *Emile* was viewed as the basic theory of *l'homme nouveau* – the renewal of man. And in this sense Rousseau was regarded as the "pioneer" of modern education.

It is in fact illuminating to consider that the time lapse between the last (Catholic) refutation of Rousseau's *Emile* in 1860[36] in France and Rousseau's first ennobling as the founding father of "modern education" in 1879[37] was only twenty years. At the end of the nineteenth century this reclassification was beyond doubt not only in Europe but also in America. "Education according to Nature" was firmly tied up with the name of Rousseau (e.g. Davidson 1898). The term "Rousseauisme" was coined at the end of the nineteenth century (Nourrisson 1903, pp. 477–507)[38] and before World War II it was common sense in the history of education that "new education" started with Rousseau and no one else (Ehm 1938 and several others).

In addition, it has often been overlooked that what Rousseau understood to be "nature" and what *progressive education* assumed were worlds apart. The reason can be summarized thus: after Darwin's theory of evolution by way of selective adaptation, Rousseau's ancient concept of nature, where nothing is repeated and everything takes its determined course, is no longer tenable as a biological model of education. Not coincidentally, none of the theories referring to Rousseau in the twentieth century goes back to the rigid concept of the ages of education.

"Development" is not a process which simply happens within the child but one to which the child actively contributes and which the child himself must make happen. If there are developmental steps, they are very different from those phases of education which Rousseau had in mind. Education is not "natural" simply due to the age of nature, and between three and twelve years there does not exist one and the same child which in principle was satisfied with one single space of learning. Learning is continual problem solving, made for feedback which to only a certain extent can be didactically controlled. The image of the "active child" becomes possible because the child's "nature" must *not* be regarded solely as rigid classifications as in botany or determined sequences as in ancient philosophy. Thus, the basic term of education would be "life," not "nature" in the sense of Rousseau.

Notes

1. From 1736 onward Haller was a professor of anatomy, botany, and surgery at the University of Göttingen and returned to his hometown of Berne in 1753, where he worked in high state positions.
2. Bonnet tells Haller about his impressions of the Second Discourse: "But it is very strange that a man who feels the advantages of good government

in such a lively way remarks that man's happiest state was that which was most similar to being unorganized" (Correspondance t. III, p. 148).

3. This is shown by Rousseau's possession of a copy of Haller's three-volumed description of the Alpes *Historia stirpum indigenarum Helvetiae inchoata,* which was published in Berne in 1768 (Cook 2003).

4. An English translation of his religious writings was published under the title *Philosophical and Critical Inquiries Concerning Christianity* (London 1787).

5. Rousseau's answer, *Lettre à M. Philopolis,* was never published during his lifetime (O.C. III, pp. 230–6). Both texts are accessible in Rousseau 1992, pp.123–32.

6. Jean-Henri-Samuel Formey attended the French Collegium in Berlin and in 1720 became the preacher of the French community in Brandenburg, and in 1731 that of the French church of Friedrichstadt in Berlin. In 1736 Formey became a professor of rhetoric at the French Collegium, and in 1739 the successor of La Corze as a professor of philosophy. Four years later he became Permanent Secretary of the newly founded Royal Academy of Sciences in Berlin. He held this position for fifty years. Formey was a follower of Wolff's philosophy, which due to him gained influence in France.

7. "You can not educate the citizen by forming the man, by doing so you will denature man and turn around his destiny. Nature is nothing else than the capability to receive the social institutions; to turn it around and make it the single object of education it will be flexed to the wrong side, perverted and finally destroyed" (Formey 1763, p. 23).

8. In 1762 Dom Jean-Joseph Cajot published *Les Larcins littéraires de J.-J. R., citoyen de Genève, ou ses plagiats sur l'éducation.*

9. As modern authors on education the theologian and philosopher Jean-Pierre de Crousaz (1663–1750) from Lausanne, the French philosopher Nicolas Malebranche (1638–1715), Etienne-Gabriel Morelly, author of *Code de la Nature* from 1755, the Abbé de Fleury (1640–1723), and others (Cojot 1766, pp. 85ff.) are mentioned.

10. Beaurieu's *Elève de la nature* was again published as an extended, two-volumed edition in 1771.

11. *L'élève de la nature, par J.-J. Rousseau, autrefois citoyen de Genève.* Genève: Chez les Frères Cramer 1768. Until 1800 eighteen different editions and translations of this book were published. Rousseau commented on the book in a letter to Charles-Joseph Panckoucke (1736–1798) from May 25th, 1764 (Correspondance t. XX, pp. 84–6).

12. Wieland's texts on Rousseau date from 1769–70. At this time Wieland was teaching at the University of Erfurt as a professor of philosophy. Here, there is a reference to the satires *Koxkox und Kikequexel,*

eine Mexikanische Geschichte as a "Beytrag zur Naturgeschichte des sit-tlichen Menschen" (1769–70) and the two essays *Betrachtungen über J.-J. Rousseaus ursprünglichen Zustand der Menschheit* (1770) as well as *Ueber die von J.-J. Rousseau vorgeschlagenen Versuche den wahren Stand der Natur des Menschen zu entdecken . . .* (1770).

13. The source is an advertisement for the recently opened Philantropin in Dessau, printed in Leipzig in 1775.

14. For example, *Auswendiglernen und Übersetzen nicht verstandner Worte* (Basedow 1775, p. 21). Analogously, it says in *Emile*: "Des mots, encore des mots, et toujours des mots" (O.C. IV, p. 346). Criticism of oral lessons is referred to Montaigne in several ways (*Essais* I, p. 26), but it is part of a common complaint on schools, for which there is numerous evidence from the eighteenth century before Rousseau.

15. The book had three more editions, the last in 1794 under the title *Théorie d' une éducation républicaine, suivant les principes de J.-J. Rousseau.*

16. Edition from 1799. This was not a single case. At the beginning of the nineteenth century the Swiss mathematician Emanuel Develey (1764–1839) made an extended attempt at writing textbooks on physics, arith-metics, and algebra according to the principles of *Emile*. As early as 1795 he presented an *Arithmétique d'Emile*.

17. The solicitor Maximilien de Robespierre became a member of the par-liament for the Third Estate. The French Estates-General came together on May 5th, 1789. Robespierre joined the "Breton Club," out of which developed the Jacobines. After Mirabeau's death on April 2nd, 1791, the Jacobines increased their influence, Robespierre, once France's most successful student, became their most successful speaker and after the split (July, 1791) led the left, radical wing. In April, 1793 Robespierre led the fight against the Girondists in the Convent; on July 27th, 1793 he joined the Committee of Public Welfare and with Saint-Just became the dominant character and propagandist of terror. On July 28th, 1794 Robespierre was executed, and half a year later the Jacobine Club was closed (see Scurr 2006).

18. *Über die Grundsätze der politischen Moral, die den Nationalkonvent bei der inneren Verwaltung der Republik leiten sollen* (Robespierre 1989, pp. 581–616). The theoretical point of reference is Rousseau's category of *volonté générale*. For Robespierre, Rousseau is the "teacher of mankind" (*ibid.*, p. 681), the founder of direct democracy (*ibid.*, pp. 426–7), and the real friend of the people. "Nobody has ever given us a better idea of the people than Rousseau, for nobody has ever loved it more" (*ibid.*, p. 176).

19. Rousseau died on July 2nd, 1778, and was – in isolation – buried on the poplar island of Hermenonville. On Robespierre's command, the

Convent in Paris decided on April 14th, 1794 to bring Rousseau's remains to Paris. In 1791 the National Assembly had decided on a former church to be a temple of honor where great men to whom the Revolution referred were supposed to be buried. In 1814 Rousseau's sarcophagus was desecrated.

20. Up to July 1791, 16,000 French copies were sold.

21. *Vindication of Natural Society: or, A View of the Miseries and Evils sharing to Mankind from every Species of Artificial Society. In a Letter to Lord *** By a Late Noble Writer.* (Second edition, 1757) (Burke 1993, pp. 8–57).

22. "It is a Misfortune, that in no part of the Globe natural Liberty and natural Religion are to be found pure, and free from the Mixture of political Adulterations. Yet we have implanted in us by Providence Ideas, Axioms, Rules, of what is pious, just, fair, honest, which no political Craft nor learned Sophistry, can entirely expel from our Breasts. By these we judge, and we cannot otherwise judge of the several artificial Modes of Religion and Society and determine of them as they approach to, or recede from this Standard" (Burke 1993, p. 30).

23. François-Louis-Thibault de Menonville (1740–1816) wrote a letter to Burke on November 17th, 1790 after having read the *Reflections*. Burke never met him in person.

24. Utilité publique (O.C. III, p. 371).

25. "It is contrary to the natural order that the greater number should govern and the smaller number be governed" (Rousseau 2004a, pp. 78–9).

26. An early study example is Claude Genoux (1856).

27. Leo Strauss (1899–1973), now mostly regarded as the intellectual force behind American "neo-conservatism," read Rousseau as the first critic of modernism and not as one of the main protagonists (Strauss 1947).

28. The third edition of Thomas Day's famous poem *The Dying Negro* is dedicated to Rousseau.

29. Rousseau knew Daniel Malthus (1730–1800), one of his admirers and a fellow-botanist, and obviously also met Erasmus Darwin (1731–1802) but did not know anything about the Lunar Society (Damrosch 2005, p. 417). Malthus translated the novel *Paul et Virginie* written by Rousseau's friend Jacques-Henri Bernardin de Saint-Pierre (1737–1814), which was published in 1788 as the fourth volume of St Pierre's *Études de la nature*. The novel was widely read throughout Europe and coined the slogan "back to nature."

30. Thomas Bicknell (1756–1787) was a barrister at the High Court. He contributed to Day's *The Dying Negro*, which was printed in 1793.

31. Algernon Sidney (1623–1683) was sentenced to death for high treason in 1683, after having made a career as a diplomat in the period of the

Restoration. Sidney was executed but rehabilitated in 1689. In 1698 his famous *Discourses Concerning Government* were published. This manifest of natural freedom influenced Day.

32. The book appeared in three volumes between 1783 and 1789 and went through 140 editions up to 1870.

33. Besides being a lady of the court and working as an educator of princes, Stéphanie-Félicité Ducrest de Saint-Aubin, Comtesse de Genlis (1746–1830) was a successful author who published numerous novels and comedies but also educational tracts and not least works on theater education (Plagnol-Diéval 1997).

34. Following various other academic positions, Jules Gabriel Compayré (1843–1913) became headmaster of the *Académie of Poitiers*. In 1895 he was offered a chair at Lyon. His *Cours de Pédagogie théoretique et pratique* (1885) became the first textbook on the history of education in France.

35. There had been more than fifteen French books against *Emile* alone in 1762, the year of publication. In the following years Rousseau was very often accused as a non-Christian. Several authors tried to "correct" him, like Formey's *Emile chrétien* (1764). The last *nouvel Emile* appeared in 1814 (see Oelkers 2002).

36. Abbé Carmagnole: *Nouvelle réfutation de l'Emile de J.-J. Rousseau*. Draguignan: Gimbert 1860.

37. Gabriel Compayré: *Histoire critique des Doctrines de l'Éducation en France depuis le Seizième siècle*. Paris: Hachette 1879. The construction in Volume II, Book 5 is as follows: Rousseau had "précurseurs" but he developed the *first real* "philosophy of education" (Compayré 1879, t. II, p. 40) which influenced "disciples" from Bernard de Saint-Pierre via Kant and the German "Philantropes" up to Germaine de Stael (*ibid.*, pp. 95–137). The opponents to Rousseau only *confirmed* "la puissance d'un grand penseur" (*ibid.*, p. 137).

38. The last book of French philosopher Jean-Félix Nourrisson (1825–1899) was completed in 1899 but only published four years after his death. Nourrisson held the chair of philosophy at the *Collège de France* after 1874.

Part 4

The Relevance of Rousseau's Work Today

6

Current Significance

In the course of his intellectual biography Rousseau gradually developed something like a "theory" which is consistent in itself and is neither a confession nor a kind of education. The term "theory" appears in the second of his posthumously published dialogs, *Rousseau Judge of Jean-Jacques* (Rousseau 1990, p. 113). Simply due to their literary form, these dialogs are a rather unique attempt at self-justification. Through dialog, Rousseau analyzes his person and his work from the point of view of somebody else. The first somebody is a converted "Frenchman" talking to the second somebody, "Rousseau," about "Jean-Jacques," himself. Thus, Rousseau is able to judge on Jean-Jacques.

In the focus of the theory is the question of self-love, himself the object. "Rousseau" makes "Jean-Jacques" out to be a man beyond *amour-propre* (*ibid.*, p. 109), a possibility which authors like Blaise Pascal or La Rochefoucauld had definitely excluded. He, Jean-Jacques, who was publicly denounced as a "madman," was in fact "a wise man in command of himself" (*ibid.*, pp. 110–11). His whole life gave weight to the theory of *amour de soi* to be not only possible but also right. *Solitude* and thus retreat from the world is the key for this: "He was ill-tempered so long as he lived in the world; he was so no longer as soon as he lived alone" (*ibid.*, p. 149).

In the first of his three dialogs with the converted "Frenchman" "Rousseau" describes what the "putative author" (*ibid.*, p. 23) of "Jean-Jacques'" works, that is he himself, had essentially said and what his enemies wanted to misunderstand. Thus, Rousseau comments on the purpose of his books and for this puts the focus on *Emile*:

He has been scorned by them and by his whole era for having always maintained that man is good although men are wicked, that his virtues came from within and his vices from outside. He devoted his greatest and best book to showing how the harmful passions enter our souls, how good education must be purely negative, that it must consist not in curing the vices of the human heart – for there are no such vices naturally – but in preventing them from being born and in keeping tightly shut the passages through which they enter. (*ibid.*, pp. 22–3)

If that is supposed to be the essence of his educational theory, it is untenable. This is suggested by practical but also moral reasons. Whoever wants to "shut" the passages through which vice reaches the hearts of children must erect a closed state of education and must rigidly control the child's entire learning environment, which was exactly what the governor does in Emile's case, filtering what will be his experiences. The idea of "pure virtue," which Rousseau indeed repeatedly brings up without connecting a unitary concept of education to it, invites this. Only the rigorism of morals is continually there. The history of totalitarian education in the nineteenth and twentieth centuries shows the failure of this rigorism, which is behind all of Rousseau's educational criticisms.

As has been shown, the criticisms themselves are very different from each other. In the political writings that which is called "good education" is education toward the fatherland, which cannot operate negatively but only positively. It communicates republican virtues to society and does not maintain the state of nature. In *Nouvelle Héloise* natural education is put into the context of an economy of the house which does not demand growing up outside society and is only very indirectly connected to the theory of self-love. This kind of education is negative only insofar as it is supposed to prevent a premature education of intellect. In his letters Rousseau comments on education at several passages, often without taking the doctrine of *éducation négative* into consideration. Finally, his own education was not "purely negative" and it was still a good education, as he himself has judged.

But Rousseau's theory of education does not only allow for variants and does not only lead to contradictions; it is untenable by itself if, as most of its readers have done, it is understood empirically. Good education can never be "purely negative"; if it is supposed to be "good," there is just the demand of its *having* positive effects, that is it must try to build up morals and to communicate truths. The idea that vice intrudes the child's soul from the outside and that everything was only about controlling the ways of learning to maintain the state of innocence stylizes the "pure" child and underestimates Rousseau's own problem, that is how *virtues* are built up. Virtues without contact to vice remain abstract entities. Not coincidentally, there are lessons on constitutional law at the end of *Emile* which are supposed to communicate theoretically that which was never experienced in practice.

What drives Rousseau by his theological essence, negating Christian original sin, entices him to that construction of education he chooses for *Emile*.

Being free of sin, the child is supposed to stay in the natural state as long as possible, but natural state is nothing other than the Christian version of innocence. It is the potentially corruptible child which must be protected but not formally taught. A child *independent* of the doctrine of original sin is not all in Rousseau's mind. His strong child of nature cannot simply discover the world and develop by his own experiences. To give protection, a closed and controlled space is necessary, which determines what is experienced and what is not. Sin has simply been shifted into society, and the price is that it is much more concrete than the Christian tradition of original sin.

In a learning environment which was only supposed to prevent them from vice, real children would have no stimulations for their cognitive and emotional development. Rousseau trusts in the course of ages of education which, however, serves only to maintain the doctrine by avoiding any kind of "premature instruction." But for that alone Rousseau had no convincing arguments. Reason is by no means composed of all other faculties, and if children's judgments are different from those of adults, this does not mean that their judgments have no cognitive weight. In their own way, they judge "reasonably," that is they draw conclusions from their experiences, they determine causalities, and act according to intentions which look plausible to them.

As shown by his perception of child prodigies, by "nature" Rousseau does not mean the special talents of children but the ages and spaces of their experience. Neither is individualized in his educational theory but put in the form of a plan. Thus, the theory does not justify how children learn emotionally and cognitively. Rousseau wants to avoid contact to that which causes vice, but virtue will only develop if children and adults know about its opposite. Without noticeable instruction by social experience virtue will stay what, according to Rousseau, it is *not* supposed to be, that is an abstract appeal without any consequences and which does not find, to use Rousseau's words, the approval of the heart.

If, however, the concept of the theory of education – from today's point of view – misses its subject, why is it that Rousseau holds an outstanding position in the history of modern education? One is well advised to distinguish Rousseau, the contemporary author, from how he was later perceived. The contemporary author writes and stylizes himself against the background of a certain situation which he cannot shove away, although he wants to solve it. That which the Frenchman in the dialogs calls "all these obscure fictions" (*ibid.*, p. 13), that is Rousseau's works, developed as a reaction to people, topics, and theories whose constellation will not come again. Stylizing himself as the only author of his time without personal interest and committed only to "public interest" (*ibid.*, p. 53) must be explained by his time and by how it was perceived by him.

But this makes Rousseau neither a madman nor an eccentric; much more, he was right to mistrust the "passions of (his) judges" (*ibid.*, p. 58). Whoever is suddenly accused by the voice of the public as "being an abominable monster" (*ibid.*, p. 61) has a reason to defend himself, and it says something for Rousseau that he tries to do this by way of an analysis of accusation and defense or by way of the structure of criminalization (*ibid.*, pp. 28ff., 56ff.). Whoever sees himself subjected only to the "interest of truth" (*ibid.*, p. 53) does not say by this that he cannot be wrong and also that he does not recognize his errors. From today's point of view, however, there is the question of how this work shall be estimated if the "greatest and best book" develops a theory which is untenable as far as it is connected to empirical facts.

If, however, one starts with *Emile* as a literary fiction which neither describes a concrete case nor examines a practical possibility from which there might result a new reality of education, one evades Rousseau's own intention. Not coincidentally, at the end of his life he insists on the basic idea of negative education because it is a practical solution of his problem of alienation. The essential thought is strikingly simple: if education prevents a child from experiencing vice, man will remain good. But this is only the reversal of the doctrine of original sin, not a concept which could stand the test of practice. There is not one successful experiment of *éducation à la Jean-Jacques*.

This is not supposed to underestimate the effect of fiction. Like no other author in the history of education before, Rousseau stimulated the imagination of education. The ideas of perfect morals, of strict protection for children, and of total avoidance of every kind of vice, have resisted criticism and are still there. They describe ideals of perfection, in complete contrast to Rousseau's own criticism of *perfectibilité*, which obviously is not true for the moratorium of childhood. This way, education becomes a field of high expectations which can hardly be affected by disappointment. Not only *Emile*, but all of Rousseau's educational writings increase expectations; they offer plausibility where probabilities do not play a role. "Good nature" is a strong imagination which controls educational discourses from the background.

But the thorn of Rousseau goes even deeper. Criticism of negative education must be distinguished from that part of *Emile* which Rousseau himself said to be the systematic essence of his book. This means not only natural religion and the criticism of materialism in the confession of the Savoyard vicar but also the theory of self-love and the transition from education to society. If one wants to evaluate *Emile* from today's point of view, one must read the sequence of problems in reverse, that is starting out from the question of society and ending with the question of how man becomes a citizen. This question is decided at the end of the novel; more precisely, it is gone through several times before the failure of all educational intentions is certain.

Thus, it remains unresolved how education could adjust to society in such a way that the power of nature is maintained while still in need of development. Making education and society fit together is not successful. In the end Emile and Sophie go out into the world; they do not become citizens but definitely man and woman, if in a different sense than announced at the beginning of *Emile*. Their way into society does not make fate happen. If happiness of life does *not* depend on the result of education, then this is also true for unhappiness. Both is possible, and it is not within the power of education. Due to this, the attempt to understand the course of nature to be the course of history fails.

But if life does not follow nature, how could education do this? Rousseau's answer of simply understanding early education to be a kind of pre-form of life is not very convincing, as education would have to anticipate that which it cannot possibly know. It says something for Rousseau that he clearly recognizes the problem of anticipating the future without finding a solution which meets the problem. The course of nature is introduced to keep education independent of historical time. But there is no preparation for life which would not be life itself. And really this, reflecting on the form and the course of life, is the strength of Rousseau's theories.

Rousseau had more to say about unhappiness being the price of life than any other author in the history of education. Only he discusses loneliness as a positive way of life, the advantage of being alone, and experiencing a kind of nature which does not need any didactic introduction to touch the human soul. Life is not a program of hope, like education, but by its course demonstrates the obstacles of happiness. Even stronger than Montaigne Rousseau reflects on the mercilessness of experience, which at the end is not paradoxical anymore but terminates learning, as from life nothing new is to be expected. The prophet of the child concludes his work being the philosopher of age.

This is not about fleeing from the world, as in Christian antiquity, when the rigorous new faith suggested asceticism and physical renunciation. Rousseau describes a "solitary by taste and by choice" (*ibid.*, p. 99), that is a way of life which does not need any society because it does not want to depend on anyone. Love of oneself is enough, as it reduces the needs to the space of experience: "The man who is not dominated by amour-propre and who does not go seeking his happiness far from himself is the only one who knows heedlessness and sweet leisure, and J. J. is that man as far as I can determine" (*ibid.*, p. 144).

The question of self-love is at the core of Rousseau's philosophy. That he considered himself a model of how to solve the problem does not affect the relevance of the question. And his own way of life which summed up the problem, like the description of a stoic everyday life,[1] is not an objection which might devaluate the center of his philosophy. This question is also behind the concept of education pursued by Rousseau. How could education adjust to self-love if by nature there is no need at all for this, as and as far as self-love is enough of itself? The answer to this is, as already said, *éducation négative*, which is supposed to protect self-love by excluding *amour-propre* as long as possible and as far as possible.

Social isolation results in the child not comparing himself to others, but due to this also not being able to develop himself, as all feedback except that which is didactically intended is missing. Rousseau's rigid theory of comparison is misleading; it is not that every comparison affects love of oneself, just as it is not that every first step which is wrong leads to unhappiness. This domino theory does not take into account the possibility of correcting or even self-correcting the process of education; for Rousseau education happens like fate but still may get out of control if one is not careful and does not nip things in the bud.

Rousseau's educational version of the ancient *principiis obsta*[2] assumes that the start – the first step toward the wrong direction – can be identified. Each development of nature has a definite start which determines the effects. Coincidence is excluded, but this is only true for the ancient concept of growth which Rousseau follows. With every non-fictional kind of education it is possible to recognize errors and to correct mistakes, as far as *not* nature alone is decisive. However, not all effects are controlled, so that every education has to do with weighing risks, something which seems to be unnecessary only in Rousseau's landscape garden or is not suggested at all, as indeed the course of nature may be pursued.

If this idea is given up, there remains the question of what is the significance of man's love of oneself for his education. Rousseau's insistence on this problem cannot be refuted by pinning him down to some of his answers which do not really fit this. Rousseau changed a topic of the literature on virtue, which – although much read – did not receive much philosophical attention, into an intellectually demanding theory which turns educational options upside down. Self-love is not the same as *amour-propre*; without love of oneself one would not be able to live because there would be no emotional reason, and *amour-propre* is not a temptation which could be educationally worked on.

Rousseau presents the last version of this theory in the second dialog, that is not in an educational context. Once more he deals with his criticism of sensualism and emphasizes that the soul could not be found within the nerve cells (*ibid.*, pp. 111–12). The principle of sensualism is not denied: "Sensitivity is the principle of all action" (*ibid.*, p. 112). But there had to be a distinction between a "passive" and an "active" kind of sensitivity. The first one is of *physical* and *chemical* nature; it protects the body by directing pleasure and pain. The second one is of *moral* nature; it controls emotions toward other beings.

The second kind of sensitivity cannot be deduced from the first one, as it has a special function. It organizes the emotions between one's self and the environment, as far as souls are concerned. In analogy to the movement of bodies, this is about attraction and repulsion, which, however, is done by the soul itself. It has no physical basis, but it works in a similar way to a magnet.[3] More precisely: "The positive or attracting action is the simple work of nature, which seeks to extend and reinforce the feeling of our being; the negative or repelling action, which compresses and diminishes the being of another, is a combination produced by reflection. From the former arise all the loving and gentle passions, and from the latter all the hateful and cruel passions" (*ibid.*).

Here, only the process is described, not a way to influence it. Attraction and repulsion are the two basic processes of the emotional control of relationships; from them come the passions which are thus not a subject of education. They are not created, neither can they be taught, but develop by relationships themselves. Neither is it stated in this passage that one kind of passion could be supported to the exclusion of another. The core of the theory is about something different, that is proving why a state is dangerous which has moved from satisfying the needs and encouraging reflection.

At first, the conceptual dualism is explained once more, which combines the two stages of self-love and *amour-propre* and which is the basis of the theory. Both stages come from "active" and "moral" sensitivity which is now split up into positive and a negative parts:

> *Positive sensitivity* is directly derived from love of oneself. It is very natural that a person who loves himself should seek to extend his being and his enjoyments and to appropriate for himself what he feels should be a good thing for him. This is a pure matter of feeling in which reflection plays no part. But as soon as this absolute love degenerates into amour-propre and comparative love, it produces *negative sensitivity*, because as soon as one adopts the habit of measuring oneself against others and moving outside oneself in order to assign oneself the first and best place, it is impossible not to develop an aversion for everything that surpasses us, everything that lowers our standing, everything that diminishes us, everything that by being something prevents us from being everything. (*ibid.*; italics J.O.)

How does the disposition of comparing oneself to others develop? *Amour-propre* is not a relief but a constant irritation of emotions. It results in dissatisfaction, thus the thesis from *Emile* is repeated: "its wish is that each person prefers us to all else and to himself, which is impossible" (*ibid.*, p. 113). But if the wish behind *amour-propre* is impossible, why does it exist? It causes constant irritation. "It is irritated by the preferences it feels others deserve even when they don't obtain them. It is irritated by the advantages someone else has over us, without being appeased by those for which it feels compensated" (*ibid.*). The feeling of inferiority in the one case poisons the feeling of superiority in a thousand other cases, and that which one really had "more" in the past has been forgotten because one has only the loss in mind.

In other words, Rousseau sketches the image of a psyche which not only constantly compares but by comparison to others also wants to be best. This results in the wish of being superior by comparison and of loving oneself only for this to move the reflection, as the fulfilling of that wish is constantly threatened and thus always demands new opportunities which themselves increase irritation. *Amour-propre* is the risk-factor of Rousseau's theory. It exists because social relationships are made for comparison, because ideas progress, and because there is provision for cultivation of the mind. This way, the needs become differentiated. "As society becomes more closely knit by the bond of mutual needs, as the mind is extended, exercised, and enlightened, it becomes more active, embraces more objects, grasps more relationships, examines, compares" (*ibid*).

Thus, society means multiplying the possibilities of comparison, which are the more used, the more they are available. "Once we have started to measure ourselves this way, we never stop, and from then on the heart occupies itself only with placing everyone else beneath us" (*ibid.*). *Emile* was written to prevent the chain of increasing dissatisfaction from starting at all. Not only is the wish behind *amour-propre* impossible, but also the wish behind *Emile*. Thus, what is finally left for Rousseau is self-reference. He himself is the application of his theory (*ibid.*, pp. 113–14), and it is true for him and for his way of life when he notes: "The sensual man is the man of nature. The reflective man is the man of opinion; it is he who is dangerous" (*ibid.*, p. 114).

The thorn which Rousseau is for the theory of education comes from the way in which he goes through the paradigmatic case of education. His fiction assumes that "good education" is at all possible only under special conditions, that these conditions will never be in reality, and that in the end even fiction must state that life will correct education. Rousseau's solution is *solitude*; such a solution is not allowed for any imaginable theory of education. It must start out from the best possible case and at the same time must claim that in principle this case could happen everywhere. According to Rousseau, such a case cannot be, even if simulated. That which society makes of man's nature contradicts it.

His own biography is the model not of the theory of education but that of life. In old age, it says in the second dialog, all wishes have gone. Nothing is able any longer to soothe his heart. When he was young, his heart had been filled with enthusiasm for desires, some he had been able to shape in a way as to make them come to life, but seldomly had they lasted long and they failed because of insurmountable obstacles which he had always had to fight. "Desiring much, he obtained very little" (*ibid.*, p. 152). Why should this be only his fate, and why should he be the only one to always overcome obstacles by imagination? "When his destiny was such that he found in it nothing that was agreeable for him to remember, he lost all memory of it, and going back to the happy times of his childhood and youth, he went over them again and again in his recollections" (*ibid.*, p. 153).

Thus, life would be a cycle, returning to its beginnings without exposing the happy times of childhood to negative education. In the whole of *Emile* there is never any mention of the end of life; it says something for Rousseau that he is able to reset the beginning in a way that differs from his educational doctrine, which is supposed to have to do as little as possible with the course of life. But solely because of this, life is able to catch up so easily with "negative education."

Notes

1. "Nothing is more uniform than his way of life. He gets up, goes to bed, eats, works, goes out and returns at the same hours, without willing it and without knowing it. All days are cast in the same mold. The same day is always repeated. His routine takes the place of all other rules: he follows it very precisely without fail and without thought" (Rousseau 1990, p. 144).
2. Ovid: *Remedia amoris*, V. 91 (*principiis obsta, sero medicina paratur*).
3. "Its strength is in proportion to the relationships we feel between ourselves and other beings, and depending on the nature of these relationships it sometimes acts positively by attraction, sometimes negatively by repulsion, like the poles of a magnet" (Rousseau 1990, p. 112).

Bibliography

Rousseau

Rousseau, J.-J. (1826) *Oeuvres complètes avec les notes de tous les commentateurs.* Nouvelle édition ornée de quarante-deux vignettes, gravées par nos plus habiles artistes, d'après les dessins de déviria. Tomes XX–XXV: *Correspondance.* Paris: Chez Dalibon, Librairie.

—— (1924–1934) *Correspondance général.* T. I–X. Ed. by P.-P. Plant and T. Dufour. Paris. (Quoted as "C.G.")

—— (1937) *Citizen of Geneva: Selections from the Letters of Jean-Jacques Rousseau.* Ed. by C. W. Hendel. Oxford: Oxford University Press.

—— (1959) *Oeuvres complètes.* T. I: *Les Confessions: Autres textes autobiographiques.* Ed. by B. Gagnebin and M. Raymond. Paris: Editions Gallimard. (Quoted as "O.C. I")

—— (1964) *Oeuvres complètes.* T. III: *Du Contrat Social: Ecrits politiques.* Ed. by B. Gagnebin and M. Raymond. Paris: Editions Gallimard. (Quoted as "O.C. III")

—— (1965–1984) *Correspondance complète de Jean-Jacques Rousseau.* Edition critique établie et annotée par R. A. Leigh. Vols I–XLII. (Quoted as "Correspondance" with "t." for the volume)

—— (1969) *Oeuvres complètes.* T. IV: *Emile: Education – Morale – Botanique.* Ed. by B. Gagnebin and M. Raymond. Paris: Editions Gallimard. (Quoted as "O.C. IV")

—— (1990) *The Collected Writings of Rousseau.* Vol 1: *Rousseau Judge of Jean-Jacques.* Transl. by J. R. Bush *et al.* Ed. by R. D. Masters and C. Kelly. Hanover, NH, and London: University Press of New England.

—— (1991) *Correspondance avec Malherbes.* Paris: Flammarion.

—— (1992) *The Collected Writings of Rousseau.* Vol. 3: *Discourse on the Origins of Inequality (Second Discourse), Polemics, and Political Economy.* Transl. by J. R. Bush *et al.* Ed. by R. D. Masters and C. Kelly. Hanover, NH, and London: University Press of New England.

—— (1992a) *The Collected Writings of Rousseau.* Vol. 2: *Discourse on the Sciences and the Arts (First Discourse).* Transl. by J. R. Bush *et al.* Ed. by R. D. Masters and C. Kelly. Hanover, NH, and London: University Press of New England.

—— (1993) *Emile.* Transl. by B. Foxley. Intr. by P. D. Jimack. London and Rutland, VT: J. Dent, Charles E. Tuttle.

—— (1997) *The Collected Writings of Rousseau.* Vol. 6: *Julie, or The New Héloise: Letters of Two Lovers Who Live in a Small Town at the Foot of the Alps.* Transl. and annot. by P. Stewart and J. Vaché. Ed. by R. D. Masters and C. Kelly. Hanover, NH, and London: University Press of New England.

—— (2000) *Confessions.* Transl. by A. Scholar. Ed. and intr. by P. Coleman. Oxford: Oxford University Press.

—— (2000a) *The Collected Writings of Rousseau.* Vol. 8: *The Reveries of the Solitary Walker, Botanical Writings, and Letter to Franquières.* Transl. by C. E. Butterworth *et al.* Ed. by C. Kelly. Hanover, NH, and London: University of New England Press.

—— (2001) *The Collected Writings of Rousseau.* Vol. 9: *Letter to Beaumont, Letters Written from the Mountain, and Related Writings.* Transl. by C. Kelly and J. R. Bush. Ed. by C. Kelly and E. Grace. Hanover, NH, and London: University of New England Press.

—— (2004) *The Collected Writings of Rousseau.* Vol. 10: *Letter to d'Alembert and Writings for the Theater.* Transl. and ed. by A. Bloom, C. Butterworth, and C. Kelly. Hanover, NH, and London: University Press of New England.

—— (2004a) *The Social Contract.* Transl. by M. Cranston. London: Penguin Books.

—— (2005) *The Collected Writings of Rousseau.* Vol. 11: *The Plan for Perpetual Peace, On the Government of Poland, and Other Writings on History and Politics.* Transl. by C. Kelly and J. R. Bush. Ed. by C. Kelly. Hanover, NH, and London: Dartmouth College Press, University Press of New England.

Other Sources

Andry, N. (1741) *L'Orthopédie, ou l'Art de prévenir et de corriger dans les enfants les difformités du corps.* Ed. by B. Gagnebin and M. Raymond. Vols I–II. Paris: Veuve Alix, Lambert et Durant.

Anon. (1782) *Remarks on Mr R's Emilius.* London.

Aristotle (1998) *The Nicomachan Ethics.* Transl. by D. Ross. Rev. by J. L. Ackrill and J. O. Ursom. Oxford: Oxford University Press.

Basedow, J.-B. (1775) *Für Cosmopoliten Etwas zu lesen, zu denken und zu thun.* In Ansehung eines in Anhalt-Dessau errichteten Philanthropins oder Pädagogischen Seminars von ganz neuer Art, die schon alt seyn sollte. Ein Antrag an Eltern, an Studirende, an solche, welche die

Nothwendigkeit guter Werke practisch glauben, an Wohlthäter armer zur Pädagogie geschickter Genies, und an Staatsmänner, die ihren Monarchen von etwas Anders, als von Finanzen und Miliz, Vorstellungen thun dürfen. Mindestens zum Anlasse einiger Discourse aufgesetzt und wiederholt. Leipzig: Crusius.

Beaurieu, G. de (1771) *L'Elève de la Nature*. Nouv. éd., augmentée. T. I–III. Amsterdam and Lille: Henry.

Bermingham, M. (1750) *Manière de bien nourrir et soigner les enfants nouveaunés*. Paris: Barrois.

Bonnet, C. (1755) Lettre de M. Philopolis au sujet du Discours de M J.-J. Rousseau de Genève sur l'origine et les fondements de l'inégalité parmi les hommes. In: *Mercure de France* (Octobre), pp. 71–7.

Boswell's London Journal 1762–1763. (1950) First Published from the Original Manuscripts. Ed. by F. A. Pottle. Preface by C. Morley. New York, London, and Toronto: McGraw-Hill Book Company, Inc.

Boyd, W. (1911) *The Educational Theory of Jean-Jacques Rousseau*. London, New York, and Bombay: Longman, Green and Comp.

Brouzet, N. (1754) *Essai sur l'éducation médicinale des enfans, et leurs maladies*. T. I–II. Paris: Chez la Veuve Cavelier & Fils.

Burke, E. (1993) *Pre-Revolutionary Writings*. Ed. by I. Harris. Cambridge: Cambridge University Press. (Cambridge Texts in the History of Political Thought. Ed. R. Geuss and Q. Skinner)

—— (1999) *Reflections on the Revolution in France*. Ed. and intr. by L.G. Mitchell. Oxford: Oxford University Press.

Cadogan, W. (1753) *Essay Upon Nursing and the Management of Children, from their Birth to Three Years of Age*. In a Letter to one of the Governors of the Foundling Hospital. Published by Order of the General Committee for transacting the Affairs of the said Hospital. The Sixth Edition. London: J. Roberts.

Cajot, J.-J. (1766) *Les plagiats de M. J. J. R. de Genève, sur l'éducation*. La Haye: Chez Durand, Libarire.

—— (1769) *Eloge de l'asne, par un docteur de Montmartre*. Londres et Paris: Delaguette.

Compayré, G. (1879) *Histoire critique des Doctrines de l'éducation en France depuis le Seixième siècle*. Ouvrage couronné par l'Académie des Sciences morales et politiques. T. I–II. Paris: Librairie Hachette et Cie.

—— (1901) *J.-J. Rousseau et l'Éducation de la Nature*. Paris: Paul Delaplane Editeur.

Davidson, T. (1898) *Jean-Jacques Rousseau and Education According to Nature*. New York: Scribner.

Dewey, J. (1916/1985) *The Middle Works 1899–1924*. Vol. 9: *Democracy and Education 1916*. Ed. by J. A. Boydston. Intr. by S. Hook. Carbondale and Edwardsville: Southern Illinois University Press.

Dewey, J. and Dewey, E. (1915/1985) *Schools of To-Morrow: The Middle Works of John Dewey 1899–1924*. Vol. 8: *Essays on Education and Politics*. Ed. by J. A. Boydston. Intr. by S. Hook. Carbondale and Edwardsville: Southern Illinois University Press.

Dubois, P. V. (1726) *Nouveau traité des scrofules*. Paris: Paulus-du-Mesnil.

Dumas, L. (1732) *La Bibliothèque des enfans ou les premiers élémens de lettres*. Cont. Le sistème du Bureau tipographique: Le nouvel ABC Latin; Le nouvel ABC françois . . . A l'usage de Monseigner le Dauphin . . . Vols 1–4. Paris: Simon.

DuPeyrou, P. A. (1765) *Recueil des Pièces relatives à la persécution suscitée à Môtiers-Travers contre M. J.-J. Rousseau*. Yverdon: F. B. de Félice.

Duvoisin, J.-B. (1798) *Défense de l'ordre social contre les principes de la Révolution françaises*. Londres.

Edgeworth, R. L. (1821) *Memoirs; Begun by himself and Concluded by his Daughter Maria Edgeworth*. Vols I–II. London: Hunter and Baldwin.

Ehm, A. (1938) *L'éducation nouvelle: Ses principes, son évolution historique, son expansion mondiale*. Préface d'A. Ferrière. Paris: Editions Alsatia.

Epinay, L. F. P., Marquise d' (1759) *Lettres à mon fils*. Génève: Gauffecourt.

—— (1774/1996) *Les conversations d'Emilie*. Ed. by R. Davison. Oxford: The Voltaire Foundation.

Exposé succinct de la contestation qui est élevée entre M. Hume et M. Rousseau avec les pieces justificatives (1766). Londres.

Falconet, N. (1723) *Système des fièvres et des crises, Selon la doctrine d'Hippocrate, Des Febrifuges, des Vapeurs, de la Goute, de la Peste, etc. Singularitez importantes sur le petite Verole. De l'Education des enfants. De l'abus de la Bouielle*. Paris: Chez Antoine-Urbain Coustelier.

Fénelon, F. (1983) *Oeuvres I*. Ed. by J. Le Brun. Paris: Editions Gallimard.

Formey, J.-H.-S. (1763) *Anti-Emile*. Berlin: Chez Néaulme.

—— (1764) *Emile chrétien consacré à l'utilité publique*. Berlin: Chez Néaulme

—— (1789) *Souvenirs d'un citoyen*. T. I–II. Berlin: La Garde.

Fritz, T. (1843) *Esquisse d'une histoire de l'éducation (et de la Pédagogique) depuis les temps les plus reculés*. Strasbourg.

Genlis, St.-F. du Crest, Comtesse de (1782) *Adèle et Théodore ou Lettres sur l'éducation*. http://visualiseur.bnf.fr/Visualiseur?Destination= Gallica&O=NUMM-88451

Genoux, C. (1856) *Les enfants de J.-J.Rousseau*. Paris: Serrière.

Gerdil, G. S. (1764) *Réflexions sur la théorie & la pratique de l'éducation, contre les principes de Mr R., par le P.G.B.* Génève: Em. Du Vilard.

Girardin, R.-L. (1992) *De la composition des paysages: suivi de Promenade ou itinéraire des jardins Erménonville*. Seyssel: Edition Champ Vallon.

Hilaire, A. (1873) *Nos maîtres, hier. Etudes sur les progrès de l'éducation et sur les dévelopements de l'instruction populaire en France depuis les temps les plus reculés jusqu'à Jean-Jacques Rousseau*. Paris: Hachette.

Hume, D. (1994) *Political Essays*. Ed. by K. Haakonsson. Cambridge: Cambridge University Press. (Cambridge Texts in the History of Political Thought. Ed. by R. Geuss and Q. Skinner)

Iconographie (1908) *Iconographie de Jean-Jacques Rousseau: Portraits, scènes, habitations, souvenirs par le Comte de Girardin. Préface du Vicomte E.-M. de Vogüe.* Paris: Librairie Centrale d'Art et d'Architecture.

James, R. (1747) *Dictionnaire de Médecine*. Trad. par D. Diderot *et al*. T. IV. Paris: Briasson, David et Durand.

Jauffret, L.-F. (1794) *Les charmes de l'enfance et les plaisirs de l'amour maternel.* 4th éd. rev. et augm. Paris: Didot.

Labat, J.P. (1722) *Nouveau voyage aux isle de l'Amérique, contenant l'histoire naturelle de ces pays, l'origine, les mœurs, la religion & le gouvernement des Habitans, anciens & modernes* ... T. I–VI. Paris: Chez Pierre-François Giffart.

Lanson, G. (1905) Quelques documents inédits sur la condemnation et la censure de l' *Emile* et sur la condemnation des *Lettres écrites de la Montagne.* In: *Annales de la Société Jean-Jacques Rousseau.* Tome I, pp. 95–178.

La Rochefoucauld, F. de (2001) *Maximes, Réflexions diverses, Portraits Apologie de M. le Prince de Marcillac, Mémoires.* Ed. par J. Truchet *et al*. Paris: La Pochothèque Le livre de poche, Classiques Garnier.

Latifau, J. F. (1974–1977) *Customs of the American Indians Compared with the Customs of Primitive Times.* Vols I–II. Ed. and transl. by W. N. Fenton and E. L. Moore. Toronto: The Champlain Society.

Le CD-Rom Jean-Jacques Rousseau (1999). Prod. by INCOPROM SA (Geneva), l'INSTITUT de FRANCE (Paris), and CYBELE PRODUCTIONS (La Muraz). General conception by C. Richardet.

The Letters of David Hume (1932). Two Volumes. Ed. by J. Y. T. Greig. Oxford: The Clarendon Press.

Locke, J. (1975) *An Essay Concerning Human Understanding*. Ed. and intr. by P. H. Nidditch. Oxford: Clarendon Press.

—— (1989) *Some Thoughts Concerning Education.* Ed. by J. W. Yolton and J. S. Yolton. Oxford: Clarendon Press.

Mandement de Monseigneur l'Archevêque de Paris, Portant condamnation d'un Livre qui a pour titre: Emile, ou de l'Education, par J.-J. Rousseau, Citoyen de Genève. (1762) A Amsterdam, chez Jean Néaulme, Libraire/Paris: C. F. Simon.

Möbius, P. J. (1889) *J.-J. Rousseaus Krankheitsgeschichte.* Leipzig: Vogel.

Montaigne (1958) *The Complete Essays.* Transl. by D.M. Frame. Stanford, CA: Stanford University Press.

Montesquieu (1989) *The Spirit of the Laws.* Transl. and ed. by A. M. Cohler *et al*. Cambridge: Cambridge University Press.

Moreau de Saint-Elier, L.-M. (1738) *Traité de la communication des maladies et des passions, avec un essai pur servir à l'histoire naturelle de l'homme.* La Haye: Van Duren.

Morelly (1743) *Essai sur l'esprit humain, ou principes naturels de l'Education*. Paris: Chez C. Jean-Bapt. Delespine.

—— (1745) *Essai sur le coeur humain, ou Principes naturels de l'éducation*. Paris: Chez C. Jean-Bapt. Delespine.

Nörkow, P. M. (1898) *Das Aktivitätprincip in der Pädagogik Jean-Jacques Rousseaus*. Leipzig: B. O. Schmidt.

Nourrisson, J.-F. (1903) *Jean-Jacques Rousseau et le Rousseauisme*. Publ. par P. Nourrisson. Paris: Albert Fontemoing, Editeur.

Oltramare, A. (1879) Les idées de J.-J. Rousseau sur l'éducation. In: *J.-J. Rousseau jugé par les Genevois d'auhourd'hui*. Conférences faites à Genève. Genève, Neuchâtel and Paris: Jules Sandoz, pp. 67–133.

Pascal, B. (s.a.) *Pensées et opuscules*. Ed. et intr. by L. Brunschvicg. Paris: Librairies Hachette.

Pope, A. (1961) *The Twickenham Edition of the Poems*. Vol. IV: *Imitations of Horace. With an Epistle to Dr Arbuthnot and The Epilogue to the Satires*. Ed. by J. Butt. Second, revised edition. London and New Haven: Methuen & Co., Yale University Press.

—— (1993) *Vom Menschen. Essay on Man*. Englisch-deutsche Ausgabe. Übers. v. E. Breidert; hrsg, v. W. Breidert. Hamburg: Meiner Verlag.

Plutarch (1992) *Lives of the Noble Grecians & Romans*. Vol. 1. Transl. by J. Dryden and A. H. Clough. Ed. by A. H. Clough. New York: The Modern Library.

Quick, R. H. (2003) *Essays on Educational Reformers*. Reprinted from the 1909 edition. Honolulu, Hawaii: University Press of the Pacific.

Saint Augustine (1998) *Confessions*. Transl. and intr. by H. Chadwick. Oxford: Oxford University Press.

Serane, P. (1774) *Théorie de J.-J. R. sur l'éducation, corrigée et réduite en pratique, par M. Serane, ci-devant professeur d'histoire et d'éloquence à Paris*. Toulouse: Robert.

—— (1789) *L'heureux naufrage, ou l'on trouve une idée de législation conforme à l'humanité, à la nature, au bien public . . .* Paris: Imp. De Demonville.

Seward, A. (1804) *Memoirs of the Life of Dr. Darwin, Chiefly During his Residence at Lichfield. With Anecdotes of his Friends, and Criticisms of his Writings*. London: J. Johnson.

Toussaint, F.-V. (1748) *Les Moeurs*. Troisième Edition. n.p.

Tronchin, J.-R. (1761) Discours sur la justice. Prononce au Magnifique Conseil du deux-cent de la République de Genève. In: *Journal Helvétique* (août), pp. 359–72.

Vernes, J. (1764) *Lettres sur le christianisme de Mr. J.-J.Rousseau, adressées à Mr. L. L.* Amsterdam: A. Néaulme.

Voltaire (1756) *Oeuvres Complètes. Essai sur les moeurs et l'Esprit des nations*. http://www.voltaire.integral.com/Html/11/04INT_10.html#17.

—— (1756a) *Poème sur le desastre de Lisbonne, et sur la loi naturelle; avec des préfaces, des notes* . . . Nouvelle Edition. Genève: En May.

—— (1961) *Mélanges.* Introduction by E. Berl. Text written and commented by J. van der Heuvel. Paris: Gallimard.

—— (1983) *Correspondance.* Tome VIII (avril 1765–juin 1767). Ed. T. Besterman. Paris: Gallimard.

Von Salis-Marschlins, U. (1775) *Briefe an Väter und Kinderfreund.* n.p.

Walpole, H. (1798) A Narrative of what passed relative to the quarrel of Mr. David Hume and Jean Jacques Rousseau, as far as Mr. Horace Walpole was concerned with it. In: H. Walpole: *Works.* Vol. 4. London: Robinson and Edwards, pp. 247–56.

Wille, H. J. (1937) *Träume und Tränen. Das Leben von Therese Lavasseur mit Jean Jacques Rousseau.* Leipzig und Wien: Johannes Günther Verlag.

Secondary Literature

Astier, R. (1984) François Marcel and the Art of Teaching Dance in the Eighteenth Century. In: *Dance Research.* Vol. II, No. 2, pp. 11–23.

Aurenche, L. (1934) *Jean-Jacques Rousseau chez Monsieur de Mably.* Paris: Société française litteraire et technique.

Blanc, P. (2006) *Franquières, essai sur l'histoire du château et de ses occupants.* St-Martin-d'Hères: Messiodor. http://pierre.blanc38.free. fr/frq/franq7.htm

Bocquentin, F. (2003) *Jean-Jacques Rousseau, femme sans enfants? Essai sur l'analyse des textes autobiographiques de J.-J. Rousseau à travers sa "lange des signes."* Paris: L'Harmattan.

Brown, P. (2000) *Augustine of Hippo: A Biography.* New Edition with an Epilogue. Berkeley, CA: University of California Press.

Bürchler, F. (2004) *"Méthode" im "Jahrhundert der Methode." Ordnung, Forschung, Vermittlung und Anweisung in der Pariser Encyclopédie.* Diss. phil. Universität Zürich, Pädagogisches Institut (Fachbereich Allgemeine Pädagogik). Unpublished manuscript. Zürich.

Burgelin, P. (1959–1962) L'éducation de Sophie. In: *Annales de la Société Jean-Jacques Rousseau.* Tome 35, pp. 113–37.

Caron, M. (2003) *Conversation intime et pédagogie dans Les conversations d'Emilie de Louise d'Epinay.* http://www.theses.ulaval.ca/2003/20994/20994.html

Cassirer, E. (1932) Das Problem Jean-Jacques Rousseau. In: *Archiv für Geschichte der Philosophie.* Band XLI, S. 177–213, 479–513.

Cook, A. (2003) Jean-Jacques Rousseau's Copy of Albrecht von Haller's Historia stirpum indigenarum Helvetiae inchoata (1768). In: *Natural History* 30 (part I), pp. 149–56.

Coontz, St. (2005) *Marriage, A History: From Obedience to Intimacy, or How Love Conquered Marriage.* New York: Viking Press.

Cornut-Gentille, P. (2004) *Madame Roland: une femme en politique sous la Révolution,* Paris: Perrin.

Cottret, M. and Cottret, B. (2005) *Jean-Jacques Rousseau et son temps.* Paris: Perrin.

Courtois, L. J. (1923) Chronologie critique de la vie et des oeuvres de Jean-Jacques Rousseau. In: *Annales de la Société Jean-Jacques Rousseau.* Tome Quinzième. Geneve: Chez A. Jullien, Editeur.

Cranston, M. (1991) *Jean-Jacques: The Early Life of Jean-Jacques Rousseau, 1712–1754.* London: Allen Lane.

—— (1997) *The Solitary Self: Jean-Jacques Rousseau in Exile and Adversity.* London: Allen Lane.

—— (1999) *The Noble Savage: Jean-Jacques Rousseau 1754–1762.* London: Allen Lane.

Damrosch, L. (2005) *Jean-Jacques Rousseau: Restless Genius.* Boston: Houghton Mifflin.

Daston, L. and Vidal, F. (Eds.) (2004) *The Moral Authority of Nature.* Chicago and London: The University of Chicago Press.

Douthwaite, J. V. (2002) *The Wild Girl, Natural Man, and the Monster: Dangerous Experiments in the Age of Enlightenment.* Chicago and London: The University of Chicago Press.

Edmonds, D. and Eidinow, J. (2006) *Rousseaus's Dog: Two Great Thinkers at War in the Age of Enlightenment.* Hopewell, NJ: The Ecco Press.

Eigeldinger, F. S. (1992) Histoire d'une ouevre inachevée. In: *Annales de la Société Jean-Jacques Rousseau.* Vol. XL, pp. 153–84.

Essner, R. and Fuchs, T. (Hrsg.) (2003) *Bäder und Kuren der Aufklärung. Medizinalkurs und Freizeitvergnügen.* Berlin: Berliner Wissenschaftsverlag.

Farrell, J. (2006) *Paranoia and Modernity. Cervantes to Rousseau.* Ithaca, N.Y.: Cornell University Press.

Favre, L. (1912) Le Manuscrit Favre de l'Emile. In: *Annales des la Société Jean-Jacques Rousseau.* Tome VIII, pp. 233–54.

Gerhardi, G. C. (1983) Hortus Clausus. Funktionen der Landschaft bei Jean-Jacques Rousseau. In: *Zeitschrift für Ästhetik und allgemeine Kunstwissenschaft.* Vol. 28, No. 1, pp. 34–61.

Goulemot, J. M. (2002) L'Enfant et l'adolescent, objets et sujets du desir amoureux dans le discours des lumières. In: *Modern Language Notes* Vol. 117, No. 4 (September), pp. 710–21.

Guyot, C. (1958) *Un ami et défenseur de Rousseau: Pierre-Alexandre DuPeyrou.* Neuchâtel: Ides et Calendes.

—— (1962) *Plaidoyer pour Thérèse Lavasseur.* Neuchâtel: Ides et calendes.

Hartle, A. (1983) *The Modern Self in Rousseau's Confessions: A Reply to Saint Augustine*. South Bend Indiana: University of Notre Dame Press.

Hastier, L. (1965) La Gouverneuse de J.-J. Rousseau. In: L. Hastier: *Vieilles histoires Etranges énigmes*. Septième série. Paris: Librairie Arthème Fayard, pp. 111–259.

Havens, G. R. (1933) *Voltaire's marginalia on the pages of Rousseau. A Comparative Study of Ideas*. Columbus, OH: Ohio University Press.

Hofmann, M., Jacottet Isenegger, D., and Osterwalder, F. (Eds) (2006) *Pädagogische Modernisierung. Säkularität und Sakralität in der modernen Pädagogik*. Bern: Haupt Verlag.

Horowitz, A. (1987) *Rousseau, Nature and History*. Toronto: University of Toronto Press.

Jimack, P. D. (1960) *La genèse et la rédaction de l'Emile*. Geneva: Institut et Musée Voltaire, les Delices. (Studies on Voltaire and the Eighteenth Century. Ed. T. Besterman, Vol. XIII).

Lanson, G. (1912) L'unité de la pensée de Jean-Jacques Rousseau: In: *Annales de la Sociéte Jean-Jacques Rousseau*. Tome VIII, pp. 1–32.

Lecercle, J.-L. (1976) Un homme dans toute la vérité de la nature. In: *Revue des Sciences Humaines*. Vol. XLI, pp. 5–17.

Lefebvre, P. (1966–1968) Jansénistes et catholiques contre Rousseau. Essai sur les circonstances religieuses de la condemnation de l'"Emile" à Paris. In: *Annales de la Société Jean-Jacques Rousseau*. T. 45–8, pp. 129–48.

Lévi-Strauss, C. (1963) Rousseau, Father of Anthropology. In: *Courier*, UNESCO (March 1963), pp. 10–15.

Lyons, T. (2003) *The Education Work of Richard Lovell Edgeworth, Irish Educator and Inventor, 1744–1818*. Lewiston, NY: Edwin Mellen Press.

Mall, C. (2002) *Emile ou les figures de la fiction*. Oxford: Voltaire Foundation.

Martin, J. R. (1981) Sophie and Emile: A Case Study of Sex Bias in the History of Educational Thought. In: *Harvard Educational Review*. Vol. 51, No. 3, pp. 357–73.

Martin, W. (2006) Consience and Consciousness. Rousseau's Contribution to the Stoic Theory of *Oikeiosis*. Unpubl. Paper. Wivenhoe Park, Colchester: University of Essex.

Meld Shell, S. (2001) Nature and the Education of Sophie. In: P. Riley (Ed.) *The Cambridge Companion to Rousseau*. Cambridge: Cambridge University Press, pp. 272–301.

Mercier, R. (1961) *L'enfant dans la société du XVIIIe siècle (before Emile)*. Thesis for the doctorate ès lettres presented to the Faculté des Lettres, University of Paris. Paris: Université de Paris. Faculté des Lettres et Sciences Humaines.

Mossner, E. C. (1980) *The Life of David Hume*. 2nd Ed. Oxford: Clarendon Press.

Muller, R. (2000) *The Uncommoded Calvin: Studies in the Foundation of a Theological Tradition.* Oxford: Oxford University Press.

Oelkers, J. (2002) Rousseau and the Image of Modern Education. In: *Journal of Curriculum Studies.* Vol. 34, No. 6, pp. 679–98.

—— (2006) Die Rationalisierung des Lernens und die Entwicklung des Konzepts der "Zivlgesellschaft" im 17. Jahrhundert. In: J. Oelkers, R. Casale, R. Horlacher, and S. Larcher Klee (Eds) *Rationalisierung und Bildung bei Max Weber. Beiträge zur Historischen Bildungsforschung.* Bad Heilbrunn: Verlag Julius Klinkhardt, pp. 17–40.

—— (2006a) Reformpädagogik *vor* der Reformpädagogik. In: *Paedagogica Historica.* Vol. 42, Nos. 1–2, pp. 15–48.

Osterwalder, F. (1995) Die pädagogischen Konzepte des Jansenismus im ausgehenden 17. Jahrhundert und ihre Begründung. Theologische Ursprünge des modernen pädagogischen Paradigmas. In: *Jahrbuch für Historische Bildungsforschung.* Vol. 2. Weinheim und München: Juventa Verlag, pp. 59–83.

—— (2002) Jansenismus und pädagogische Reformen im ausgehenden 17. Jahrhundert. In: *Zeitschrift für pädaogische Historiographie.* Vol. 8, No. 1 (2002), pp. 43–9.

Pearson, R. (2005) *Voltaire Almighty: A Life in Pursuit of Freedom.* London: Bloomsbury Publishing PLC.

Plagnol-Diéval, M.-E. (1997) *Madame de Genlis et le théâtre d'éducation au XVIIIe siècle.* Oxford: The Voltaire Foundation.

Py, G. (1997) *Rousseau et les éducateurs. Etude sur la fortune des idées pédagogiques de Jean-Jacques Rousseau en France et en Europe au XVIIIe siècle.* Oxford: Voltaire Foundation.

Ravier, A. (1941) *L'éducation de l'homme nouveau. Essai Historique et Critique sur le Livre de l'Emile de J.-J. Rousseau.* Vols I–II. Issoudun: Editions Spes.

Rosenblatt, H. (1997) *Rousseau and Geneva. From the "First Discourse" to the "Social Contract."* Cambridge and New York: Cambridge University Press.

Rudolf, G. (1969) Jean-Jacques Rousseau und die Medizin. In: *Sudhoffs Archiv zur Wissenschaftsgeschichte.* Vol. 53, No. 1 (July), pp. 30–67.

Scurr, R. (2006) *Fatal Purity: Robespierre and the French Revolution.* London: Metropolitan Books.

Shanks, L. P. (1927) A Possible Source for Rousseau's Name *Emile.* In: *Modern Language Notes* XVII, pp. 243–4.

Starobinski, J. (1980) *Jean-Jacques Rousseau: Transparency and Obstruction.* Transl. by A. Goldhammer. Intr. by R. Morrisey. Chicago and London: The University of Chicago Press.

Strauss, L. (1947) On the the Intention of Rousseau. In: *Social Research* 14, pp. 455–87.

—— (1953) *Natural Right and History.* Chicago: Chicago University Press.

Terrasse, J. (1970) *Jean-Jacques Rousseau et la quête de l'âge d'or*. Bruxelles: Palais des Académies.

—— (1992) *De Mentor à Orphée. Essais sur les écrits pédagogiques de Jean-Jacques Rousseau*. Québec: Hurtubise.

Thiery, R. (Ed.) (1992) *Rousseau, l'Emile et la révolution*. Actes du colloque international de Montmorency 27 septembre–4 octobre 1989. Paris: Universitas et Ville de Montmorency.

Todorov, T. (1996) Living Alone Together. In: *New Literary History*. Vol. 27, No. 1 (Winter), pp. 1–14.

Trousson, R. (1988–1989) *Jean-Jacques Rousseau*. T. I: *La marche à la gloire*. T. II: *Le deuil éclatant du bonheur*. Paris: Tallandier.

—— (1995) *Défenseurs et adversaires de Rousseau. D'Isabelle de Charrière à Charles Maurras*. Paris: Champion.

Trousson, R. and Eigeldinger, F. S. (1998) *Jean-Jacques Rousseau au jour le jour*. Paris: Honoré Champion Editeur.

—— (Eds.) (2001) *Dictionnaire de Jean-Jacques Rousseau*. Paris: Honoré Champion Editeur.

Turnovsky, G. (2003) The Enlightenment Literary Market: Rousseau, Authorship and the Book Trade. In: *Eighteenth-Century Studies*. Vol. 36, No. 3 (Spring), pp. 387–410.

Uglow, J. (2003) *The Lunar Men: A Story of Science, Art, Invention and Passion*. London: Faber & Faber.

Van Berkel, K. and Vanderjagt, A. (Eds.) (2006) *The Book of Nature in Early Modern and Modern History*. Vols I–II. Leuven: Peeters Publishers. (Groningen Studies in Cultural Change, Vol. 17)

Variot, G. (1926) La doctrine de J.-J. Rousseau en puériculture et les opinions des médecins de son temps. In: *Bulletin de la Société française d'histoire de la médecine*, pp. 339–49.

Internet Sources

Editions

A Dissertation on the Origin of Inequality (1754)
  http://www.constitution.org/jjr/ineq.htm
  http://www.wsu.edu:8001/~dee/ENLIGHT/DISC2.HTM
  http://www.marxists.org/reference/subject/economics/rousseau/
    inequality/ch01.htm
A Discourse on Political Economy (1755)
  http://www.constitution.org/jjr/polecon.htm
Emile On Education (1762)
  http://www.ilt.columbia.edu/pedagogies/rousseau/Contents2.html

The Social Contract (1762)

http://www.constitution.org/jjr/socon.htm

http://www.marxists.org/reference/subject/economics/rousseau/
social-contract/index.htm

http://www.classicreader.com/author.php/aut.124/

Constitutional Project for Corsica (1765)

http://www.constitution.org/jjr/corsica.htm

Considerations on the Government of Poland (1772)

http://www.constitution.org/jjr/poland.htm

The Confessions (1782)

http://oregonstate.edu/instruct/phl302/texts/confessions/
confessions.html

http://philosophy.eserver.org/rousseau-confessions.txt

Lettres 1728–1778

http://classiques.uqac.ca/classiques/Rousseau_jj/lettres_1728_
1778/rousseau_lettres.pdf

Lettres à Malesherbes

http://membres.lycos.fr/jccau/ressourc/rousseau/oeuvres/
malesher.htm

http://pedagogie.ac-toulouse.fr/philosophie/textesdephilosophes.
htm#rousseau

Person

Lucidcafe's profile of Jean-Jacques Rousseau:

http://www.lucidcafe.com/library/96jun/rousseau.html

A brief discussion of the life and works of Jean-Jacques Rousseau:

http://www.philosophypages.com/ph/rous.htm

http://www.philosophers.co.uk/cafe/phil_jun2003.htm

http://oregonstate.edu/instruct/phl302/philosophers/
rousseau.html

http://www.blupete.com/Literature/Biographies/Philosophy/
Rousseau.htm

http://www.radicalacademy.com/philenlightenment.htm#rousseau

http://cepa.newschool.edu/het/profiles/rousseau.htm

http://www.classicreader.com/author.php/aut.124/

http://www.infed.org/walking/wa-rousseau.htm

http://www.online-literature.com/rousseau/

http://kirjasto.sci.fi/rousse.htm

http://www.philosophersnet.com/magazine/article.php?id=438&
amp;el=true

http://www.trincoll.edu/depts/phil/philo/phils/rousseau.html

Jean-Jacques Monnet, La vie et l'oeuvre de Rousseau en cartes postales:

http://www.asso-etud.unige.ch/cite-uni/rousseau/

http://www.geneve.ch/fao/2003/20030815.asp

http://www.silapedagogie.com/jean_jacques_rousseau.htm

MEMO le site de l'histoire: http://www.memo.fr/dossier.asp?ID=37

http://ahrf.revues.org/document1548.html

http://www.cosmovisions.com/Rousseau.htm

Colette Kouadio, SOS Philosophie, ≪ Rousseau: 1) Les sources de sa pensée; 2) La vie de Rousseau; 3) L'apport conceptuel; 4) Les principales oeuvres.

http://perso.orange.fr/sos.philosophie/rousseau.htm

Encyclopédie Microsoft Encarta 1999,

http://www.cvm.qc.ca/ccollin/portraits/rousseau.htm

Rousseau, Jean-Jacques (Internet Encyclopedia of Philosophy):

http://www.iep.utm.edu/r/rousseau.htm

http://atheisme.free.fr/Biographies/Rousseau.htm

http://agora.qc.ca/mot.nsf/Dossiers/Jean-Jacques_Rousseau

http://pages.globetrotter.net/pcbcr/rousseau.html#bio

http://www.evene.fr/celebre/biographie/jean-jacques-rousseau-108.php

http://www.rousseau-chronologie.com/

Index